JOHN F. KENNEDY

Half a century after his assassination, John F. Kennedy continues to evoke widespread fascination, looming large in America's historical memory. Popular portrayals often show Kennedy as a mythic, heroic figure, but these depictions have often obscured the details of the president's actual achievements and failures. Despite the briefness of his presidency, Kennedy dealt with many of the issues that would come to define the 1960s, including U.S. involvement in Vietnam, the wider Cold War, and the growing Civil Rights movement at home.

In *John F. Kennedy: The Spirit of Cold War Liberalism*, Jason K. Duncan explains Kennedy's significance as a political figure of the 20th century in U.S. and world history. Duncan contextualizes Kennedy's political career, and addresses his complex personal life and his enduring legacy. In a concise narrative supplemented by primary documents, including presidential speeches and critical reviews from the left and right, Duncan builds a biography that illuminates the impact of this iconic president and the history of the United States in the mid-twentieth century.

Jason K. Duncan is Professor of History at Aquinas College in Grand Rapids, Michigan.

ROUTLEDGE HISTORICAL AMERICANS

SERIES EDITOR: PAUL FINKELMAN, ALBANY LAW SCHOOL

Routledge Historical Americans is a series of short, vibrant biographies that illuminate the lives of Americans who have had an impact on the world. Each book includes a short overview of the person's life and puts that person into historical context through essential primary documents, written both by the subjects and about them. A series website supports the books, containing extra images and documents, links to further research, and where possible, multi-media sources on the subjects. Perfect for including in any course on American History, the books in the Routledge Historical Americans series show the impact everyday people can have on the course of history.

Woody Guthrie: Writing America's Songs
Ronald D. Cohen

Frederick Douglass: Reformer and Statesman
L. Diane Barnes

Thurgood Marshall: Race, Rights, and the Struggle for a More Perfect Union
Charles L. Zelden

Harry S. Truman: The Coming of the Cold War
Nicole L. Anslover

John Winthrop: Founding the City upon a Hill
Michael Parker

John F. Kennedy: The Spirit of Cold War Liberalism
Jason K. Duncan

Forthcoming:
Laura Ingalls Wilder: American Writer on the Prairie
Sallie Ketcham

Ronald Reagan: Champion of Conservative America
James Broussard

Bill Clinton: Building a Bridge to the New Millennium
David H. Bennett

Sojourner Truth: Prophet of Social Justice
Isabelle Kinnard Richman

Woodrow Wilson: Progressive President or Moral Crusader?
Kelly A. Woestman

John F. Kennedy
The Spirit of Cold War Liberalism

JASON K. DUNCAN

For Will,
check out
3307 N
street in
Georgetown
sometime!
best,
Jason Duncan

R Routledge
Taylor & Francis Group

NEW YORK AND LONDON

www.routledge.com/cw/HistoricalAmericans

First published 2014
by Routledge
711 Third Avenue, New York, NY 10017

and by Routledge
2 Park Square, Milton Park, Abingdon, Oxon OX14 4RN

Routledge is an imprint of the Taylor & Francis Group,
an informa business

Library of Congress Cataloging-in-Publication Data

Duncan, Jason K.
John F. Kennedy : the spirit of cold war liberalism / Jason K. Duncan.
    pages cm. — (Routledge historical Americans)
    Includes bibliographical references and index.
  1. Kennedy, John F. (John Fitzgerald), 1917–1963.   2. Presidents—United States—
Biography.   3. United States—Politics and government—1961–1963.   I. Title.
    E842.D85 2013
    973.922092—dc23
    2013014461

ISBN: 978-0-415-89562-0 (hbk)
ISBN: 978-0-415-89563-7 (pbk)
ISBN: 978-0-203-08162-4 (ebk)

Typeset in Minion Pro
by Apex CoVantage, LLC

Printed and bound in the United States of America by Sheridan Books, Inc. (a Sheridan Group Company).

To Amy and Leo

CONTENTS

Acknowledgments

I am in debt to the many people who have supported and aided me in the preparation of this book. Paul Finkelman of Albany Law School, editor of the Historical Americans series at Routledge, invited me to write this short biography of John F. Kennedy, in whom I have been interested as long as I can remember. Paul's advice and insight has been valuable along the way. The professional staff at Routledge—Kimberly Guinta, Rebecca Novack and Genevieve Aoki—have been a pleasure to work with. At the John F. Kennedy Presidential Library and Museum in Boston, Dr. Karen Abramson and Mr. Steve Plotkin welcomed me during my visit in the summer of 2011, and have been very helpful since in answering my inquiries. In Grand Rapids, Charles Brown, a scholar, gentleman and accomplished biographer of Reinhold Neibuhr, provided valuable assistance all the way through the writing process; my debt to him is considerable. I also owe much to the many scholars, biographers and historians, too numerous to mention here, who have done such valuable work on the life and presidency of John F. Kennedy. Any errors, shortcomings or notable omissions in this biography lie solely with me.

Progress toward completion of the book was speeded up when I was awarded a sabbatical by Aquinas College for the Fall 2012 semester, for which I am most grateful. I also appreciate the financial support that the college provided me at various stages of this project. Chad Gunnoe, Provost of Aquinas College, has supported this project, as have my outstanding colleagues in the History Department, John Pinheiro and Bethany Kilcrease. I owe special thanks to Anne Marie Ferratt, and Chad Buczkowski of Aquinas for their technical assistance, to Jeanine Weber of the college library staff, as well as to Cynthia Miskura, formerly of the college, for their valuable assistance.

I also want to thank Gleaves Whitney, director of the Hauenstein Center for Presidential Studies at Grand Valley State University, for his promotion of my work on John F. Kennedy. My family in Albany, New York, especially my parents Kay and David Duncan, have continued to support me and my academic work over the years.

My biggest debt goes to my wife, Amy Richards Duncan, whose support and encouragement in countless ways has given me a second life, including an academic one. A serious scholar in her own right, in addition to caring for our one-year-old son Leo, she has found time to help me with this book. It is with love that I dedicate this biography of John F. Kennedy to Amy and Leo.

Introduction

On January 20, 1961, John Fitzgerald Kennedy removed his topcoat and hat despite the sharply cold—though sunny—weather in Washington, and took the oath of office as the thirty-fifth president of the United States. With his family and the political leadership of the nation assembled on the platform before the U.S. Capitol, Kennedy addressed the vast crowd present as well as the tens of millions watching and listening across the country. With the advent of electronic mass media earlier in the twentieth century, first radio and later television, national broadcasts of inaugural addresses became great opportunities for new presidents to set the tone for their administrations. Kennedy took full advantage of being on display before a national audience; few presidents are more associated with their inaugural address. Jabbing the freezing air with his forefinger, he was at his most forceful and confident, his New England accent distinct but not quite as distinct as it had been earlier in his life. Highlighting the generational theme he had emphasized since his first run for public office 15 years earlier, Kennedy declared that the "torch had been passed to a new generation of Americans, born in this century."

The moment Kennedy took the oath of office he inherited not only the leadership of his own nation, but also the leadership of the Western alliance which was well into the second decade of its struggle with the communist world that was the Cold War. The chief rival of Kennedy's America was the Union of Soviet Socialist Republics, i.e. the Soviet Union. Both nations, born in revolution, sprawled across a continent and were home to diverse peoples. Both aspired to demonstrate the superiority of their model of establishing justice and organizing modern life. The United States of America was born out of a revolt against British colonial power, establishing a republic in 1776 based on representative government, individual rights, and private property. By the twentieth century, the United States had become the world's leading power.

On the other side of the world, communists seized power in what had been until a few months earlier the centuries-old Russian Empire in 1917, the year of Kennedy's birth. The Communist Party, influenced by the writings of nineteenth-century European thinker Karl Marx and interpreted by Russian revolutionary Vladimir Lenin, established the Soviet Union. It had as its goal nothing less than reshaping human nature and creating a classless society. For the Communist, history was defined by the struggle between economic classes. Soviet ideology dismissed the political and economic systems of the West as structures of oppression to benefit the rich and powerful. Further, Soviet leaders declared that there was no God and that religion too was a structure of oppression used to pacify the masses in order to benefit the rich and powerful. In the Soviet understanding of history, the American "Revolution" was no such thing; rather it was a war of independence in which one ruling class merely replaced another. These were the contrasting visions of revolution polarizing the Cold War rivals. Kennedy saw it differently, reminding his fellow Americans in his inaugural, "we are the heirs of that first revolution." By that he meant that it was the United States, and not the Soviet Union, that had the greatest claim on speaking for freedom and democracy in the 1960s.

Despite being Cold War rivals, the two nations had been allies in World War Two. Their cooperation was based on a shared desire to defeat Nazi Germany, which had invaded the Soviet Union in 1941. The latter eventually prevailed, paying a horrific human and economic cost for their victory in the most destructive war in history. The Soviets' unprecedented burden was eased somewhat by aid, military and other, from the United States. As the war drew to a close, this alliance floundered, however, as major differences between the leading nations emerged, destroying hopes for postwar cooperation. To the consternation of the United States and Great Britain, among others in the Western alliance, the Soviets imposed their communist system on lands in Eastern Europe that the Red Army had liberated from Nazi tyranny. Winston Churchill, the British wartime leader, denounced this as an Iron Curtain descending across the region, separating east from west. Two rival political and military blocs soon developed, one led by the United States as it abandoned its traditional isolationism, the other by the Soviet Union. By the time Kennedy was elected, each bloc presided over growing arsenals of nuclear weapons, with the United States holding a substantial advantage and the Soviets enjoying a significant advantage in troops and conventional weaponry. A global struggle for power and influence ensued. Military forces of the Soviet Union and the United States had not engaged each other in combat during the Cold War, although American troops had engaged soldiers of the People's Republic of China (a communist state since 1949) in the Korean War of 1950–1953.

Elected president as a Democrat, Kennedy was heir to an American liberal tradition dating back in the twentieth century to the Progressive Era, as well as the Cold War Liberal tradition. Theodore Roosevelt, Woodrow Wilson, Franklin Roosevelt, and Harry S. Truman, all Democrats except the first Roosevelt, pressed the federal government to regulate the economy, relieve the most crushing burdens of poverty, create opportunity where it could, and smooth the rough edges of capitalism. That economic system had produced enormous wealth in the United States, but with it came great inequities, some of them quite striking. At the dawn of the Cold War there was a broad consensus across the political spectrum on the necessity of containing communism. It was Harry Truman, a domestic liberal, who presided over the establishment of the key institutions of the Cold War. Where Cold War liberals differed from more conservative anti-communists was in their belief that a democratically elected national government, acting within constitutional limits, also had responsibility for solving domestic social and economic problems.

As the liberal tradition evolved in the Cold War era, it faced a new threat from the American right. Joseph McCarthy, a U.S. Senator from Wisconsin, alleged that events such as the stalemate in the Korean War and the coming to power of communists in China were not coincidences. He claimed that there were those on the American left, in positions of influence, who were working secretly for the communists. Although McCarthy's charges grew ever wilder and eventually collapsed under their own weight, he had managed to create doubts about the patriotism of liberal and left-leaning Americans. Conservatives more honorable and more serious than McCarthy feared that what Kennedy described in the 1960 campaign as "effective governmental action" was the slippery slope to totalitarian planning. They were influenced by the Austrian economist Friedrich Hayek's *The Road to Serfdom,* published in 1944.

In the wake of World War Two and in the global struggle of the Cold War, liberals in both parties began to understand the question of equality and justice for African-Americans as a moral cause long neglected. For the Democrats, with their longstanding base of support in a South where the Jim Crow system of white supremacy still reigned in 1961, this was a particular dilemma. As Kennedy assumed the presidency, the matter of racial equality was far from resolved. Kennedy thought that too much attention in the inaugural address on divisive domestic issues would not be appropriate. Nevertheless, at the urging of his civil rights advisors, Kennedy did proclaim his commitment to human rights, both around the world and "at home," and warned, "If a free society cannot help the many who are poor, it cannot save the few who are rich."

John F. Kennedy was not the most obvious Democrat to become the great champion of Cold War liberalism.[1] Born into a wealthy, rambunctious, and highly competitive Irish-American family in Boston, he was elected to Congress in 1946 from a strongly Catholic, working-class district. He was shaped in part by an Irish-American political tradition that included elements both liberal and conservative. His powerful father, Joseph P. Kennedy, a controversial businessman and diplomat for whom Kennedy had enormous respect, was an isolationist before and after World War Two. As a young politician, Kennedy was not drawn to those who initially crafted Cold War liberalism in the late 1940s. Its distinguished intellectual originators included historian Arthur M. Schlesinger Jr. (who later served in the Kennedy White House), diplomat George F. Kennan, and Christian theologian Reinhold Niebuhr. As he climbed the political ladder, winning election to the U.S. Senate in 1952 and becoming a national figure by the middle of the decade, he began to change. Broadening the scope of his staff, he hired people outside the familiar Irish Catholic orbit of Boston. He jettisoned some of his earlier positions on church-state relations. However, some liberals in the Democratic camp still had reservations about Kennedy. Although he early on broke with Joe Kennedy on foreign policy to become an internationalist, he remained his father's son. He had not endeared himself to liberals by his absence during the censuring of McCarthy in the Senate and in equivocating on civil rights. Other contenders for the Democratic presidential nomination in 1960, most notably Hubert Humphrey of Minnesota, had more distinguished and longer-standing records in championing the causes of workers, farmers, and African-Americans that were at the heart of American liberalism for much of the twentieth century.

There were others reasons for Democrats and liberals to be wary of a Kennedy candidacy. He was barely into his forties when he began to seek the presidency. Despite his youth, and the concerns it raised, he had suffered from poor health since childhood. There were ongoing rumors about his philandering, many of which were all too true. While in Congress, Kennedy had not distinguished himself either as a leader or a legislator. He was not readily identified with any major legislation that became law in his name, nor was he widely associated with any significant issue of the time. His criticism of U.S. foreign policy as not sufficiently attentive to the rising expectations of the emerging nations of the Third World attracted little attention. None of this dissuaded Kennedy, however, from offering himself to the nation in 1960 as an inspirational figure who could, in his words, "get the country moving again."

Kennedy had much to overcome in his bid for the White House. Although the Catholic Church was adamant in its opposition to communism, Kennedy found himself having to defend his patriotism and his loyalty to the United States during both the contest for the Democratic presidential nomination and the general election campaign of 1960. In the latter, he managed on the central issue of the Cold War to get to the right of his Republican opponent, Vice President Richard Nixon, who had a well-deserved reputation for anti-communism. Kennedy charged that the nation's Republican leadership had allowed the United States over the previous eight years to slip into complacency and fall behind the Soviet Union in many critical areas. He claimed a narrow victory, becoming the youngest man ever elected president, and the first Catholic, overcoming centuries of antipathy in America toward his religion.

During the long history of the Cold War, no president was as eloquent as Kennedy in holding out both the olive branch of peace and the arrows of potential war, both held tightly by the eagle on the Great Seal of the United States. Offering a resounding defense of the Western tradition and its freedoms as he took office, Kennedy made clear the determination of the United States and its allies to resist aggression. Affirming his belief in a strong national defense, Kennedy, a decorated veteran of World War Two, said of potential enemies of the United States, "We dare not tempt them with weakness." In tones that later seemed grandiose and even dangerous, he further proclaimed:

> Let every nation know, whether it wishes us well or ill, that we shall pay any price, bear any burden, meet any hardship, support any friend, oppose any foe, in order to assure the survival and success of liberty.

He welcomed the responsibility of what he described as "defending freedom in its hour of maximum danger," which given the immediate circumstances of January of 1961 was a slight exaggeration, but only that. Although Joseph Stalin, the murderous Soviet dictator, had been dead for nearly a decade, his successors remained committed to the triumph of the communist system around the world. Shortly before Kennedy became president, Soviet leader Nikita Khrushchev declared his support for "wars of national liberation." Even so, Kennedy devoted much of his inaugural address to appeals for cooperation, asking that both Cold War camps, "begin anew the quest for peace" in the face of a potential nuclear war.

After his memorable inaugural address, Kennedy had a difficult first year in office. The Cold War worsened, in part due to his mistakes, and in October of 1962 the conflict reached its most dangerous moment. The United States and the Soviet Union narrowly averted nuclear war over Cuba. By his third year in the White House, Kennedy was on steadier ground in managing the Cold War, and he and Khrushchev reached agreement in a historic arms control treaty. On the domestic side, after an extended period of hesitation and caution, he put the full powers of his presidency behind the greatest social movement for change in American history, the modern civil rights movement.

Kennedy also had success in encouraging leaders of the emerging nations of Asia, Africa, and Latin America to look on the United States as a partner in building a prosperous future together. He understood that the United States had to present more to the wider world than reflexive anticommunism. He ultimately infused Cold War liberalism with new energy and idealism, taking it "across the globe" and beyond, into outer space. Not all the ventures that he originated succeeded as hoped, but Kennedy's efforts to reclaim for the United States the banner of progress and democracy were nonetheless a noble and important undertaking.

In Vietnam, a war-torn land distant from the United States and one unfamiliar to nearly all Americans, Kennedy expanded a military commitment he had inherited. He never did, however, settle on a definitive U.S. policy toward that nation. The subsequent dramatic escalation of U.S. involvement in Vietnam by his successor proved to be quite costly for Kennedy's party, for Cold War liberalism, and the nation as a whole. It remains one of the more controversial and ambiguous parts of his legacy. In the late fall of 1963, a politician at the peak of his powers, he was struck down in an instant, leaving a stunned and saddened nation and world in his wake. The contrast of that dark day in Dallas with the hopes that Kennedy gave rise to at his inauguration nearly three years earlier could not have been starker.

Kennedy once said that complex problems of the modern world demanded politicians who "communicate[d] a sense of conviction and intelligence, and rather, some integrity."[2] At his best, he did just that. He inspired many, especially the young, to think of government service, in pursuit of the common good and a better world, as an honorable endeavor. Although he saw himself as an introvert, any such reticence did not keep him from establishing a strong bond with much of the nation and even with large parts of the wider world. His personal charisma proved to be an asset for him not only at home but also abroad. Many in Europe, South America, and elsewhere were fascinated by the young American president and his wife, Jacqueline. Closer to his immigrant roots than any modern U.S. president, Kennedy came to personify American optimism and vitality around the world.

After his death, revelations of his extramarital affairs, some of them appalling in their recklessness, have complicated the image of a man who while he lived seemed almost too good to be true. Kennedy has become something of a flawed hero in the American imagination, which may have only added to interest in him in an American culture that has changed enormously since the early 1960s. The shock of his assassination, still part of the national psyche, and the many conspiracy theories surrounding his death have also contributed to the Kennedy mystique. Much of this has obscured the fact that, underneath the charisma, charm, glamor, and an intense desire to enjoy the pleasures of life on his own terms, John F. Kennedy was at heart a serious man.

The fall of the Berlin Wall in 1989, erected during Kennedy's presidency, became the iconic event symbolizing the collapse of the Soviet Union and the communist regimes in Russia and Eastern Europe. With it came the end of the Cold War, with a couple of small nations, namely North Korea and (ironically) Cuba, holding on to their original models of communism into the twenty-first century. John F. Kennedy used the Cold War as an organizing principle around which he summoned the United States to greatness. That long struggle is now an important chapter in world history. His efforts to defend the Western alliance, bring assistance and hope to "those struggling to break the bonds of mass misery," as he said on January 20, 1961, and his willingness to step back from the abyss of nuclear war remain among the most riveting and memorable episodes in the "long twilight struggle" that was the Cold War.

PART I

JOHN F. KENNEDY

CHAPTER 1

"ANCIENT HERITAGE"

In 1897, U.S. Congressman John Fitzgerald of Boston, Massachusetts, met at the White House with President Grover Cleveland, a fellow Democrat. The subject of their meeting was a bill recently passed by Congress that would require all immigrants entering the United States to prove their literacy in English and demonstrate knowledge of the U.S. Constitution. The bill emerged out of one of the periodic outbursts against immigrants that have marred American history. Fitzgerald, whose grandson and namesake John Fitzgerald Kennedy was elected president of the United States more than 60 years later, had denounced this legislation as aimed at "thousands of Irish and Jewish girls," among others, denied educations by the oppressions of the British and Russian governments, respectively.[1] In his final days in office, Cleveland vetoed the bill, and immigration to the United States from southern and eastern Europe, as well as from Ireland, continued apace. In the Gilded Age of the late nineteenth century, American politics was often a clash of competing religious, cultural, and regional identities. Catholics, especially Irish immigrants and their American-born children, were often in the center of this politics in the decades after the Civil War. Four years earlier, Republican presidential nominee James Blaine, a charismatic politician of Irish descent, was poised to pry some Catholic and Irish-American voters from their usual loyalty to the Democrats. These efforts ran afoul when he appeared on stage late in the campaign with a minister who denounced the Democrats as marked by "Rum, Romanism and Rebellion," implying, and not in a complementary way, that the party consisted of drinkers, Catholics, and southern ex-Confederates. As no religious ethnic group in the United States had a stronger allegiance to a political party than Irish-American Catholics did to the Democrats, it behooved party leaders to solidify that loyalty in 1888. Those Irish-American Democrats included P. J. Kennedy, the son of two immigrants who left Ireland in the face of the devastating potato famine of the middle of the nineteenth century. He was part of an American political tradition that was still very much in the making, one of nineteenth-century immigrants, their children, and their descendants to follow, striving to make their mark on the nation.

It begins with the history of Ireland. The Kennedys (the name means "ugly head" in the Irish language) had been a moderately important clan on the island, one that had emerged out of its medieval struggles as allies of Brian Boru, who had nearly united Ireland as its High King, about 1000 AD. The Kennedys, who emerged in the west of Ireland, eventually made their way eastward, losing power and prestige like virtually all Irish Catholics in the early modern era. At the start of the seventeenth century, the last and most important bastion of traditional Irish power and culture, Ulster, in the north of the island, had fallen to English forces and been "planted" or colonized by Protestant settlers from England and Scotland. This occurred as English colonialists established their first successful colonies in America. Many of the Kennedys eventually settled in County Wexford and other counties in southeast Ireland. They and other Catholics in Ireland suffered much from the effects of the penal laws which the English government enacted in the late seventeenth century with the goal of making Ireland a Protestant land, one loyal to the crown in London. As they and other Irish Catholics would have understood this history, these laws were a culmination of centuries of English efforts to pacify Ireland. They were a new departure only in their thoroughness and detail, denying as they did Irish Catholics all manner of civil, political, and religious rights. The great eighteenth-century British statesman Edmund Burke, himself of Irish birth, summarized the penal laws aptly: "a machine of wise and elaborate contrivance and as well fitted for the oppression, impoverishment, and degradation of a people, and the debasement in them of human nature itself, as ever proceeded from the perverted ingenuity of man."[2]

A century after these laws were imposed, Ireland saw more upheaval. Inspired by revolutions in America and France, the United Irishmen, proclaiming themselves republicans, rebelled in 1798. Republicans in Ireland in the late eighteenth century, both Protestant and Catholic, sought to liberate the island from British rule and establish an independent republic. County Wexford was the scene of some of the most intense fighting. The Kennedys of Wexford fought for this first attempt to build an independent Irish republic, one which ultimately failed in its efforts to replicate the success of American and French revolutions.[3] A half-century later, a fungus severely damaged much of the island's potato crop, on which most of the rural Catholic Irish had become dependent. This most devastating crisis, still spoken of in Ireland as Famine Times and the Great Hunger, directly killed 1 million people and forced another 1.5 million into exile. Among those leaving were Patrick Kennedy and Bridget Murphy, who emigrated from County Wexford in the late 1840s; a few years later, as the famine neared its end, Thomas Fitzgerald also left Ireland. There had been food in Ireland during those catastrophic years, however, including on the very ships taking starving Irish to English port cities, where some rested briefly before heading to America. British officials in London and Ireland itself were slow to react to the emerging disaster, which further embittered relations between the English and Irish. It is no wonder that one historian described these mid-nineteenth-century immigrants to America this way: "The Catholic Irish were more communal than individualistic, more dependent than independent, more fatalistic than optimistic, more prone to accept conditions passively than to take initiatives for change, and more sensitive to the weight of history than to innovative possibilities for the future."[4] However, one Irish immigrant at the time, Richard O'Gorman, saw less passivity and a potential for creativity; as soon as Irish immigrants arrived in the United States, he claimed, they seemed "to be imbued with miraculous energy for good and evil."[5]

Like most Irish immigrants who arrived in Boston in the middle of the century, the Kennedys were stalked by starvation, disease, and the burdens of exile and poverty. In the North Atlantic basin, Boston, Massachusetts, was a direct sea voyage from Ireland. As scholars of the Irish Catholic experience have long noted, however, Boston was probably the least welcoming place on earth for those seeking to escape the famine. It was a city dominated since its founding in 1630 by Protestants in the Puritan tradition. Catholicism was banned in colonial Massachusetts, the first Catholic Church not opening in Boston until the 1780s, after the American Revolution had generated a new religious freedom. There were Catholics of Irish birth and ancestry in Boston and other places in the United States before the Great Famine. There was also a resurgence in nativist and anti-Catholic sentiment beginning about 1830 in many parts of the United States. This arose in large part from the Protestant revivals of the Second Great Awakening, when some evangelically minded saw an increase in Catholic immigration from Ireland as a threat to their renewed efforts to build a truly Christian commonwealth in the United States.

Soon after arriving in the United States, Patrick Kennedy and Bridget Murphy, John F. Kennedy's great grandparents, married and moved to Noddle's Island, a poor Irish neighborhood in East Boston. They lived among other Irish Catholics in an ethnic world, the chief institutions of which were the Catholic parish and neighborhood saloons. Most Irish immigrants faced difficult lives marked by grueling physical labor, poor health, crime, and all the miseries that come with poverty. There was also the matter of discrimination. The first Kennedys born in the United States were listed in the 1855 Boston city census as "foreigners." Patrick Kennedy died in 1858, the year his son "P.J.," the future state senator, was born, but Bridget Murphy Kennedy kept the family together by working as a maid, as many Irish immigrant women did in the homes of the growing middle class in the United States during the nineteenth century. She later bought a small shop that sold stationery, and grew her small business by selling groceries and alcohol.[6] She sent her son to Catholic schools in the 1850s, a time when the openly anti-Catholic and anti-immigrant party, the Know-Nothings, had its greatest success in Massachusetts. P. J. Kennedy, quiet and reserved but ambitious, advanced through work and education, graduating from Boston College, a Jesuit institution that served primarily working-class Irish Catholics and other immigrants. He acquired ownership of several bars and also operated in the liquor trade, reflecting the Irish cultural tradition of drinking and socializing. What Irish Catholics and immigrants in the United States did possess—at least the adult men in those groups—was the right to vote, claim citizenship, and run for public office. The U.S. Constitution was clear on this point: "no religious test shall ever be required as a qualification to any office or public trust under the United States." The constitution of Massachusetts, however, written in 1780, effectively barred Catholics from holding office by requiring them to take an oath renouncing all foreign religious authority. In 1820, the oath of office was revised, allowing Catholics to take it in good conscience. These efforts were advanced and then protected by American Catholics and their political allies, usually Jeffersonian Republicans and later Jacksonian Democrats, in the decades after the American Revolution. By the middle of the nineteenth century, most Catholics, especially Irish immigrants, cast their votes for the Democratic Party.

Besides running small businesses, the Kennedys, like many other Irish immigrants in the United States, turned to politics to climb the social ladder. This tendency has been assumed to be something natural, a function of the Irish innate gift of gab and gregariousness that does not need to be explained. The roguishly corrupt and outrageously gregarious Irish ward heeler and political boss is a staple of American political lore. Despite its long life, Daniel Patrick Moynihan, an Irish-American politician and scholar, rejected its validity, arguing, "There is no greater nonsense than the stereotype of the Irish politician as a beer-guzzling back-slapper."[7] If there was anywhere that this image reflected reality, however, it was in Boston. In that city and around Massachusetts from the mid-nineteenth century onward, Irish-American politicians emphasized their ethnicity, sometimes to great lengths, in a political arena defined by the rivalry between Protestant Republicans, known as Yankees, and Irish Americans and immigrant groups, largely Catholic, who made up the Democratic Party.

There are also specific historical circumstances out of which this supposed Irish skill at politics emerged. During the eighteenth century, Catholics were effectively banned from civic and political life in Ireland by the penal laws. For example, from the middle of the seventeenth century no Irish Catholics served in Irish or British parliaments until Daniel O'Connell was elected in 1829. It was the struggle for Catholic political emancipation in Ireland, organized by O'Connell, that is most relevant. Irish Catholics formed political committees, attended meetings, canvassed their neighbors, read (if they were literate), and were more interested in politics than other European immigrants.[8]

And so it was politics that proved to be central for the Kennedys in Boston, as it was for the Fitzgeralds. After a brief attempt at farming, Thomas and Rosanna Cox Fitzgerald, (John F. Kennedy's grandparents) moved into Boston's north end. The Fitzgerald name carried historical weight in Ireland; it had roots going back to an Old English-Norman family that had been prominent since medieval times. Much like P. J. Kennedy, John F. Fitzgerald showed early ambition and drive, graduating from the prestigious Boston Latin School. Fitzgerald, such a voluble talker that his speech became known in Boston as "Fitzblarney," personified the image of the sentimental and extrovert Irish-American politician that Moynihan thought simplistic. "Honey Fitz," as he was called, also went into Democratic Party politics, serving briefly with P. J. Kennedy in the Massachusetts Senate before being elected to the U.S. House of Representatives in 1894, winning re-election twice in an era when few Catholics served in Congress. While in Washington, it was awareness of his family's history and that of many of his constituents that led him to oppose the anti-immigration bill.[9] He was later elected mayor of Boston, but his political career stalled in 1916 when he lost to Henry Cabot Lodge, a member of a prominent Yankee political family, for a seat in the U.S. Senate. His oldest child, Rose, was quite close to her father and she acted as Mayor Fitzgerald's "hostess-companion-helper," traveling often with her father, meeting President Taft at the White House, and attending the 1912 Democratic Convention.

It was Democratic Party politics in Boston that brought together the Kennedys and the Fitzgeralds. The two families vacationed together in North Carolina as early as the 1890s, and after the turn of the century, did so closer to home at Old Orchard Beach, Maine. Honey Fitz had invited P. J. Kennedy and other Boston Irish political figures to build alliances and strengthen ties between them. It was at one such gathering that Rose Fitzgerald and Joseph Kennedy, son of P.J., first met, as children. Years later, as teenagers, they found themselves on another political vacation at Old Orchard together, and this time a romance was begun. Young Joseph, or Joe, Kennedy went to schools beyond the Catholic institutions of Boston, most notably graduating from the prestigious Latin School, and then Harvard University, class of 1912. The powerful Cardinal William O'Connell urged Boston Catholics to avoid Harvard University, much as he urged Honey Fitz not to send his daughter Rose to Wellesley College, which was not Catholic. Mary Hickey Kennedy, however, was independent-minded, a supporter of women's suffrage in the early twentieth century. At Harvard her son Joseph was industrious and active, made many friends, and showed extraordinary ambition and drive. He had an entrepreneurial bent, starting a bus company that took tourists to historic sites in and around Boston. A great moment of disappointment, however, came when he was passed over for selection at Harvard's most exclusive eating clubs, which were akin to fraternities. Kennedy often wondered if the snub stemmed from anti-Catholicism or bigotry against Irish-Americans; he would never know for sure. Rose Fitzgerald was more sanguine about any prejudice or social rivalry that existed between Boston's old established families and the city's Irish-Americans, saying that she "accepted it as one of those elementary facts of life not worth puzzling about."[10]

After graduation from Harvard, Joseph Kennedy chose not to follow his father's path into local politics, considering it time consuming and ultimately not worth the trouble. Instead, he set his sights on the business world and on making a fortune. He did use his father's connections at the start, landing a job as a clerk at a small bank that P. J. Kennedy had helped to establish years before. It was Joe's potential as a businessman that allowed Honey Fitz to drop his opposition to his daughter marrying Kennedy. The union of these two prominent and rising Irish-American families was represented in the marriage of Joseph Kennedy and Rose Fitzgerald. Rose was a lifelong devout Catholic and, in 1914, she and Joe were wed by Cardinal O'Connell, afterwards moving into a new home in the comfortable Boston suburb of Brookline. Joseph Kennedy's next big break came with some assistance from his father-in-law, then mayor of Boston. Joe told Honey Fitz that no Irish Catholic had ever been a state bank examiner; Mayor Fitzgerald brought this information to the governor and threatened to make it public. Kennedy was subsequently selected, after having passed a test. His new position allowed him to learn the banking industry across Massachusetts in great detail, and he parlayed that knowledge into launching a brilliant financial and business career. After helping the bank to fend off a hostile takeover by a larger financial institution, the board of directors made him its president, at the age of 25. As Kennedy himself put it, "banking was the basic business profession" that would allow him to gain a fundamental understanding of that world as a whole.[11] Investing and working in several different areas of business, Kennedy never fully committed to one field. His overriding goal was to make money, which would give him and his family the freedom to live as they wished, without financial worries.

He and Rose began their family right away, with Joseph Patrick Kennedy Jr. the first, born in 1915; Honey Fitz was disappointed that his daughter's first child was not named for him, but he masked that enough to predict, and not entirely tongue in cheek, that little Joseph would someday be President of the United States. Two years later, on May 29, 1917, Honey Fitz got his wish when the Kennedys named their second child John Fitzgerald Kennedy, in honor of his grandfather. Jack, as he was known from early on, was not a very healthy baby, suffering from a variety of ailments. His birth came several weeks after President Woodrow Wilson, a progressive Democrat who had greatly expanded the regulatory role of the federal government during his first term, persuaded Congress to declare war on Germany, and enter the conflict on the side of Great Britain, France, and Russia. This leap into the Great War in Europe marked a departure for the United States from its longstanding tradition of avoiding direct involvement in European affairs of this magnitude. Jack Kennedy's birth also came between the two Russian revolutions of 1917, the second of which eventually resulted in the establishment of the Union of Soviet Socialist Republics, a new type of nation, based on the ideology of Karl Marx and Vladimir Lenin and founded in the name of the workers and peasants of the old Russian Empire. And in the land of Kennedy's ancestors, a different type of insurrection, one based on nationalism and anti-colonialism, took place the previous April. The Easter Rising of 1916, a turning point in the history of modern Ireland, eventually brought about a divided island, with 26 counties forming the Irish republic, and 6 northern counties remaining in the United Kingdom.

Joseph Kennedy, unlike some of his friends and business associates, did not volunteer for the war. His focus was on his family; he said as he gazed into his infant son Joseph's face, "this is the only happiness that lasts."[12] His second son, Jack, grew up in affluent circumstances in suburban Boston. The Kennedys' large family enjoyed, as it grew, much closeness, material wealth, and the opportunities that came with the fortune that Joe Kennedy was busy accumulating. Rose Kennedy talked about the "family enterprise" that she and her husband had embarked on; it involved help from a bevy of maids, cooks, chauffeurs, and others, but also a great commitment from the parents, financially and emotionally. Rose was determined to raise her children as strong Catholics, but also encouraged their worldly success. Joe's main priority was to instill in his children the desire to get ahead, to win and achieve, and not to be restricted by the rules others had set. The Kennedys, for an Irish-American family, were an unusual mix of wealth and privilege, yet still set apart in Boston by their Catholicism and ethnicity. Joe was denied membership at a local golf club in 1926, and reacted strongly when described as an "Irishman" in a newspaper, famously protesting: "I was born here, my children were born here, what the hell do I have to do to be an American?"

While still quite aware of their heritage, the Kennedys were determined at the same time to distance themselves from Boston's large Irish Catholic population. The climb to acceptance by what Rose Kennedy once called "Boston's better people" was not easy. The Kennedys eventually left Boston altogether, or so it seemed, when in 1927 Joe and Rose moved their growing family, in a private railroad car, to the affluent Riverdale section of the Bronx, in the northernmost part of New York City. Two years later they moved again, this time further north to equally affluent Bronxville, in suburban Westchester County. Joe Kennedy later said of the decision to leave Boston, that it was "no place to bring up Irish Catholic children."[13] It was also true that proximity to New York City made sense, given his business interests on Wall Street. The family, however, did buy the vacation home they had been renting at Hyannis Port, Massachusetts, on Cape Cod.

Young Joe and Jack attended several different schools; the latter did quite well at Riverdale Country Day School, an exclusive private school not far from the Kennedys' home. Jack's mother wanted them to receive a Catholic education, but their father insisted that his sons be educated alongside the most influential and affluent of northeastern society. A compromise of sorts was reached when Jack enrolled at the Canterbury School, in Connecticut, then still a fairly new institution which enrolled primarily the sons of wealthy New England Catholic families. Among Jack's classmates in 1930 was Robert "Sarge" Shriver from Maryland, who remembered his future brother-in-law as a "very wiry, energetic peppy youngster."[14] Forced to leave Canterbury because of an appendicitis, he never again attended a Catholic school.[15]

As the family expanded and the children grew, the Kennedys exuded a unique energy. Joe prided himself on the family being exceptionally close-knit, one friend saying, "the Kennedys had a feeling of being heightened and it rubbed off on the people who came in contact with them. They were a unit. I remember thinking to myself that there couldn't be another group quite like this one."[16] However, along with their wealth and energy, there were some serious problems. Joe Kennedy's extramarital affairs were apparently numerous. In 1920, just after the birth of Rosemary, their fourth child, Rose left her husband, in part due to his infidelities. Her father, however, told her to "go back where you belong."[17] Before doing so for good, she attended a Catholic retreat and there resolved to focus on raising her children and accepting her marriage as permanent. The troubles continued, however. Most famously, after moving to Hollywood part-time in the late 1920s to invest in low budget movies, Joe began a brief but intense business relationship and romantic affair with Gloria Swanson, then one of the country's most famous movie stars. Kennedy even brought Swanson to family gatherings and vacations; as she later said of Rose, "she was either dumb, or a better actress than I was."[18] Joseph Kennedy's life had become quite different to that of the Irish Catholics he had grown up with. He might have easily, given his education and ambition, gone into law and politics, making a comfortable living and staying within the orbit of Boston. Instead, he pursued his business career with extraordinary vigor, going to New York and then Hollywood. This presented him with opportunities, and temptations, that were beyond the imagining of his father, for example. Joe Kennedy largely abstained from drinking, showed great interest in all matters financial, operated as something of a lone wolf in his career, and also pursued women outside of marriage. All this made him atypical among Irish-Americans of the time.

Both Kennedys took time away from home and their large family, especially Joe on business and vacations, and Rose on extended shopping trips, often to Europe. By the middle of the 1930s, they were apart some 300 days a year.[19] After the birth of their last child, the sexual intimacy between them ended, at Rose's insistence. Joe Kennedy, in a way that was unusual for fathers in the early decades of the twentieth century, especially among the wealthier classes, took an intense interest in the details of his children's lives. When he was home he devoted much time and attention to each child, asking them endless questions about school and their friends and encouraging their interests.[20] His parenting came in intense bursts, and included the long, individual letters he wrote to each child. As his children got older, he urged them toward achievement and action, encouraging them to compete and, above all, to win—his sons especially. Joe Sr. prided himself as a tough competitor, one who did not abide by rules if he found them an obstacle to his ambitions.

His second son, Jack, was less robust than his older brother; more than the usual bouts of childhood illnesses marked his early years. Not growing up with good health made dealing with sickness an ingrained part of his character. His parents both warned against self-pity and he learned not to complain. When he was three, Jack had a serious case of scarlet fever, which required a hospital stay and then convalescence at an institution in Maine. His nurse there became attached to the sick little boy, so much so that when he was discharged and sent home, she arranged to visit her former patient at the Kennedy home in Brookline. His father prayed fervently for his son's recovery and, when Jack survived, he donated half of his growing fortune to a Catholic charity.[21] Young Jack battled an array of ailments, some traceable to structural problems with his skeletal frame, and others more internal and related to his intestinal system; he also had a weak immune system, which made him susceptible to any number of diseases. It was Joe Kennedy who oversaw Jack's illnesses and his many visits to the doctors and to hospitals. Being with Jack at those times tied the father and son together closely.[22]

Despite his frailties, Jack Kennedy was energetic and active when healthy and eager to play sports. He also developed, in part from being bedridden so often, an extraordinary love of books and reading. Some of his boyhood favorites lay outside children's books and included histories and legends, such as *King Arthur and the Round Table*. One Kennedy family friend visited Jack when he was in the hospital and was astonished to see the young boy, about 12 at the time, surrounded in his bed by books and reading Winston Churchill's history of World War One, *The World Crisis*.[23] Rose encouraged Jack's interest in books, and she also observed in her second oldest son a tendency toward daydreaming: "I often had a feeling that his mind was only half-occupied with the subject at hand, such as doing his arithmetic homework or picking his clothes off the floor.[24] She also remembered that her second child had "his own thoughts, did things his own way, and somehow just didn't fit any pattern."[25] Young Jack also had an irreverent streak; when Rose told him about Jesus riding into Jerusalem on a donkey on Psalm Sunday, he asked her what happened to the donkey after Jesus dismounted from it.[26]

Rose Kennedy's influence on her children has perhaps been underestimated by biographers of the family—her religious devotion too easily dismissed. Because her husband was often away from home, building his career and fortune, Rose, especially in the early years of their first children, was chiefly responsible for raising them. By all accounts her Catholic faith was real and strong, and at its heart was more than simple obedience to rules such as no meat on Friday (which she followed and insisted her children did too). A major theme of her Catholic faith, one that she emphasized to her children, was belief in the Christian Resurrection, when all who are to be saved are raised from the dead in a perfected form. While Rose freely admitted she had worldly ambitions for her children, she also inspired in them a distinctly hopeful outlook on life, one based firmly on that Christian faith. How deeply that resonated with her children, including Jack, is not possible to know exactly; it may well have been, however, an essential part of what the family would come to call their "Kennedy confidence."

Jack Kennedy, although overshadowed by his older brother in sport and grades, had a way of winning people over that his brother, who could be rigid and even abrasive, did not fully enjoy. Jack later said, "Joe had a pugnacious personality," which eventually "smoothed out but was a problem in my boyhood."[27] At Choate School in Connecticut, where Joe was enrolled and became a campus leader and sports hero, Jack was a promising student in those subjects he had a genuine interest in, such as history and English, but was indifferent to the rest, especially math and foreign languages. He played many sports, although his poor health and slight frame prevented him from becoming a star. Despite being an ethnic and religious outsider at Choate, Kennedy, according to one student of the family, "was afraid of no one and held no one in awe."[28] Unlike his older brother, Jack Kennedy was not a student leader in the conventional sense. He was the unofficial chief, however, of a band of Choate students who quickly developed a reputation for mischief and hijinks. The school's headmaster, George St. John, labeled them "the Muckers." The head of the Student Council had brought a Muckers' plan to disrupt a special weekend at the school to the attention of the headmaster. Kennedy could seem, to those in authority, irresponsible and even delinquent: habitually late, unable or unwilling to keep a clean room, and defiant, although often in a humorous way. One of the pranks he organized was to take all the pillows in the dorm and stuff them into a single room. The headmaster, driven to distraction by the band, came to the brink of expelling Kennedy and 12 of his friends. St. John met with Joe Sr. and decided to give Jack one more chance. In this episode, young Jack Kennedy appears as the leader of a prep school Animal House troupe. But those who knew him best saw the potential and seriousness behind the mischief and rebelliousness. LeMoyne Billings, Kennedy's lifelong friend from Choate, said of him: "He read a great deal of history generally while he was at school. . . . I don't remember any other boy subscribing to the *New York Times*, but Jack did—and he read it every day."[29] Eventually, Jack Kennedy won over even George St. John, who despite being exasperated by his antics and his lack of focus, was impressed by Kennedy's "clever and individualist mind," saying that "when he learns the right place for humor and learns to use his individual way of looking at things as an asset instead of a handicap, his natural gift of an individual outlook and witty expression are going to help him."[30]

As he completed his studies at Choate, Jack Kennedy came across as an intelligent, talented, humorous, somewhat restless and unfocused young man, with a great capacity for friendship and reveling in his outsider status. Not all of his classmates, however, appreciated his sense of humor, especially not those who bore the brunt of his sometimes sarcastic wit.[31] Being the *second* son of Joseph P. Kennedy gave him one advantage; he did not bear the full weight of his father's high expectations as his older brother did.[32] Despite his rather mediocre academic record at Choate, Kennedy had a promising future—even selected by his classmates as "Most Likely to Succeed." This honor had its ironies, however; it came out of a campaign that Jack organized in part to spite the teachers and administration of the school with whom he had been in trouble so often, and not surprisingly preferred that another student earn that particular distinction.

Just as Jack was graduating from Choate, his father entered public service. Joe Kennedy moved to Washington to become the first chairman of the Security and Exchange Commission, established in 1934 as part of President Franklin Roosevelt's New Deal. Kennedy had raised money for Roosevelt during the 1932 campaign and made known his interest in a prominent position in his administration. The irony of Roosevelt tapping Kennedy to be the first chairman of a new agency charged with overseeing Wall Street was apparent to all who knew the financial world of the 1920s and early 1930s. Joe Kennedy's reputation as a wily and ruthless investor who took considerable advantage of a largely unregulated financial industry was well known; as Roosevelt himself said of his choice, "it takes a thief to catch a thief." The appointment was a major shift in the trajectory of Joseph Kennedy's career, away from private and capitalist ventures and into public life. He had come to believe that the future no longer belonged to the business world, now fallen into some disrepute with the onset of the Great Depression, but that "in the next generation the people who run the government would be the biggest people in America."[33] Joe Kennedy wanted his sons to study politics and history in preparation for careers as leaders in the public arena, all the while harboring his own ambitions for high office.

But first things first. In 1935, the summer after graduating from Choate, Jack traveled to London on his first European trip, to study with Harold Laski, a socialist and a brilliant teacher at the London School of Economics. Although Joe Kennedy was often overbearing and domineering in his relations with others, paradoxically he did not demand that his own children see the world just as he did. He often questioned them on public affairs, encouraging them to form their own judgments. His second son in particular responded to that freedom. While in London, Jack was most interested in the plentiful social life that was available to him. Another bout of illness, however, sent him back to the United States. When it came to choosing a college, Jack first sought to follow his own path, enrolling at Princeton University instead of Harvard, his father's alma mater and where Joe Jr. was already studying. He was also interested in attending college with his friend LeMoyne Billings. But once again, illness interfered with his plans, bringing his time at Princeton to an end after only a month; he also found the campus remote and the lodgings not to his liking. He turned to Harvard, enrolling in the fall of 1936. Jack's record there bore similarities to his time at Choate: a certain popularity, recurrent illness, an uneven academic record, and concerns that he would not live up to his potential. As before, his older brother Joe, who made the varsity football team and achieved stellar grades, overshadowed him. Jack was a fiercely competitive athlete himself: "He played for keeps, he did nothing half way," said his football coach at Harvard, but his slight frame and poor health kept him on the junior varsity.[34]

These physical limitations also prevented him from becoming much of a drinker, another traditional way to prove one's manhood on a college campus. Even so, he made quite an impression at Harvard. John Kenneth Galbraith, a young professor, described Jack as "handsome . . . gregarious, given to various amusements, much devoted to social life and affectionately and diversely to women."[35] Another teacher remembered many years later "his bright young face which stood out in the class."[36] His wit and sense of humor led to many friendships and romances, and although the son of a rich and increasingly powerful father, his contemporaries noted that Kennedy seemed refreshingly unpretentious and irreverent.

At Harvard, Jack Kennedy became known as a ladies' man (or "Play-boy", as he wrote in a letter to LeMoyne Billings).[37] He was very much influenced by his father's behavior in this regard. It was in relations with young women that his generally weak health was not a handicap, as it was in sports. Jack Kennedy could succeed here on his own terms, as it were. Behavior of this kind was not unusual during the 1920s and into the 1930s, especially among the rich, who were perhaps less concerned about keeping up the appearance of traditional moral behavior than were the middle classes. Although the Great Depression struck the United States and much of the world in the late 1920s and deepened during the 1930s, the Kennedys were immune to the hardships and anxieties it created. Joe Sr. had cagily figured out before most others that the great stock boom of the 1920s would end. His second oldest son told a journalist many years later: "I have no firsthand knowledge of the depression. I really did not learn about the depression until I read about it at Harvard."[38] Jack Kennedy had a well-earned reputation of rarely carrying cash or being concerned about expenses; his father's accountants would pay all debts eventually, although Jack's friends in the meantime often had to foot the bill. Servants and others among their father's array of employees were usually available to clean up the children's messes, both literal and otherwise. George Thomas, an African-American valet, began looking after Jack at Harvard and then for many years after. Years later, Joe Kennedy said: "None of my children has the slightest interest in making money; not the slightest."[39] That had been his aim, to free his children from financial worries so that they could focus on developing their potential for public and political leadership.

One of the great opportunities that the Kennedy's wealth afforded them was travel. In the summer of 1937, between years at Harvard, Jack and LeMoyne Billings went on an extended tour of Europe. Their interest was in history and contemporary politics, which were of great moment in Europe in the late 1930s as the Spanish Civil War raged and fascist governments in Italy and Germany militarized their societies. Jack Kennedy's views on world affairs were shaped initially by those of his father, an isolationist whose first loyalty, as he made clear, was to his family. Joe Jr.'s thinking was much in the same mold. During the latter part of that decade, Joe Kennedy added to his accomplishments in public life. After a productive stint at the Securities and Exchange Commission, in which he oversaw the implementation of new federal regulations of the financial industry, he became a nationally known figure. In the fall of 1937, *Fortune* magazine featured him on its cover. Joe Kennedy's career in government reached its peak when President Roosevelt named him, despite his having no such experience, to the most important and coveted position in the diplomatic corps: U.S. ambassador to Great Britain, at the venerable Court of St. James. The new ambassador took his entire family to London, and the Kennedys made a great splash with their numbers, exuberance, and vitality. As Joe said to Rose as they dressed for dinner with the King and Queen, "this is a helluva way from East Boston, isn't it?"[40] It was, and Kennedy's new assignment was all the more significant to him because he was the first Irish-American Catholic to represent the United States in London as ambassador.

After his second year at Harvard, Jack worked at the U.S. embassy, traveled around Europe, met and greatly enjoyed the company of the English aristocracy (and they his), and pursued his strong interest in the European political and military scene. Back at Harvard, he turned his attention to studying in depth a member of the U.S. House of Representatives. The professor, Arthur Holcombe, suggested that Kennedy investigate Bertram Snell, from St. Lawrence County in northern New York, the Republican Minority Leader in the House during the 1930s and a staunch opponent of Roosevelt's New Deal. Holcombe's idea of politics was to study it dispassionately, looking primarily at the facts, as it were, and not relying on emotion or preconceived notions. This clinical approach appealed greatly to Jack Kennedy and, after traveling to Washington to see his subject in his place of work, he wrote a final paper that Professor Holcombe found to be a "masterpiece." Jack's grandfathers had learned about politics as young men in their respective neighborhoods in Boston. That world was not unknown to their grandson, but Jack also studied politics in the classrooms of Harvard and in the corridors of Washington. His college professors noted that Kennedy was not primarily interested in specific domestic issues or social causes (he never joined the College Democrats, for example), but was fascinated by the process of politics and the character of individual politicians.

Jack's own reading reflected his interest in personalities and political leadership; he preferred history written from a heroic perspective, thus his keen interest in Churchill's writings as one who also took part in history. Another of his favorite books was David Cecil's biography of the nineteenth-century English statesman, Lord Melbourne: he admired the mixture of high politics and rollicking social life that Melbourne enjoyed.

Cecil was also the uncle of William Cavendish, a member of the English aristocracy and a Protestant, who in 1944 married Kathleen "Kick" Kennedy against Rose Kennedy's wishes. In contrast to the sibling rivalry with his older brother Joe, Jack was close to Kick, his younger sister and the fourth of the Kennedy children. They shared a love of the social scene of London, especially its young aristocratic circles. Their closeness also had its roots in Kick's dissenting from their parents in insisting that Jack, not Joe, was the most promising of her two older brothers. It was in London in the late 1930s that Jack met David Ormsby-Gore, a member of the British aristocracy and another second son of an influential family, who similarly appeared, at least to his parents, to lack a certain ambition. The two began an enduring friendship, "a twenty-five-year conversation," as Ormsby-Gore described it, primarily about the nature of political leadership in a democratic setting.

Jack's interest in Great Britain and international affairs intersected when he chose a topic for his senior thesis at Harvard. As fascinated as he was with history, it was what was happening in the present that captivated him most completely. In researching what he originally entitled "Appeasement at Munich," Jack had access to government documents due to his father's position in London, and typists to help him. Focusing intensely on his topic, Kennedy produced a 148-page thesis that was granted honors, despite some problems with sloppiness and repetition. Jack himself said he had never worked harder on a project. In 1940, after much revision, Kennedy's manuscript was published as *Why England Slept,* a clear nod to Winston Churchill's book of two years earlier, *While England Slept,* in which he denounced Britain's failure to re-arm in the face of the mounting threat from Nazi Germany. It is rare for undergraduates to publish their senior thesis as a book. Jack Kennedy was assisted in polishing his prose by his father's friend, Arthur Krock, a *New York Times* journalist. As World War Two had now begun in Europe, however, Kennedy's topic had obvious relevance for an American audience, and his father, ambitious as always, pushed Jack toward publication, writing to him: "You would be surprised how a book that really makes the grade with high class people stands you in good stead for years to come."[41] The elder Kennedy took an active role in the preparation of the book, which may explain why Jack largely absolved the British political leadership—especially Prime Minister Neville Chamberlain—of its mistakes. At times Jack seemed to place the blame for Britain's dangerously slow reaction to the Nazi re-armament on democracy itself. Joseph Kennedy had said, indiscriminately, that "democracy was finished" in Britain, words that led to his recall as ambassador. Henry R. Luce, publisher of *Time* magazine and a family friend, wrote the book's foreword. In it, he praised Kennedy effusively: "If John Kennedy is characteristic of the younger generation—and I believe he is—many of us would be happy to have the destinies of this Republic handed over to this generation at once."[42]

Jack Kennedy was increasingly attracted to Churchill's view that Britain had made a potentially disastrous error in choosing to overlook Nazi Germany's growing military strength. He admired the heroic leader who guides his people with courage and wisdom in times of danger; for him, Winston Churchill clearly met that standard. In the concluding chapter, entitled "America's Lesson," he speculated further about the weakness and danger inherent in democracy being that people generally prefer peace and are reluctant to prepare for war when it is not obviously imminent; dictatorships, it is presumed, are much less concerned with public opinion. This was a reasonable enough assertion, and for one so young, Jack Kennedy demonstrated a remarkable levelheadedness about war and peace; he wrote: "We must always keep our armaments equal to our commitments."[43] He emphasized that point further in a letter to *The Harvard Crimson,* the student newspaper, in June of 1940, urging America to learn from England's bitter lesson.[44] In keeping with his belief in the power of the individual hero and perhaps influenced by his father's pessimism about the future in a world where totalitarian governments were on the march, Kennedy argued that "if a democracy cannot produce able leaders, its chance for survival is slight."[45] How to reconcile the promise and decencies of democracy with the often harsh realities of the world was a question Jack Kennedy would continue to ponder. Educating himself through travel, he toured the Middle East and Soviet Union, describing the latter as a "crude, backward, hopelessly bureaucratic country."[46] The outbreak of war in Europe in 1939 influenced his growing internationalism. At Harvard, his course of study was Government, with his specific field International Law and Relations; he also took many courses in economics and history, especially European history. When he graduated in 1940, aged 23, his father cabled him from London: "Two things I always knew about you one that you are smart two that you are a swell guy. Love Dad."[47]

Joseph Kennedy's diplomatic career came to an unhappy end. In an interview with a Boston newspaper in 1940, he managed to criticize Churchill for his drinking, King George VI for his stuttering, and Queen Elizabeth for her less than glamorous appearance, in addition to declaring the "death of democracy" in Britain.[48] Shortly afterwards, President Roosevelt, to the surprise of no one, accepted his resignation. The senior Kennedy was an isolationist, as were many Americans at the time, but as a diplomat he had the responsibility to be careful in his public statements. Joe had harbored plans to succeed Roosevelt as president if FDR chose not to run for a third term in 1940, despite not having been previously elected to any office. There was a recent precedent for such a thing, however. Herbert Hoover was elected president in 1928, never having held elective office, after a distinguished career in international business and disaster relief aid and nearly eight years as Secretary of Commerce. But Kennedy had damaged himself so badly, especially in light of England's heroism during the Battle of Britain and the subsequent unfolding of World War Two, that any talk of him seeking the presidency ended once and for all. Some of Kennedy's friends had tried to warn him, before he accepted the assignment to London, that despite his many talents and achievements he did not have the experience or personality for high-level diplomacy.[49] They were right. His failure was such that it is a wonder the family's reputation ever recovered.

Joe Kennedy and his family were not quite finished with politics, however. Over the years he had cultivated Democratic leaders in the cities, most of whom were Irish-American. When Roosevelt decided to break with tradition and run for a third term in 1940, his oldest son, Joseph Kennedy Jr., a delegate to the Massachusetts Democratic Convention at age 25 (almost certainly with his father's blessing), dissented by supporting James Farley, an Irish-American Catholic from New York. But with the publication of *Why England Slept*, Joe's younger brother was also beginning to establish himself within their highly competitive family—and beyond. Jack Kennedy had garnered national attention, on his own, for the first time. He had also demonstrated sounder judgment about important matters than his father. Despite his fragile health and the concerns of his parents and others that an inclination toward rebelliousness and laziness might thwart his potential, he was poised to take his place in the world.

CHAPTER **2**

"Tempered by War"

After Harvard, Jack Kennedy was uncertain about his future plans. Free of the financial concerns that most Americans faced, he thought first of continuing his education. Although he listed himself as pre-law in his senior yearbook at Harvard, his interest in that field proved fleeting. Joe Jr. was already at Harvard Law, so Jack, of course, first looked at Yale, but a recurrence of illness put those plans on hold as he was sent to the Mayo Clinic for treatment. He had continued to have serious digestive and stomach problems, and his back, never stable, was giving him more trouble. Partly in the hope that the good weather of California would benefit his health, Kennedy obtained permission in the fall of 1940 to audit classes at Stanford School of Business Administration, in Palo Alto, California. One strong impression he made at Stanford was that of a rich playboy from the East, tooling around campus in the green convertible he had bought with royalties from his book. He continued to have a very active social and dating life. But as always there was also a serious side and his interest in the war and foreign affairs remained high. One of his girlfriends noted: "he was fascinated with the news. He always turned it on in the car, on the radio. . . . He was intrigued by what was going on in the world."[1] Kennedy's time at Stanford does not fit neatly into the bigger story of his life; he seems to have been somewhat adrift, but not necessarily lost. Making friends easily as he always did, he spoke frequently to them of his family, especially his father. Stanford drew the wealthy and well heeled of the West Coast. Jack Kennedy, although part of the gaiety of that social scene, frequently reminded others that a war had begun and America would soon be in it. He did not do so out of despair but rather as a realist who saw the direction in which things were moving. Along the same lines, he registered with the U.S. government for the draft in the fall of 1940, and publicly supported the idea of a draft as necessary in light of possible U.S. entry into the conflict. Kennedy's action here was consistent with the theme of military preparedness he emphasized in *Why England Slept*. He also brought his knowledge of the situation in Europe to bear in advising his father on how to repair his damaged reputation following his resignation as the U.S. ambassador to Britain. He urged Joe to support President Roosevelt's program of military aid to Great Britain, known as Lend-Lease, which most isolationists vigorously opposed. The father was beginning to trust the son's judgment on such matters and was eventually won over to Jack's point of view.[2] In January of 1941 he gave a nationally broadcast radio address in which he came out in favor of Lend-Lease. He and Jack were of different minds on the crucial question of war and peace, though. Joe, an important figure in European diplomacy on the eve of the conflict, was charged in many quarters with being defeatist and unduly isolationist. His second oldest son had published a book urging the United States not to repeat the mistakes of Great Britain and in the end brought his father around to a more internationalist position, albeit too late to salvage the elder Kennedy's public career. But differences of opinion between the two, even on such important matters, were not divisive or personal. Their common goal remained, as Joe demanded, unity within the family and a collective effort to advance its interests and reputation in the wider world. Joe Kennedy could ask a very great deal of his children. But at the same time he managed, as one observer of the family saw it, to do so "without ever breaking their spirits."[3]

Jack remained close to his family while out west, traveling with his mother and sister Eunice to South America. Eunice was four years younger than Jack and became a fierce protector of her brother. Even closer to Jack in age was Rosemary, born in 1918. Rosemary's mental and social capacities were not at the level of the other children and in her early twenties she began to show signs of emotional problems, to the point that the family grew deeply concerned. On one ghastly occasion she even attacked her elderly grandfather, Honey Fitz.[4] Whether or not she suffered from mental retardation, as the phrase then had it, her family believed that she was not developing into a functioning adult. Some of her rage and anger may also have stemmed from her frustration at not keeping up with her dynamic siblings. Although the family, including Jack, generally treated Rosemary with kindness and respect, it was becoming clearer that she most likely would not grow out of her disabilities. At the urging of Joe Sr., in the fall of 1941 the Kennedys took the dramatic step of having a radical new surgery known as a lobotomy performed on Rosemary. It was a success in that it quieted her rages and wanderings, but also a calamity in that it took away virtually all of her personality. At the suggestion of Richard Cushing, Auxiliary Bishop of Boston, Rosemary was sent to a Catholic convent in Wisconsin, where according to the Kennedy family she would work with retarded children at the institution. In fact, she herself was a patient. Rose Kennedy later said that Rosemary's operation and subsequent placement in the Wisconsin convent was "the first of the tragedies that were to befall us."[5] Some of the Kennedy women, especially Rose and Eunice, would visit her there over the years; her father and brothers did not.

In the wider world, Joe Kennedy's biggest fear was that the United States would be drawn into the war, and with it his family; this became a reality with the Japanese attack on Pearl Harbor in December of 1941. The Kennedy family would come to learn more of what Joe Kennedy had eerily prophesied when he said of his large family that he and Rose "had given nine hostages to fortune." Even before the Japanese attack on Hawaii, Joe Jr. had successfully volunteered for the Navy, but for Jack, with his ongoing health problems, it would not be so easy to enter the military. Due to his persistent back, stomach, and other ailments and his family's connections to the government, Kennedy could have almost certainly avoided military service altogether. This would have been in keeping with his father's decision to remain a civilian during World War One 25 years earlier. But Jack was single, without a wife and small children, unlike his father in 1917, and, as he had already demonstrated by his writings and his public support of the draft, he did not share his father's isolationism. He was also looking to his future and how the war might shape it. As he told his friend LeMoyne Billings, "they will never take me into the army—and yet if I don't [serve] it will look quite bad."[6]

His initial effort to enter military service failed when he could not pass the Army's physical exam. As usual, his first instinct had been not to follow his older brother, who had joined the Navy. He tried that next, but the Navy also turned him down for health reasons. Jack then used his father's influence and willingness to help his children advance (although Joe was not enthusiastic about his son enlisting) to arrange for him to pass, despite his medical history, a physical and he entered the Navy as an officer in August of 1941. At the end of October he was assigned to the Office of Naval Intelligence in Washington, having been commissioned an ensign. Such an assignment would presumably keep him out of harm's way, which probably explains why Joe Kennedy was willing to arrange for Jack to join this branch of the Navy. Kennedy's first assignment was a desk job in Washington, where he was able to maintain his usual brisk social life. His sister Kathleen (Kick) worked for a newspaper there, and by then she was an important part of Jack's world.

It was Kick who introduced her brother to one of her colleagues at the *Washington Herald*, Inga Arvad, a Danish woman four years older than Jack and separated from her second husband after divorcing her first. The two almost immediately began an intense love affair; it became perhaps the deepest of Jack's life. But she would not have been easily accepted by the Kennedys as a potential wife for Jack. In addition to being twice married and not a Catholic, Inga had met leading Nazis, even interviewing Adolf Hitler at the Berlin Olympics in 1936. By the time she met Jack, Inga had already drawn the attention of agents at the Federal Bureau of Investigation, who feared she might be, of all things, a spy for Nazi Germany. That she was now dating an officer in Naval Intelligence raised their suspicions. After Pearl Harbor, the United States declared war on Japan and finally entered the global conflict. The federal government jettisoned its relatively easygoing pre-war security procedures and moved to tighten them at every turn. Among the targets was the striking Washington-based Danish journalist with apparent connections to the Nazi leadership. This, together with Joe's (and presumably Rose's) strong displeasure at their son's seemingly serious intentions toward Inga Arvad, made their relationship increasingly difficult. The romance hit the Washington gossip columns, though without mention of Inga's fleeting connection with Hitler. Even so, the family, in the aftermath of the damaging statements Joe had made while ambassador, could not afford anything remotely like a Nazi scandal. Ensign Kennedy was immediately transferred to a naval station at Charleston, South Carolina; although the official records do not reflect it, Joe Kennedy may have maneuvered to have his son moved out of Washington and away from Inga. Inga visited Jack in Charleston, but the two eventually agreed, under continued pressure from Joe, to end their relationship.[7]

With the United States now fully engaged in the war, Jack Kennedy sought to escape life at a desk for duty at sea. This was despite a back that gave him so much trouble when he first entered the Navy that he had to sleep on a piece of wood. A position on the front lines seemed unlikely. With his various ailments and his family connections, Jack could have remained stateside, had that been his goal. But Joe Jr. had already earned his wings at flight school as a naval aviator and many of Jack's friends were either in combat or preparing for it. Jack had never shown a lack of physical courage, on the athletic field or anywhere else. He was also an enthusiastic supporter of the U.S. war effort, following its progress with great interest, exulting when news arrived of American victories over the Japanese in the Pacific. And Kennedy also understood that his ambitions were in some way tied to proving himself in war, poor health notwithstanding. While his father's political hopes remained primarily invested in Joe Jr., Jack had his own hopes for the future. He had confided to Inga Arvad his desire to enter politics, with the presidency itself as the goal. Despite his uneven academic record, his struggles to remain healthy, and his skepticism of institutions and authority, he had a genuine confidence in his own abilities and an abiding, if not always obvious, determination to make his mark on the world. Although Kennedy had endured more than his share of health problems since early childhood, he and his family refused to view him as defined by those struggles. Outwardly easygoing, with a casual attitude toward many things, he also had, as Inga Arvad put it, "two backbones. Your own and your father's."[8]

Kennedy continued to use his family's influence to advance in the Navy. Despite his reservations about his son seeing active duty, Joe saw to it that Jack gained assignment to a naval base near Chicago to learn how to command and operate motor torpedo boats, or PT boats, as they were commonly known. Naval men from the upper class of U.S. society, especially those who had sailed growing up, as Jack Kennedy had, were drawn to the PTs. They offered independence, excitement, and a chance for heroism. For anyone with a troublesome back, however, these "Bucking Broncos," as they were known, were far from ideal.[9] Even so, Kennedy did well in training and made a positive impression on his superiors, but was then transferred to Rhode Island to become a PT boat instructor. This was not the path to glory that Jack Kennedy envisioned for himself. He thus enlisted his grandfather, Honey Fitz, to intercede with U.S. Senator David Walsh of Massachusetts, chair of the Naval Affairs Committee, on his behalf. Senator Walsh, along with Joe Kennedy (who perhaps did not understand the dangers of such an assignment), helped to get Jack the command of a PT boat in the Pacific in early 1943.[10] In a way that showed the moral unity of the American people in World War Two, and Jack Kennedy's own commitment to the conflict, he used his family's considerable influence not to stay out of harm's way but, as one naval officer put it, "to get into combat."[11]

By the middle of 1943, the U.S. Navy, Marine Corps, and Army were grinding their way across the Pacific, pushing the Japanese slowly back toward their home islands. Kennedy, now a Lieutenant Junior Grade, had been assigned to command a PT boat, the 109, and its crew of 12 junior officers and sailors. The 109 was part of a large squad of PT boats that was deployed for aggressive operations against the Japanese Navy in the vicinity of the Solomon Islands in the South Pacific, northeast of Australia. Jack made a strong impression in the Navy on those who knew him best. His fellow officers and sailors found him engaging, warm, and ambitious; possessing charisma and confidence but not the pompous manner that can accompany those traits. Yet at the same time they noted a certain shyness and reserve. Jack wrote long letters back home about the war to family and influential people he or his father knew. He also discussed in depth the politics of the state and the locales of the other sailors and officers. One naval man said of Jack: "it was written all over the sky that he was going to be something big. He just had that charisma. You could just tell by his nature, by the way people would stop by and visit with him."[12] Another said of him years later, "There was an aura about him that I've never seen duplicated in anybody else. He was an extraordinary fellow."[13] Freed from direct comparisons with his brother, some of his best qualities became apparent to those around him. His casual air toward some naval regulations, however, was more appreciated by the men under his command than by his superiors. Far from his family and from the immediate privileges of his upbringing, in situations he had never previously faced, Jack Kennedy was showing that he could adapt and survive in difficult circumstances and lead other men in serious matters.

The PT boats, despite the heroic aura around them, proved not very useful militarily due to poor design and antiquated weaponry. Kennedy himself saw their limitations in the Pacific War: "The glamour of the PTs just isn't except to the outsider."[14] Jack was not experienced with such boats and neither were the young men under his command. This mattered little, though, and the PT boats were thrown into the fray, charged with tracking down and sinking Japanese destroyers. In early August 1943, Kennedy's crew and 14 other PT boats were sent into combat. A Japanese ship, the *Amagiri,* smashed into PT 109 in the darkness of night. Two of the thirteen men on board PT 109 were killed outright, disappearing in the chaos of the collision, never to be seen again. Lt. Kennedy, who barely missed being crushed to death by the destroyer, scrambled to save the lives of his remaining men and his own; he later said of the moment of impact, with his usual detachment: "this is how it feels to be killed."[15] The survival chances of the remaining crew, sent out without radar, looked slim. Some were injured, including Kennedy, who aggravated his already fragile back during the collision. Injured and swallowing gas as he swam, Kennedy led the survivors to an island where they could avoid the enemy, pulling along one badly burned sailor, Patrick McMahon. After reaching a safe island, he risked his own life by swimming out into the ocean to look for help. At the PT base camp, the working assumption was that Kennedy and his crew had been lost. Mass was said for the crew at the base and the Kennedy family on Cape Cod were officially informed by the Navy that Jack was missing. Back in the South Pacific, Kennedy and his crew met up with some island men who knew the area well. Jack wrote a message on a coconut that the islanders brought to the base island of the PT boats. A successful rescue followed; Lt. Kennedy had improvised, led, and willed his surviving men to safety after a harrowing week, forging a lifelong bond of loyalty between them.

But despite the leadership qualities and courage which Kennedy undeniably showed after the encounter with the Japanese destroyer, some questions loom. The Navy decorated him for valor in the rescue of his men, awarding him a Purple Heart, among other citations. The collision between enemy vessels that night might be understood as a random event, one of the fortunes of war.[16] Furthermore, Kennedy's superiors did not devise an effective battle plan, which contributed to the fog of war that enveloped Kennedy and his men. It was, however, the only recorded incident of its type in the Pacific theater, raising the possibility that Kennedy, as commanding officer, might have been at fault. The Lieutenant had not put his ship and crew in the ideal position before coming into the proximity of the Japanese destroyer: two of his men were asleep, two others lying down, and only one engine was in gear. In this regard, he was not following proper procedure for combat; that is to say Kennedy and his crew were caught by surprise by the much larger Japanese ship.

After recovering, at least partially, from his ordeal, Kennedy took command of another PT boat, seeking to repay the Japanese Navy for what he saw as his humiliation at its hands. He had earned the right to go home, due to his injuries and in accordance with the Navy's tradition that shipwrecked officers be allowed an honorable discharge.[17] Remaining on active duty in the South Pacific is an indication that Kennedy was not satisfied with his performance, notwithstanding his valiant efforts to secure rescue for his men. Kennedy later looked back with his ironic sense of humor when asked how he had become a hero: "it was involuntary, they sank my boat." But it was the courageous part of the story that his father made sure was publicized in U.S. newspapers and magazines and which later became a central part of Kennedy's biography.

Jack Kennedy was changed by his experience in World War Two, as were millions around the world, especially the young. He had followed the principles he articulated while a college student, that democracy and Western civilization were worth defending. Even before Pearl Harbor he had volunteered for military service, got himself to the front despite health concerns, and even continued to fight after the smashing of PT 109. If he ever had any illusions about the romance of war, he lost them forever in the South Pacific. While he continued to believe in the righteousness of the Allies' cause and the necessity of U.S. involvement in the war, he saw the disconnect between its stateside enthusiasts and those overseas fighting for it. Nearly all the men Kennedy served with wanted to meet their responsibilities to country and comrades. But their overriding goal was to return home safely, in one piece, to the family, friends, and lives they had left behind. And never one to accept authority without questioning it, after all he had seen the young naval officer also came to view the senior officers above him with some skepticism.

The Kennedy family rejoiced at the news of Jack's rescue. On leave at home at the time, Joe Jr. was also relieved, of course, but at the same time felt jealous and fearful that his younger brother was becoming the family favorite. He became upset by the focus on him and vowed that he would match, at least, Jack's exploits. Returning to duty, he volunteered for a highly dangerous secret operation, even though he had already flown enough missions to earn an honorable discharge. Flying a plane packed full of explosives toward German V-1 rocket sites in Belgium (an early version of cruise missiles and drones) the plan was for him and his co-pilot to parachute out before the plane reached its target. Before embarking, he said to a friend, "if I don't come back, tell my father, despite our differences, that I love him very much." Mistakes made by high command made the flight even riskier than it should have been, although that was not known until much later. As the plane approached the point where the crew were to parachute out, transferring control to those who would remotely guide the bomb-packed plane into the V-1 base, it blew up in a massive explosion, killing the two aviators instantly. The news, when it reached the Kennedy family on Cape Cod, was a blow beyond words; Joe, who had placed such hope in and made such great demands on his eldest son, never fully recovered from the death, telling one associate that he thought of it every morning.[18] During the presidential campaign of 1944, Joe, referring to President Roosevelt, said to vice-presidential candidate Harry Truman, "What are you doing campaigning for that crippled son of a bitch who killed my son Joe?"[19] Even years later, when Joe Jr.'s name came up in conversation at a lunch with friends, he suddenly burst into tears and was wracked by sobs. One friend remarked of the impact on Joe: "it was one of the most severe shocks … that I have ever seen registered on a human being."[20] Rose, also devastated, took solace in her Catholic faith, but her grief too would never fully subside. On one occasion she broke down in public while speaking of her lost son. For a family that prided itself on stoicism and maintaining a strong public face, this public grieving revealed the depth of the wound. Jack, home recuperating from a back operation, went for a long solitary walk on the beach after hearing the news. He later gathered and edited a series of recollections about his brother entitled *As We Remember Joe,* published privately. Like countless other families across the United States and around the world in the 1930s and 1940s, the Kennedys, despite their wealth, power, and glamour, had suffered the anguish of losing one of their own to the violence of war.

As he recuperated from his wartime injuries and illnesses, Jack Kennedy pondered his future. He was educated, wealthy, and quite interested in and informed about the world scene as war began to give way to peace. Although still in his twenties, his overall health was poor. He suffered from severe back problems, made worse by his service in the Navy, and by chronic problems with his stomach and digestive and adrenal systems. He had been taking experimental steroids to help with his back for several years; they in turn apparently contributed to his contracting a form of Addison's disease, in which the body has a lessened ability to fight disease and infection. This put a cloud over this future, and the Kennedys were concerned that Jack's life span would be considerably shorter than the norm. Even so, he accepted an offer from the Hearst newspaper chain (his father had suggested the idea to a contact there) to cover the initial United Nations conference in San Francisco in the spring of 1945. While enjoying the nightlife in San Francisco, he also worked hard, filing 17 stories over the span of a few weeks under headings such as "Serviceman Looks at Conference." Their main theme was the gradual deterioration of the U.S.-Soviet alliance. Kennedy saw fairly clearly what the immediate Soviet goals were after the war in Europe, writing in the same week Nazi Germany surrendered: "The Russians have a much greater fear of a German come-back than we do. They are therefore going to make their Western defenses secure. No governments hostile to Russia will be permitted along her borders. They feel they have earned the right to security. They mean to have it, come what may."[21] Kennedy had no illusions about Soviet intentions, perceiving clearly that national security, even more than Marxist-Leninist ideology, was at the heart of the U.S.S.R.'s post-war aims. At the same time, he understood that the wartime alliance between the West and the Soviet Union would be difficult to maintain now that their common enemy, Nazi Germany, had been vanquished. He did not, however, think that a new war was imminent, noting privately: "I think the clash with Russia will be greatly postponed."[22]

The Hearst newspapers, satisfied with Kennedy's work, sent Kennedy to Europe in the summer of 1945, directing him to report on the aftermath of the war he had fought in on the other side of the world. He saw the devastation resulting from the conflict, especially in England and Germany, and it added to his education in war and peace. Kennedy met many world leaders, and became reacquainted with members of the British aristocracy he had met before the war. Among those he met in Germany were General Dwight Eisenhower, whose mixture of great achievement and humility he noted; these encounters only added to his growing belief that he too might play an important role in the emerging postwar world. Kennedy's eye for politics was evident in his dispatches from England. He raised the possibility that Winston Churchill and the Conservative Party, despite their wartime leadership, would be defeated in the 1945 elections; they were. Continuing to fight his weak back and a severe case of malaria, he found himself at the center of action in Europe, attending the Potsdam Conference, visiting devastated Berlin with prominent U.S. officials, and making a tour of Hitler's mountain retreat in Bavaria. His chief interests were the domestic politics of nations (including Ireland, which he visited for the first time), and the international scene.

Now that the war was winding down, however, the question of Kennedy's future loomed, health problems and all. His flair for writing, and his dispassionate approach to issues and events might have made him an accomplished journalist or perhaps a professor of government or history. Jack, however, was not necessarily in training for a career as a journalist, especially now that his older brother was deceased and Joe's enormous political ambitions for his family were now focused on him. Unlike his grandfather however, Boston was to be the beginning, not the endpoint, for the political career that Joe Kennedy had in mind for Jack.

Was this Jack's plan as well? Joe Jr., the family had assumed, was the obvious one to run for elective office, with his extroverted personality, high energy and drive. His sudden death took away that possibility. Joe Sr. perhaps underestimated his second son's potential for politics, thinking Jack more suited by temperament for a life of writing or teaching. But while the young Jack Kennedy has often been described as shy or reserved, he also possessed charisma, intelligence, and ambition, and a confidence of his own—the latter quality of a quieter sort than his brother's. Jack was beginning to feel pressure from his father to enter politics, to be sure. He said to a friend at the time: "I'll be back here with Dad trying to parlay a lost PT boat and a bad back into a political advantage."[23] As a veteran returning from war and entering public life, Jack joined a tradition that went back to George Washington and the earliest days of the republic. Other young veterans around the country were doing the same, among them Richard Nixon, a young attorney in Southern California, who ran for Congress in 1946; Joseph McCarthy, a former Democrat and war veteran elected to the Senate from Wisconsin as a Republican; and naval veteran Gerald Ford, who won a House seat two years later in Grand Rapids, Michigan. Kennedy's decision to enter politics as a standard bearer himself ("The Candidate" became his tongue-in-cheek nickname among intimates) was shaped by several factors: coaxing from his father, a sense of obligation to his family to replace his fallen brother, and his own ambitions and eagerness to play an active role in the world. His interest in writing remained, but ultimately he did not see it as his life's work, saying to a friend, "A reporter is *reporting* what happened. He is not *making* it happen."[24] Service in the Navy had deepened his already considerable interest in politics and world affairs, making newly apparent to him the seriousness of life.

Boston, Massachusetts was the natural political base for John Fitzgerald Kennedy. Although the Kennedys had maintained their residence in suburban New York City until the 1940s, and bought an ocean-front estate in Florida in the early thirties, they had also kept their summer home on Cape Cod in Massachusetts. Boston itself, however, had never been home to Jack in that he had never lived in the city proper. In the fall of 1945 Jack gave a public address at a fundraising dinner there that caught the eye of some local politicians. For his part, Joe made sure to keep the Kennedy name before the voters of Boston, making a high-profile financial donation. He also took a job that allowed him to travel around the city and state, meeting key leaders, with an eye to helping his son's fledgling campaign. Most importantly, he helped persuade Boston political legend James Michael Curley, hugely popular with many of the city's Irish Catholics but now past his political prime, into forgoing re-election in Massachusetts' Eleventh Congressional District and to run once again for Mayor of Boston. There was talk of Jack running for Lt. Governor of Massachusetts, but with his interest in international affairs and the world scene, a seat in Congress at the dawn of the Cold War was more appealing. The Eleventh was the most Democratic district in the state; Honey Fitz had represented part of it in Congress at the turn of the twentieth century. Although Brookline, Jack's birthplace and boyhood home, was just outside the border, it did encompass East Boston, where Joe was raised, the North End, home of the Fitzgeralds and Honey Fitz's old political base. The district contained a considerable number of working-class and poor neighborhoods, as well as Cambridge, home of Harvard University. There was a significant Catholic population, especially Irish-Americans and Italian-Americans, along with a small group of African-Americans, most of whom lived in a Cambridge neighborhood. In the mid-1940s the economy of Boston and indeed much of New England was not flourishing. Boston's seaport lagged behind other major cities on the East Coast, and workers in New England textile factories faced the loss of their jobs as businesses moved to the South in search of cheaper, non-union labor.[25]

As Jack's bid for the Democratic nomination in the district began, an old Boston political hand and Kennedy cousin, Joe Kane, coined its slogan: "The New Generation Offers a Leader." The Kennedy campaign also promoted Jack as a "Fighting Conservative," invoking his service in the South Pacific by mailing voters copies of an article about his heroism that had appeared in a leading magazine. It also appealed to the traditional, religious ethos of many voters in his district. The campaign was comprised of veterans of Boston politics, with ties to the Kennedys and Fitzgeralds, as well as newcomers drawn to it by their prior connections to Jack and his appeal to their sense of public service. The Democratic Party in Boston and surrounding towns was not a very strong institution. The Kennedys shrewdly built their own organization, one that came into being solely for the purpose of electing John F. Kennedy to Congress. As one Boston politician saw it, the Kennedys were in effect building their own political party of sorts, even as Jack ran in the Democratic Party's primary. Joe Kennedy, not wishing to overshadow his son, worked behind the scenes. He did, however, spend a part of his fortune to ensure that Jack would win the Democratic nomination in a crowded field, which meant near-certain election to Congress in November. The official campaign manager, Mark

Dalton, a naval veteran like Jack and a young lawyer, said later that Joe was the true mastermind of the campaign, and undoubtedly the financial power behind it.[26] The field of ten candidates included a woman, Catherine Falvey, a rarity in the politics of the 1940s; she (and others) dismissed Kennedy as "the poor little rich kid."[27] Jack Kennedy was also accused at various times of being a carpetbagger, and of being too inexperienced, too skinny, too sickly, and even too British. It was a long list, but none of the charges gained much traction in the face of the many advantages of the Kennedy campaign. The "carpetbagger" charge against him was potentially the most serious, but the deep roots of both the Kennedy and Fitzgerald families in Boston made the allegation look somewhat petty, especially against a decorated war veteran. One of his older, more experienced opponents said that if Jack endorsed him he would take him on his staff in Washington should he be elected. Most young men still in their twenties seeking a career in politics would probably have jumped at this opportunity, but neither the candidate nor his father were looking for such a conventional way for Jack to climb onto the political ladder.

The 1946 campaign was not without its mistakes; at one scheduled event in Cambridge, after hundreds of invitations had been sent out, not one potential voter appeared. But as Mark Dalton said, "We were very disappointed, but John Kennedy was not discouraged."[28] Jack was not a natural campaigner but he overcame a certain shyness and reserve with determination and resolve. Dalton later reflected: "He was always shy. He drove himself into this. It must have been a tremendous effort of will."[29] His early speeches were not memorable; he tended to do better when answering questions and speaking to voters in small groups. His early rhetorical style was unadorned, especially by the standards of more flamboyant Boston politicians such as James Michael Curley or Jack's grandfather, Honey Fitz. He usually won over his audiences with his self-deprecating humor and infectious grin, matched by a genuine seriousness. At one campaign stop, addressing a crowd of Gold Star Mothers (women who had lost a child in wartime), Kennedy said quietly that he had some understanding of their grief, as his mother was also a Gold Star recipient. And while Kennedy was not a conventional extrovert in the political sense, neither did his basic personality hamper him while campaigning. Dave Powers, who signed on with Kennedy in 1946 and remained with him thereafter, described him then as "aggressively shy."[30]

The focus of his campaign (after an initial emphasis on the post-war scene in Europe, which generated little interest in the constituency) was the economic concerns of those he hoped to represent in Washington. Although astounded that the emerging Cold War rivalry between the United States and the Soviet Union was not of greater importance to voters, he recognized that reality and shifted his attention to questions of economic security. As the weeks wore on, Jack became a stronger candidate. Not having a day job he was able to campaign for hours on end. He shook hands at factory gates both morning and evening, visited barbershops, fire stations, grocery stores—wherever he could find potential voters.[31] At night there were house parties across the district, dozens of them, and short speeches to various community groups. The hard work took its toll on Jack's health and he eventually collapsed after a parade, his shortness of breath and other symptoms frightening those who tried to help him. He recovered, but healthy men in their twenties generally do not fall ill in that way; it was a sign of the Addison's disease that later plagued him.

Jack's campaign in 1946 also included his family; Rose, herself well known in much of the district, hosted the first of the Kennedy campaign receptions for women. Jack's dynamic younger sister Eunice and Rose were especially important in helping draw the votes of women, as Catherine Falvey was one of the more experienced candidates in the race, having twice been elected to the Massachusetts legislature. Jack Kennedy proved highly popular among much of the district's Irish-American community, with its long history of electing their own to office: his family names were major assets. Kennedy's political debut also hearkened back to an even older tradition in American politics, perhaps best exemplified by Thomas Jefferson, whom the historian Richard Hofstadter styled "The Aristocrat as Democrat."[32] He joined a long line of wealthy, well-born individuals who entered politics as representatives of common people.

John F. Kennedy also confronted the question of race in America in his first run for office. In his campaign literature he commended the service and valor of Americans of all races who had fought for their country. It followed from that, Kennedy continued, that a nation that had stood up to the evils of Nazism and its racist ideologies must guarantee to protect the rights of all its citizens. And with the Cold War emerging, the United States could not afford to fall behind the communists on the matter of racial justice. Kennedy also offered his support for reform measures such as the elimination of the poll tax in southern states, often used to keep African-Americans from voting, and for new laws to guard against racial discrimination in business.[33] While not a priority, Kennedy's interest in winning the votes of black voters showed his campaign's thoroughness, his awareness of the potential importance of the issue of race in postwar America, and the need to overcome the legacy of racial discrimination that was alive in the North as well as the South.

On Primary Day in June 1946, John F. Kennedy won the Democratic nomination with just over 40 percent of the vote, an impressive showing in a crowded field. His strategy of campaigning hard across the whole district (which included not only parts of Boston but also several other cities and towns), in the expectation that the other candidates would mainly win votes in their home communities, had worked. In November, despite being all but assured of victory, Kennedy continued to campaign vigorously, as the Republican Party was poised to make major gains in New England and around the country in the first postwar election. It did, but that was no matter in the Eleventh Congressional District of Massachusetts as Kennedy won easily and prepared to move to Washington to take his seat in the House of Representatives. The United States and Soviet Union were at that moment seeing their wartime alliance continue to deteriorate and turn into a much more adversarial relationship.

John F. Kennedy was not interested in a long career in the House of Representatives (the "people's house," as its champions like to think of it) where his grandfather had served. His interest from the start was beyond his own district, even though he and his staff established and maintained strong constituent services. Kennedy was himself not much interested in listening at length to the problems of those he represented, but he hired people who ably served him in that task. Jack Kennedy's attitude in the House was not that of a wide-eyed newcomer. He brought his casual attitude with him to Congress. Even on his first day he was deliberately late to a meeting called by John McCormack of Massachusetts, a powerful leader among the House Democrats. Often walking onto the House floor in ill-fitting, even sloppy clothes, he was so youthful in appearance that he was mistaken for a Congressional page. His attendance for votes and committee hearings was less than stellar; his attentions were often elsewhere, including on the enjoyments that any young, rich man might experience. He lived in a rented house in the historic Georgetown district of Washington, with housekeepers and cooks attending to his needs. Even though he might appear to be a dilettante, however, Kennedy could on occasion demonstrate seriousness and independence. In his first year in Congress he was the only member of the Massachusetts House delegation not to sign a petition asking that Boston Mayor James Michael Curley, in prison for corruption, be pardoned and released. The Kennedys and Curley had been political rivals for decades, but Jack sought to distance himself from the old-school ways of Boston politics. In another instance, he criticized leaders of the American Legion on the floor of the House for their opposition to federally subsidized housing for veterans, which Kennedy supported. These remarks generated some intense condemnation of his alleged slandering of a venerable patriotic organization.

In the House of Representatives, Kennedy supported efforts by the liberal wing of the Democratic Party and President Truman to protect and even extend New Deal policies. He voted against the successful Republican-led effort to override Truman's veto of the Taft-Hartley bill, which organized labor strongly opposed. And while in the main he did agree with the goals of unions—one major labor group gave him a perfect score for his Congressional voting record—in private he conceded that unions could act selfishly at times and without regard to the national interest, as he understood it. But his voting record and public statements showed clearly that Kennedy represented the economic concerns of most of his constituents, working-class people who had supported the New Deal and wanted to see it preserved in American life and law. A seat on the influential Committee on Education and Labor (apparently secured with his father's help) and another on the Committee on Veterans Affairs gave him platforms that were of great importance to many of those he represented in Congress. Kennedy also encountered the emerging issue of civil rights for African-Americans, supporting bills to abolish the poll tax for racial equality in employment law and for home rule for the District of Columbia, a city with a large African-American population.[34] His politics here were not rooted so much in a sense of the injustice of racial discrimination as in his understanding that the fight for racial equality was part of the larger Cold War rivalry with the Soviet Union.

And it was foreign policy that Kennedy was primarily interested in. In March of 1947, less than three months into his first term in Congress, he spoke at the University of North Carolina in Chapel Hill, where he declared his support for President Truman's call for $400 million dollars of aid to be sent to Greece and turkey to help them rebuff internal threats from groups sympathetic to communism. Placing the issue in historical terms, Kennedy said this was not a radical departure from the best traditions of U.S. foreign policy but "a new interpretation of the Monroe Doctrine," one which he claimed gave "the Greeks an opportunity to rebuild their country; and to the Turks an opportunity to maintain their security."[35] He also supported the ambitious Marshall Plan, through which the United States invested heavily in restoring Western Europe's economic vitality. Joe Kennedy, in contrast, still held to his isolationist views and opposed the thrust of postwar U.S. foreign policy. Congressman Kennedy accepted the basic premise of the Cold War from the American perspective, which held that there was an international communist conspiracy, centered in Moscow, to spread Marxist-Leninism across the globe and eventually destroy the Western capitalist democracies. His internationalist view of foreign policy, the heavily Catholic ethos of his district, and his own inclinations as the son of a wealthy man contributed to his anti-communism. The House of Representatives is not the institution in which U.S. foreign policy is primarily crafted, but even so, Congressman Kennedy made his mark in this area. In 1951 he took an extensive trip to the Middle East and Asia, taking in

Vietnam, or French Indochina, as it was usually called in the United States. Soon after landing at the Saigon airport, Jack and his brother Bobby and sister Patricia were greeted by gunfire from the Vietminh guerrillas and were told it was too dangerous to venture far beyond the city limits.[36] Jack spoke to diplomats and reporters about the situation on the ground and left Southeast Asia highly skeptical of the United States aiding France in its bid to re-impose colonial rule in the region. In a radio address on his return to Boston, Kennedy told his listeners: "in Indochina we have allied ourselves to the desperate efforts of the French regime to hang on to the remnants of an Empire."[37]

Maintaining his longstanding interest in Europe, Kennedy traveled there in the summer of his first year in the House as part of a fact-finding trip related to the Marshall Plan. He visited Ireland for the second time, vacationing with his sister Kathleen at a castle and touring the town of New Ross, in County Wexford, the home of their Irish ancestors. Jack thoroughly enjoyed visiting his Irish cousins and connecting with his ancestry. During his campaign the year before his political opponents had claimed that the Kennedys' wealth and power made them something other than Irish-American, that there was something almost British about them. Jack Kennedy himself had a lot of admiration for the British aristocracy. He especially identified with those nineteenth-century British who enjoyed a rollicking social life but were also serious men who took their turn serving in government. In Boston as well as in the British Isles the Kennedys were regarded, with good reason, as aristocrats. Their wealth and political influence gave them that aura. But there was no denying the humbler realities of Irish and Irish-American history that had helped to shape the family, and Jack Kennedy understood this. His latest European trip did not end well, however: he became seriously ill and was officially diagnosed with a malfunctioning of the adrenal system commonly known as Addison's disease. Its immediate symptoms include fatigue and nausea; he had suffered from the disease's effects for years. In the past Addison's disease had usually been fatal, but new drug treatments meant that by the late 1940s its sufferers had a better chance of survival. Still, it was a serious illness that threatened to considerably shorten Kennedy's life.

Jack and his sister Kick remained close, despite her living overseas; he visited her and her lover Peter Fitzwilliam, a wealthy, Protestant (and married) Englishman whom she hoped to eventually marry, despite the strong objections of her mother Rose. However, the couple was killed in a plane crash in France in 1948. Jack learned of their deaths while at his home in Georgetown; a friend with him at the time remembered how he was moved to tears by the news. Barely into his thirties, Jack Kennedy had now lost the two siblings to whom he was closest. His grief over Kick's death was real and long-lasting. But so was his determination, born in part out of his own uncertain health and the deaths of his brother and sister, to squeeze the most out of life—to live each day, as he once told a friend, as if it was his last one on earth. This may be what gave him something that those who knew him well over the years saw as a "heightened sense of being," one seemingly unique to him. And in the winter of 1950 he was also profoundly moved by a long conversation with his aging grandfather about the joys and satisfactions of a life in politics. Earlier the same day he had been among the thousands who waited in line in the cold to express his sympathies to Boston's Mayor James Michael Curley, two of whose grown children had died of natural causes within hours of each other. Kennedy was struck by both Curley's courage in facing his anguish and the genuine outpouring of feeling of the people of Boston for their mayor. These two venerable, aging figures had shown him something of the deeper possibilities of politics, ones that went beyond structures and rote formalities. This helped to renew in him a commitment to the profession toward which he often felt a certain ambivalence.[38]

As a young politician, Kennedy's most admirable traits were intellectual curiosity and a strong streak of independence. One family friend remembers him as a young congressman at Washington cocktail parties, not making idle chatter but off in a corner talking intensely with someone who knew more about an issue that interested him than he did.[39] He was also not afraid to challenge powerful interests groups that wielded great influence within the Democratic Party, including organized labor. During his first term in the House, he went after Harold Christoffel, an organizer with the United Auto Workers. Christoffel had been instrumental in a strike that shut down a defense plant outside Milwaukee in 1941. Displaying an aggressive anti-communism, Kennedy took the lead in charging that Christoffel had denied under oath before the Education and Labor Committee that he was in fact a Communist. He was eventually convicted of perjury and spent time in federal prison. Kennedy not only supported President Truman's foreign policy regarding the Soviet Union, he saw the emerging Cold War as having a domestic front too. This attitude was consistent with his father's views on communism and the Catholic Church's adamant opposition to it, as well as the thinking of most of his working-class constituents in Boston. John F. Kennedy described himself early in his political career as a "Massachusetts Democrat," a term that had a different connotation then to that which it took on later. In the middle of the twentieth century, Massachusetts, including its Democratic Party, was culturally conservative. Historically, the state had been Republican since the Civil War era. Much of the Democratic Party in the state was Catholic, especially since the arrival of Irish immigrants in the 1840s. A key turning point in the political history of the commonwealth occurred in 1948, the year in which Congressman Kennedy was unopposed for re-election. President Harry Truman won Massachusetts and the Democratic Party made major gains in the state legislative races, enough to allow them to elect Thomas P. "Tip" O'Neill of Boston as the first Democratic Speaker of the Massachusetts House. Democrats had benefitted that year from an increased turnout by Catholic voters, encouraged by their clergy to vote against repealing a ban on doctors informing their patients about artificial birth control.[40]

The postwar era was marked by a certain tension between Catholics and liberals. Paul Blanshard, a writer for *The Nation*, published *American Freedom and Catholic Power* in the late 1940s. Blanchard saw Catholics—and he singled out Boston's Irish Catholics in particular—and their connection to the papacy as a dangerous threat to traditional American values and freedoms as he understood them. Congressman Kennedy supported federal aid to parochial or religious schools, most of which were Catholic, especially in Massachusetts. And although in political agreement with much of the liberalism of President Truman's Fair Deal program in the late 1940s, he held himself aloof from actual liberals. He never joined the Americans for Democratic Action, an organization created by leading liberals in 1947 in support of the New Deal tradition and in opposition to communism, saying, "I never felt comfortable with those people."[41] In 1950, the University of Notre Dame, the nation's leading Catholic university, awarded Kennedy an honorary doctorate, citing him for his "forthright assertion of the truth and condemnation of error."[42] He also presented well-known, anti-communist Richard Nixon, a Republican with whom Kennedy was friendly when they served together in the House, with a campaign donation from Joe Kennedy when Nixon ran for the U.S. Senate in 1950. Nixon's opponent was a left-wing Democrat, Helen Gahagan Douglas. The Kennedys, father and son, clearly preferred Nixon in the U.S. Senate at that moment in the Cold War, party affiliations notwithstanding. Although supportive of much of President Truman's agenda both at home and abroad, Jack also criticized him at times for not being vigilant enough against the communist threat either internally or overseas.

Kennedy had a safe seat in the House of Representatives and might have looked forward to serving there for many years, perhaps rising in the ranks of leadership, as did John McCormack and Tip O'Neill, two other Boston Democrats in Congress in the twentieth century. But from his first years in Washington, Jack had his sights on a statewide campaign in Massachusetts, for either the U.S. Senate or governor. To that end he began to travel on weekends back to Massachusetts, not just to visit his family at their ocean-front estate on Cape Cod, but to engagements in gritty little industrial cities, home to Democratic voters. He also made sure to visit the Republican old Yankee towns of rural Massachusetts; as his aide Dave

Powers said, "no town was too small or too Republican for him."[43] As in his first run for the House, Kennedy was determined to get a head start on the opposition, to work very hard, build a network (this time across the whole of Massachusetts) of mainly volunteer supporters, and spend as much of his family's money as was necessary to gain victory. Kennedy spoke before veterans groups, civic organizations, labor unions, Communion breakfasts in Catholic parishes, and socials in non-Catholic churches and religious communities.

Eventually, Jack decided to run for the U.S. Senate against Henry Cabot Lodge Jr., an incumbent Republican. Senator Lodge was a well-established and highly regarded moderate Republican. Unlike more conservative members of his party, he largely accepted the basic premises of the New Deal, putting him at odds with leading GOP (Grand Old Party) figures such as Senator Robert Taft of Ohio. Like Kennedy he was a Harvard graduate and decorated World War Two veteran, and had bridged some of the Protestant-Catholic divide in Massachusetts politics by holding his own among Irish-American voters. His grandfather, Henry Cabot Lodge Sr., was a longtime Massachusetts senator who had defeated Jack's grandfather, Honey Fitz, in 1916. Thirty-five or so years later, his grandson worried about the possibility of being unseated by a different type of Irish-American politician, one untouched by typical corruption charges and with crossover appeal to Republicans. John F. Kennedy, with his moderate politics, wealth, and charisma, fitted that profile. Even so, defeating Lodge was far from a sure thing; Joe Kennedy in particular had great respect for the senator. When the campaign got off to a slow start, Bobby Kennedy, then 26, left his job in Washington and began organizing furiously. Joe remained highly involved, but Bobby was the campaign manager. Meanwhile, Senator Lodge was busy for much of 1952 helping General Dwight Eisenhower secure the Republican nomination for president. The two candidates agreed on many of the central issues, including the Cold War, and the race became a contest of campaign organization (in which the Kennedy side clearly had an advantage) and personality rather than profoundly clashing political philosophies. One side's campaign billboards proclaimed "Kennedy Will Do *More* for Massachusetts"; the other: "Lodge Has Done—and Will Do—the *Most* for Massachusetts."[44]

When the Kennedy campaign did point out policy differences, it was to portray Lodge as neither ardent enough in his support for the economic interests of ordinary people nor sufficiently vigilant in the struggle against communism. In other words, they attacked him from both right and left.[45] But most significantly, the 1952 Senate race reflected two distinct and oppositional ethnic and religious identities, both with deep historical roots in Massachusetts. John Fitzgerald Kennedy represented the long-held aspirations of descendants of Irish immigrants. His family tradition, and

Democratic pedigree, also gave him an edge over Lodge with members of the many other ethnic groups in Massachusetts. Henry Cabot Lodge Jr., for his part, embodied the best of a proud Yankee, Protestant, and Republican tradition that stretched back to the founding of Massachusetts Bay Colony in the seventeenth century. Lodge's grandfather was the last major northern politician to take seriously the promise made by the federal government to African-Americans and the nation in the Civil War era to ensure racial equality in matters political and legal. His efforts along those lines in 1890 had been defeated, a setback which allowed the creation of the Jim Crow system of segregation in the South.

Despite this admirable heritage, the Kennedy team sensed a potential weakness in the current Lodge's campaign history and his voting record in the Senate. He had not done well in Boston's predominantly African-American districts during his most recent Senate campaign. He had also voted against changing the filibuster rule, which southern Democrats had used for decades to block civil rights legislation by endless Senate debates. In what promised to be a very close race, the Kennedys sought out young African-American activists (the older ones were allies of the McCormack-Curley wing of the Democratic Party and thus unenthusiastic about Kennedy's bid) and brought them into the campaign.[46] Congressman Kennedy campaigned in Boston's black neighborhoods, advertised heavily in the city's main African-American newspaper, and gave two speeches devoted to civil rights, placing the question in the context of the U.S.-Soviet Cold War rivalry. He had less to say about the ways in which racial segregation and discrimination, in all parts of the country, demeaned and diminished the dignity and hope of U.S. citizens of African ancestry. But the intentional courtship of African-Americans voters, including two Kennedy teas for black women, was effective.

The Kennedys used their numbers, energy, and money in putting up a fierce challenge to Lodge. Building on a practice used in Jack's initial run for Congress, Rose Kennedy and her daughters hosted a series of teas across Massachusetts. Eunice in particular was a highly effective surrogate for her brother. A bachelor now in his early thirties, Jack had considerable appeal to women, which his campaign exploited. The teas, some attended by thousands of guests, were successful in drawing women into the Kennedy campaign and generating interest in it through word of mouth. Most of the working- and middle-class women who received the engraved invitations had not previously been so solicited, not by political campaigns or by anyone else, for that matter. The communities in which the teas were held saw a marked increase in turnout among women voters, which presumably benefitted Kennedy. In similar fashion, in the final weeks the Kennedy campaign used the emerging medium of television to reach voters. Jack took lessons on how to project his personality over the airwaves and was advised by his father, the former producer of Hollywood movies, on how to make the camera work for him.[47] Jack hosted a show entitled "Coffee with the Kennedys" and one observer noted, "Mr. Kennedy has a natural approach which comes over television very well."[48]

As John F. Kennedy awaited the results on election night, he displayed a rare nervousness. His mother recalled him pacing anxiously, taking his jacket on and off so much that he got the sleeves turned inside out.[49] In his calmer moments, however, it was clear he expected to win, speculating to a friend as to what position the incoming president, Dwight Eisenhower, might appoint a defeated Henry Cabot Lodge Jr.[50] Just over 90 percent of Massachusetts' voters, a startlingly high figure, went to the polls. Most of the gains the Democratic Party had made in Massachusetts in recent years were wiped out. Eisenhower did indeed carry the state and the nation, and the incumbent Democratic governor, Paul Dever, was defeated. Congressman John F. Kennedy, however, edged Senator Lodge, becoming only the third Massachusetts Democrat to win a seat in the U.S. Senate. As Rose Kennedy noted, her son's triumph also served to settle something of an old family score, as Jack defeated the grandson of the man who had blocked Honey Fitz's efforts to reach the U.S. Senate decades earlier.

Although the campaign had generally been conducted in a civil manner by both camps and Lodge was gracious over the defeat in public, privately he blamed his defeat on "those damn tea parties."[51] Eisenhower's view was that the Kennedys' money had made the difference. Jack Kennedy, not surprisingly, proved especially popular with Catholic voters; that vote was boosted when Archbishop Richard Cushing baptized Bobby and Ethel Kennedy's son in a well-publicized ceremony before Election Day. Kennedy also outdid Lodge's previous opponents among members of labor unions and among women.[52] Lodge's complaint about the tea parties had some merit; while many factors contributed to his defeat, the Kennedy campaign's targeted efforts to increase the turnout of women worked. And in the two wards of Boston with a large African-American population, Kennedy won well over half the vote, contributing to his crucial margin of victory.[53] And as planned, Jack was able to dent Lodge's margins among Republican voters: his dogged campaigning in Republican strongholds across Massachusetts paid off. Lodge's efforts to gain the Republican presidential nomination for Eisenhower meant that it was denied to conservative hero Robert Taft. More conservative Republicans in Massachusetts, seeing Kennedy as sufficiently anti-communist, punished Lodge by not voting in the Senate race or by supporting Jack outright. And Joe's money, never to be underestimated in his son's campaigns, was important as well. The senior Kennedy made a substantial loan to the strongly anti-communist publisher, John Fox, of the

Boston Post when his newspaper faced mounting debts. Soon after, Fox and his paper endorsed Kennedy over Lodge.

For all the historical weight of the 1952 Senate race, it also presaged the future; the Lodges, despite their public service and all their achievements, never again won an election. On the other hand, the Kennedys were now clearly a rising force in Massachusetts politics, and beyond—one of the first congratulatory phone calls Jack received after his victory came from Lyndon Johnson of Texas, who was working to become leader of the Democrats in the Senate. John F. Kennedy, at the age of 35, now prepared to take a step on the American political ladder that no other member of his family had yet taken.

CHAPTER **3**

"A HARD AND BITTER PEACE"

John F. Kennedy became a U.S. senator in January of 1953, joining a legislative body better suited to his temperament, both politically and otherwise, than the more raucous, democratic "People's House" that he had served in for six years. More so than the House, the Senate was conscious of its history, and also more given to reflective deliberations, as intended by the framers of the Constitution in 1787. They designed it to cool the more popular passions of the House of Representatives. At various times in American history, most notably in the decades prior to the Civil War, it was the Senate that was the main crucible of the national government. Kennedy did not now represent only the working-class, heavily Democratic districts of Boston and its environs but the entire state of Massachusetts, with its long and rich history. Among his new constituents were those living in aging industrial cities, residents of the wealthy suburbs of Boston, and inhabitants of small towns and farming communities. He took his seat as the Korean War was in its third year, with no end in sight. That conflict, of course, was only part of the wider Cold War to which Kennedy was committed. The Senate had greater institutional influence over foreign policy, Kennedy's primary interest, as it alone had the power to ratify treaties negotiated by the executive branch.

John F. Kennedy was now in a legislative body of 96, as opposed to the House with its 435 members. He was well liked and on good personal terms with nearly all his colleagues, Democrat and Republican, but at the same time held himself aloof from most of them. One observer of him in the Senate remembers him as "elegant and casual, he sat in the back row, his knees against the desk, rapping his teeth with a pencil and reading the *Economist* and the *Guardian*" (both British publications).[1] His Democratic colleagues included courtly and staunchly segregationist Richard Russell of Georgia, energetic northern liberal Hubert Humphrey of Minnesota, and Lyndon Johnson, the highly ambitious and larger-than-life Texan. Among Republican senators were Midwesterners Everett Dirksen of Illinois, a skilled orator; Robert A. Taft of Ohio, the legendary "Mr. Republican"; and Joseph McCarthy of Wisconsin, already launched on his anti-communist crusade. The latter's influence, still growing in the early 1950s, was beginning to shape the political culture of the decade. McCarthy was connected socially to the Kennedy family and had a strong following among his many fellow Catholics who shared his antipathy to communism. Not being close to the moderate Henry Cabot Lodge Jr., McCarthy did not campaign for him in the 1952 Senate race, which was a boon to Jack Kennedy. Among New Englanders in the Senate were Yankee Republicans Leverett Salstonstall, also from Massachusetts, and Prescott Bush of Connecticut, father and grandfather of future presidents. Another New Englander, Margaret Chase Smith of Maine, a moderate Republican, was the only woman in the Senate. There were no Republicans, however, from the South in the Senate that convened that January; the former Confederate states were represented by Democrats, most of whom were fully committed to maintaining racial segregation and white supremacy in their states and region.

As he entered the Senate, John F. Kennedy expanded his political and intellectual horizons. Modern American politicians who advance in their careers take on more responsibilities and their staff becomes ever more important to their survival and success. Kennedy was well served in the House by a team that excelled at the nuts and bolts of constituent service and Boston politics. Sensing that he needed something more, Kennedy hired Theodore (Ted) Sorensen, a young lawyer from Nebraska with an intellectual bent. Sorensen, only 24 years old, was of Danish and Jewish ancestry and a Unitarian—that is, a member of a church generally associated with liberalism. He and his family had also been shaped by progressivism of the Midwestern populist variety. At their first meeting, Sorensen was struck by Kennedy's informality and even ordinariness; he noted later that Kennedy, unlike some other politicians, did not try to overawe him with the prestige of his position but simply "seemed like a good guy."[2] Although impressed, Sorensen had some reservations about Kennedy's commitment to liberal politics, his father's reputation, and his stance on Joseph McCarthy's anti-communist crusade. After Kennedy had addressed his concerns, Sorensen accepted his offer of a staff position and declined that from another Democratic Senate freshman, Henry M. Jackson of Washington, a Cold War liberal without peer. Sorensen ignored the advice of those who told him Jackson had the brighter future; Kennedy had offered Sorensen more of substance, challenging him to develop a legislative strategy to revitalize the flagging New England economy.

In early 1953 Jack Kennedy was 36 years old and still a bachelor in an era when most men were married by their mid-twenties. His reputation around Washington and elsewhere as a confirmed playboy was well deserved. Since his wartime affair with Inga Arvad he had had many sexual relationships—his interest in sex and his capacity for making it part of his life was nearly boundless. Kennedy's attraction to women, and theirs for him, was enormous. As one of his best friends in politics, Senator George Smathers of Florida, once said simply, "Jack liked girls, and girls liked Jack."[3] If he had wanted to marry earlier, he certainly could have done so. Was it his parents' troubled marriage that delayed him from making a binding commitment? Once asked if he had ever been truly in love, Jack's answer was no, but he said he had been quite *interested* a time or two. As a politician with growing ambition in an era in America when the traditional family was held up as the ideal, it would not benefit him to remain single. Adlai Stevenson, the Democratic presidential candidate in 1952, was divorced, and this had not helped him with voters, especially in Catholic consitituencies. Joe Kennedy especially was eager to see his son marry, get on with his life, and boost his political prospects.

Jack Kennedy and Jacqueline Bouvier first met on a train between New York City and Washington in 1948. Like Kennedy, Bouvier had grown up in a wealthy Catholic family on the East Coast. In her early twenties, she was nearly 12 years younger than Kennedy. After her graduation from George Washington University she remained in the nation's capital, working as a photographer for a newspaper. She and Jack were reintroduced to each other by mutual friend Charles Bartlett at a dinner party in Washington in 1951. Jacqueline Bouvier was interested in the arts, in ideas and history; in that regard she and Jack Kennedy were a good match. Despite some advantages in life, Jacqueline, or Jackie as she was called, had also known her share of suffering. Her parents divorced when she was 12, her father having been an alcoholic and unfaithful to her mother. At that level too, perhaps, she and Jack Kennedy connected. His close friend LeMoyne Billings said that Jack "saw her as a kindred spirit. I think he saw that the two of them were alike. They had both taken circumstances that weren't the best in the world when they were younger and learned *to make themselves up* as they went along."[4]

Their courtship began, but it was interrupted by her travels in Europe and his Senate campaign. During the latter, Jackie remembered, Kennedy would "call from some oyster bar up there [in Massachusetts], with a great clinking of coins, to ask me out to the movies the following Wednesday in Washington. . . . He was not the candy-and-flowers type, so every now and then he'd give me a book." [5] The couple attended President Eisenhower's inauguration in January of 1953, became engaged that June (Jack proposing by telegram), and were married in September at St. Mary's Catholic Church in Newport Rhode Island. The ceremony was conducted by Archbishop Richard Cushing of Boston and was marked by the reading of a special blessing from Pope Pius XII. The wedding was followed by a gala reception at Jackie's stepfather's sprawling estate, with every one of Jack's new colleagues in the U.S. Senate invited and thousands of guests in attendance. From their honeymoon in Acapulco, Mexico Jack wrote his parents: "At last I know the meaning of rapture. Jackie is forever enshrined in my heart. Thanks mom and dad for making me worthy of her."[6]

Despite its fairytale beginnings, the marriage had its problems from the start. Even as a new husband, Kennedy continued his relationships with other women. He was on a pleasure cruise for that purpose while Jackie had a miscarriage; "I'm never there when she needs me," he admitted to a friend. The newlyweds also faced the challenge of Jack's health; it deteriorated further when his back condition worsened. Weary of the constant, often debilitating pain and of the crutches he increasingly had to use, in the fall of 1954 he underwent surgery that was dangerous and experimental, especially for a patient with Addison's disease. It proved to be unsuccessful, forcing a second operation. Kennedy was absent from the Senate for more than six months, recuperating mainly at his parents' estate in Florida. Kennedy also suffered from ailments related to the back surgeries, from intestinal and urinary tract infections, and problems stemming from his Addison's disease. In one period of two and a half years in the 1950s he was admitted to hospital on nine separate occasions, spending more than six weeks there.[7] A still relatively young man, Jack Kennedy faced life knowing in some fundamental way that he was not well. He once said that the best he could hope for was to be "85 percent" healthy. His illnesses bring to mind Franklin Roosevelt's struggles with polio. There is a difference, however. Roosevelt had enjoyed good health until suddenly stricken in his late thirties, when he lost forever the ability to walk. Jack Kennedy fought for survival from birth, and later fought to give at least the appearance of genuine vitality. His energy, stamina, and courage in waging these constant battles shaped his character as an adult.

It was while Kennedy was recuperating from his first back surgery that the U.S. Senate voted overwhelmingly to censure one of their own, Joseph McCarthy. Since 1950 McCarthy had been outspoken in charging that Communists had infiltrated the highest ranks of the government. He claimed they operated under the direct control of Moscow and were responsible for, among other things, the 1949 victory of the communist forces in the Chinese civil war. During these years the Cold War had intensified as North Korea launched its attack on South Korea in 1950, bringing U.S. soldiers into an actual war against Communists for the first time. The Soviet

Union continued to be led by a brutal dictator, Joseph Stalin, who through the lens of Marxist-Leninist ideology and his own increasing paranoia, was convinced that the capitalist nations, led by the United States, were preparing to launch an invasion against the world's leading communist state. In 1949, the Soviet Union, seemingly ahead of schedule, had successfully deployed its first atomic bomb. On top of all this, two U.S. citizens, Julius and Ethel Rosenberg, had been arrested, charged, and convicted of spying for the Soviet Union. In these circumstances the time was ripe in America for a demagogue to emerge and capitalize on what were some rational fears and concerns about what the nation faced in the Cold War.

To liberals, McCarthy was the worst sort of politician, one who threatened, bullied, and used his power to persecute his opponents and challenge their patriotism, all with little or no regard to facts. If McCarthyism, as critics described the tactics of the senator from Wisconsin, was allowed to flourish and even triumph, liberal politics in the United States would wither on the vine, crippled by the menacing accusations that liberals themselves were somehow aligned with the Soviet Union and international communism. Kennedy's personal and political style was quite different than McCarthy's, but they shared a common ethnic and religious heritage as Irish-American Catholics and an avowed opposition to communism. In his first year in the Senate, Kennedy went out of his way to define himself politically as one who was "not a liberal at all." [8] He did not discount McCarthy at first, saying in 1950: "Joe may well have something." [9] The Kennedy family, including Joe and Bobby, had strong social and political ties to McCarthy; for instance, Bobby worked as an aide for McCarthy's Senate committee. Jack was not as close to the Wisconsin senator as his father or brother, but he too considered McCarthy a friend—even attending his wedding. Conventional wisdom held that McCarthy was popular in Massachusetts, especially among the working-class Catholics who first elected young John F. Kennedy to Congress in 1946 as a "fighting conservative" and unabashed Cold Warrior. As much as any state, Massachusetts reflected the nation's cultural and political divisions, driven largely by the Cold War that emerged in the late 1940s and early 1950s. Kennedy was clearly aware of this. But once in the Senate, Kennedy, like most of McCarthy's colleagues, came to see him as an embarrassment at best and a danger to the nation's best traditions at worst. In the summer of 1954, Kennedy was prepared to support a motion in the Senate to censure McCarthy and to speak on behalf of it on the Senate floor, albeit in a measured manner. The motion was tabled, but when the Senate next took up the McCarthy question in December of that year, Kennedy was in the hospital recovering from back surgery and out of contact with his staff. Had he been present it seems virtually certain he would have voted to censure McCarthy, who was now even more discredited after televised hearings exposed the lack of evidence behind his wild charges of communist infiltration of the U.S. Army. Every one of Kennedy's fellow Senate Democrats—southern conservatives and populists and northern moderates and liberals—did so. Kennedy had not been a leader on this question and, after McCarthy's disgrace was complete, he chose to remain publicly silent, neither defending nor damming him. Kennedy did tell an aide privately: "if I had made a big thing about giving McCarthy an extra kick after he was censured, I would have looked cheap."[10] Jackie Kennedy's view was that "Jack thought just what everyone thought of McCarthy. But again he was never one to run in a pack against [someone]."[11] As with his refusal years earlier to sign the petition asking for clemency for Boston political legend James Michael Curley, Kennedy demonstrated a certain independence of mind in relation to the McCarthy episode, albeit one for which some would not soon forgive him.

John F. Kennedy was not a leader or a major figure in the U.S. Senate. First-term senators were expected, in accordance with long tradition, to listen and learn and defer to their senior colleagues. His initial priority was to invigorate the economies of Massachusetts and New England, as he had told Sorensen. But Kennedy's interests transcended his native region. In 1954 he voted for the St. Lawrence Seaway, a major new waterway transportation system that would benefit most immediately the Great Lakes region, at the expense of the Port of Boston. The Massachusetts congressional delegation had long opposed this project. Kennedy wrestled with the politics of this issue before deciding on support. On the Senate floor he said that to do otherwise would demonstrate "a narrow view of my functions as a U.S. Senator" and invoked the words of Daniel Webster, who had argued that "our aim should be, States dissevered, discordant [or] belligerent; but one country, one constitution, one destiny."[12] On other economic matters Kennedy could be doggedly protective of Massachusetts' interests, but with this particular high-profile matter he made it a point to demonstrate that he considered himself importantly a U.S. senator and not only a voice for Massachusetts.

Perhaps it was his vote on the St. Lawrence Seaway that prompted Kennedy to think more about political courage in American history. During his recovery from back surgery in 1955, Kennedy began work on a book of examples of courage by statesmen in the American past. One of his subjects was John Quincy Adams, who had supported Thomas Jefferson, his father's great rival, in the embargo against Great Britain in 1807, which threatened to badly damage New England's economy. Kennedy also featured seven other U.S. senators, (with briefer references to other politicians) in *Profiles in Courage,* published on January 1, 1956. It is rare for an elected official to write a work of history; it was (and is) more common for ambitious politicians to write autobiographies or publish their campaign speeches in book form. Kennedy had written a book in which politicians were the heroes. In the post-World War Two era, esteem for government and those in it was high; one of the larger points that Kennedy sought to make was that politics could be a noble profession and history provides examples that can inspire and instruct. Although the subject of the book was American politics, Kennedy, in keeping with his interest in British history, gave the opening words to Edmund Burke, whose eloquence he admired. Kennedy's profiles were of men who had, in his view, placed the national interest, as they understood it, above constituency, region, or party. He included briefer portraits of those who took principled but unpopular stands, such as John Adams in his legal defense of British soldiers accused of murder in the Boston Massacre of 1770. For Kennedy, history was full of heroes, many of whom he had read about as a boy and young man. In the early Cold War period, much of American historical writing focused on political leaders and the commonalities that bonded the nation. The best of this scholarship, which includes Arthur Schlesinger's *The Age of Jackson* (1945), Richard Hofstadter's *The American Political Tradition and the Men Who Made It* (1948), Daniel Boorstin's *The Genius of American Politics* (1953), and Louis Hartz's *The Liberal Tradition in America* (1955), was sophisticated rather than celebratory in the treatment of the American past—in Hofstadter's case, even ironic and iconoclastic. *Profiles in Courage,* whether intentionally or not, had some philosophical connection to these works. John F. Kennedy had no formal graduate training in history, as he acknowledged in the preface, and nor did his assistant Ted Sorensen, whom Kennedy generously credited for "his invaluable assistance in the assembly and preparation of the material upon which this book is based."[13] Kennedy also acknowledged assistance from leading historians such as Schlesinger and James MacGregor Burns, of Williams College in Massachusetts. *Profiles in Courage* was an immediate bestseller and Kennedy was awarded the Pulitzer Prize for Biography in 1957. Winning a Pulitzer put him in the company of a select group of American men and women of letters. Later that same year, however, a controversy arose which was to dog Kennedy and his reputation for many years. A rumor made its way around political and literary circles that Ted Sorensen was the actual author of *Profiles in Courage.* Kennedy, it is true, was not a professor working alone in his study, but a U.S. senator with a capable staff to assist him and write for him, and this might have led to some of the doubts and confusions surrounding the book's authorship. Drew Pearson, a prominent newspaper columnist, publicly aired his suspicions of Kennedy on national television. The Kennedys responded swiftly, formally threatening a lawsuit against Pearson, who recanted his allegation. Decades afterward, Sorensen said of the controversy: "Like JFK's speeches, *Profiles in Courage* was a collaboration," with authorship resting with Kennedy.[14] That appears to be as close to the truth of the matter as anything said about it.

Profiles in Courage was not a work of partisanship or a tribute to the Democratic Party. Kennedy included Republicans in his study and argued that it was a benefit to the nation that both major parties in the middle of the twentieth century were not strictly ideological, with Republicans and Democrats alike welcoming liberals and conservatives into their ranks. He lauded George Norris of Nebraska, a liberal Republican, for his courageous support of Al Smith, a Democrat and a Catholic, when he ran for president in 1928. He also devoted a chapter to Robert A. Taft of Ohio, recently deceased, a conservative Republican. Kennedy admired Taft's determination in the face of serious illness and the intellectual honesty and integrity which led him to question the legality of the Nuremberg trials of former Nazi leaders soon after World War Two. Taft, of course, held no brief for Nazism, but he maintained, in the face of ferocious public criticism, that the legal foundations of the trials themselves were dubious.

Kennedy did not directly engage the vexing question of race in his book. Had he looked, he could have found illuminating examples of politicians who had risked their careers and even their lives to advance the cause of racial justice. The revolution in writing about the American past with regard to race and African-American history arose with the civil rights movement that had barely begun when Kennedy wrote *Profiles in Courage*. Kennedy hailed efforts by Lucius Quintus Cincinnatus Lamar, a Mississippi Democrat, to heal the divisions between North and South after the Civil War. In doing so, Kennedy restated the prevailing view of the post-Civil War Reconstruction as a dangerously misguided effort that resulted in the oppression of the white South. He held up Adelbert Ames, a New England native, as the archetype of the meddling Yankee, attributing Ames' election as Governor of Mississippi to a coalition of "freed slaves and Radical Republicans, sustained and nourished by Federal bayonets."[15] Ames indeed had fought the Civil War as a Union general and was chased out of Mississippi by white Democrats determined, as they saw it, to reclaim their state. After having moved to Northfield, Minnesota, for some well-deserved peace and quiet, he had to survive Jesse James and his pro-Confederate gang's raid on the bank in that small town, after they learned that Ames had money in it. Ames's daughter, Blanche, still living in the 1950s, was offended by Kennedy's portrayal of her father and wrote to him, demanding that he revise this interpretation in any future editions of the book.[16] Senator Kennedy put off Blanche Ames's entreaties, but her determined efforts were a sign that what had once been major questions in American life—concerning racial justice and the role of government in protecting it—were not yet settled.

Having returned to the Senate in the middle of the 1950s in better health than he had enjoyed for years, John F. Kennedy's closest aides noticed a new seriousness in his commitment to his political career. He was also looking to advance his own interests, with an eye toward becoming the party's vice-presidential nominee in 1956. Kennedy endorsed Adlai Stevenson, whose intellectual and oratorical talents he admired, for a second run against President Eisenhower. To build his credibility with party leaders across the nation, Kennedy and his political advisors decided that he needed to establish control over the Massachusetts delegation to the Democratic National Convention. Apart from his own Senate campaign, Jack Kennedy had largely avoided state politics in Massachusetts, following his father's advice not to "get into the gutter with those Irish bums up in Boston."[17] Kennedy believed he had no choice, although doing so meant going head to head with John McCormack, the powerful congressman from Boston who controlled federal patronage in Massachusetts and was a Kennedy rival. McCormack's ally, William "Onions" Burke, was chairman of the Democratic state committee. From rural Massachusetts (hence the farmer nickname), Burke had a reputation as a bully, and the Kennedys saw him as the worst of the old-time political figures in the state. Most of all, he was in the way of Jack's ambition to lead the statewide party. The senator tried to broker a deal by which the statewide delegation to the national convention would be split between those supporting Stevenson and those for McCormack, who had won the Massachusetts primary as a favorite son. Burke rejected this proposal and mocked the Stevenson camp as communist sympathizers. This meant political war between the two factions, and Jack Kennedy entered the fray wholeheartedly, lobbying members of the state committee himself. The ensuing battle was unusually intense; during one meeting, Kennedy was subjected to verbal abuse and taunts, including the familiar one that he was using his father's money to buy political power. Jackie Kennedy said that during the Onions Burke episode, she never saw her husband so preoccupied, to the point of being unusually "nervous when he couldn't talk about anything else."[18]

For the climactic meeting, the Kennedy camp hired two imposing off-duty police officers, to provide muscle if need be. Pat Lynch, a Kennedy man, was elected chair of the state committee, making Jack Kennedy the new de facto boss of the Massachusetts Democratic Party. He cut a different figure to his predecessors, lacking as he did the grizzled features and trademark hat of the typical Irish-American political chieftain. Kennedy tried to avoid gloating over the victory, at least in public, paying his respects to John McCormack but also declaring "the beginning of a new era for the Democratic Party in Massachusetts."[19] In later years, Kennedy's closest political advisors frequently spoke about that fight as a turning point in his career, as important as his better-known triumphs.[20] Had he failed in his bid for party leadership in 1956, Kennedy might well have been viewed by the political pros in his home state as a pleasant and wealthy dilettante, one who wrote the occasional history book but was ultimately feckless when it came to accumulating power and wielding influence. That same year, Edwin O'Connor published *The Last Hurrah,* a novel about a fading Irish-American political boss of the old school, based on Boston's James Michael Curley. For John F. Kennedy, his latest victory in Massachusetts was another beginning, one that cleared the way for his emergence as a national political figure.

The newly empowered junior senator from Massachusetts arrived at the Democratic convention in Chicago in 1956 as the leader of his state's delegation, at a time when political conventions were largely unscripted and important decisions were made in the heat of the moment. Ted Sorensen had prepared a memorandum that spring for circulation among party leaders regarding the possibility of Kennedy joining Adlai Stevenson on the ticket. He argued, using statistical analysis, that Kennedy would be a strong vice-presidential candidate, one who could win back traditionally Democratic Catholic voters to the party. This was especially important in some of the populous northern industrial states that weighed so heavily in the Electoral College. Essentially, Kennedy's camp was claiming that there *was* a Catholic vote, and that this would be more likely return to its political home in the Democratic Party if an appealing Catholic such as John F. Kennedy were on the ticket. Stevenson was indeed looking to boost his standing among Catholic Democrats, and his campaign decided to feature Kennedy at the convention. First, Jack narrated a documentary film on the history of the Democratic Party (after Edmund Muskie of Maine, another promising young Catholic senator, turned the opportunity down). After the movie was shown to the delegates, Kennedy briefly appeared on the podium to accept their cheers. Stevenson also asked Kennedy to deliver the first speech nominating him for president; this was also an honor, but a sign too that the speaker would probably not be selected for vice president. To more loud applause, Kennedy hailed Stevenson, in a manner that also described how Jack was coming to see himself, as "a man uniquely qualified by inheritance, by training and by conviction, to lead us out of this crisis of complacency, and into a new era of life and fulfillment."[21]

Kennedy's name began to be mentioned more frequently as a potential running mate for Stevenson, with many delegates and party leaders impressed by his performance at the podium and others noting how impressive he looked on television. The *New York Times* gushingly compared Kennedy to a "movie star."[22] The three national television networks covered the 1956 convention to a greater extent than usual. This gave Kennedy an advantage over older and less telegenic politicians (including, not insignificantly,

Stevenson himself). It had been expected as the convention opened that Estes Kefauver of Tennessee, a capable U.S. senator more respected than liked, with more pledged delegates than anyone but Stevenson, would be nominated for vice president. Stevenson, however, decided to leave the decision on the vice-presidential nominee with the convention itself. This set off a brief frenzy which caught Kennedy and his team (along with nearly everyone else) by surprise. But Kennedy's ambition quickly emerged and, despite being not yet 40 and still in his first term in the Senate, he made a bid for the nomination. Joe Kennedy, vacationing in Paris, was unhappy to learn the news. He feared that if Jack were on the ticket, a Democratic defeat in November (and Stevenson was already lagging badly in the polls) would be blamed on his son's Catholicism, ending his presidential aspirations.

The question of race emerged in unexpected ways, for this was the first Democratic convention after the landmark school desegregation case, *Brown vs. Board of Education,* was handed down by the Supreme Court in 1954. A solid white Democratic South was an essential part of the national strategy of any Democrat hoping to win the White House (although Eisenhower in 1952 and Dixiecrat Strom Thurmond in 1948 had both punctured that monolith.)

In 1956, 19 of the 22 U.S. senators from the states that had comprised the Confederacy issued a statement popularly known as the Southern Manifesto. Its signatories made clear their opposition to the Brown case and their support for the Jim Crow system of segregation and white supremacy. The three senators who did not sign it, Kefauver and Albert Gore Sr. of Tennessee and Lyndon Johnson of Texas, all desired to be president, and they sensed that any southern Democrat seeking his party's nomination could not be unreconstructed on the question of race. In Chicago the two Tennesseans quickly emerged as the other main contenders for the vice presidency. Their stand on civil rights garnered them favor among northern liberals but drew rebukes from their fellow southerners, especially Kefauver, the most outspoken of the three on civil rights. The Democratic Party in its platform had stepped back from its progress on civil rights and largely avoided the question that year, much as Kennedy himself had done in *Profiles in Courage.* And the 25 African-American delegates at the 1956 convention wielded little influence.

On the convention floor, Bobby Kennedy led Jack's impromptu bid to be Stevenson's running mate. Joe, who had initially erupted in anger from Paris when Bobby called to tell him the news, changed course and called urban Democratic leaders on his son's behalf. Kefauver had an advantage in the delegates he acquired during the presidential contest with Stevenson earlier that year, but Kennedy ran a strong second to him on the first ballot. On the second ballot, Kennedy surged into the lead, gaining support from many states and building on his southern support. And though it was not quite a stampede like that for William Jennings Bryan in 1896, John F. Kennedy had clearly caught the imagination of a good many delegates and party leaders. Lyndon Johnson proclaimed from the convention floor that Texas, like other southern states with a culture that particularly honored military service, would cast its votes for "the fighting sailor who wears the scars of battle."

Beneath the excitement and hoopla, however, were some hard political realities. Kennedy, the New England Catholic, had, as early as the first ballot, won five times as many votes from the southern states as did Kefauver, a native of the region. Southern politicians in the wake of the Brown decision and at the advent of the modern civil rights movement were not easily swayed by the emotions of the moment. There was a long history, dating to before the Civil War, of northern Democrats allowing the South (meaning white people) to have its way on racial matters. More recently, Al Smith, despite being a Catholic from New York City and a "wet" on the question of Prohibition, won several Deep South states in his otherwise doomed presidential race of 1928. He said little on race beyond voicing support for "states' rights." And Franklin Roosevelt, also of New York, was enormously popular across the South, winning every state each of the four times he ran for president, some by margins of well over 90 percent. Part of Roosevelt's appeal was that he did not promote or encourage any real challenge to the system of white supremacy known as Jim Crow. Southern politicians had their distinct version of American history and they must have seen Kennedy in part through that prism. Their enthusiasm for him was genuine; James Coleman, Governor of Mississippi, said to Jack afterwards: "We are proud of having supported you, and would be happy to have the opportunity to do so again."[23]

Racial politics was not the whole story behind Kennedy's boomlet in Chicago, as Kennedy won support and generated excitement among delegates across the country. A few weeks before the convention, however, he did waver on his initial support for the Brown decision. Appearing on a network news show, he declared that Congress had no appropriate role to play in the desegregation of the nation's schools and that the Democratic platform should not explicitly endorse Brown.[24] This was apparently not lost on southern Democrats but, despite their support for Kennedy in Chicago, Kefauver eventually won the nomination. Jack went to the podium and with much grace and dignity asked that the convention make Kefauver's nomination unanimous, further endearing him to the party faithful in the hall and around the country. But the disappointment on his face as he stood at the podium, accepting more cheers from his fellow Democrats, was quite evident nonetheless. Even so, Kennedy's career as a national politician had been launched. He took close notice of his support from across the country, especially from the South, saying afterwards: "I'll be singing Dixie for the rest of my life."[25] His ambition was stronger than ever, now completely in line with his father's, and clearly focused on the presidency. Kennedy mused to Dave Powers after the 1956 convention: "with only about four hours of work and a handful of supporters, I came within three and a half votes of winning the vice-presidential nomination. If I work hard enough over the next four years, I ought to be able to pick up all the marbles."[26]

In 1957, 40-year-old Jack Kennedy became a father for the first time, to a daughter her parents named Caroline Bouvier. Jackie had given birth to a stillborn infant the previous year, a girl named Arabella, so Caroline's safe arrival after four years of marriage was especially meaningful. The Kennedys purchased a home in Washington's historic district of Georgetown, where Jack had first lived as a young congressman. Ten years later, his commitment to a career in politics was now complete. "I've learned that you don't get far in politics until you become a total politician. That means you've got to deal with the party leaders as well as with the voters. From now on, I'm going to be a total politician."[27] Kennedy was going to make the Senate the base for his presidential campaign. Only twice before in American history—when Franklin Pierce managed it in 1852 and Warren Harding in 1920—had a sitting senator been elected president, although numerous others had tried. Despite that meager precedent, the logic of the Cold War put Washington front and center, and the assumed need for a president with some expertise in foreign policy would seem to give senators an advantage.

Senators, however, had long records of taking positions on controversial public issues, making them both friends and enemies. Kennedy encountered one of the more difficult of these questions in 1957 when he was appointed to an important committee commonly known as the McClellan, after its chairman, or Rackets Committee. Bobby Kennedy served as its counsel, because the committee investigated allegations of corruption in labor unions. The Kennedy brothers waded into the doings of the Teamsters and the powerful United Auto Workers, drawing criticism both for being anti-labor and being the stooges of union bosses. Kennedy proposed comprehensive legislation aimed at eliminating criminal elements from labor unions while defending their rights to represent honest working people. His bill failed to become law, but his work on the McClellan Committee solidified his ties with a key constituency in the Democratic Party. This had been achieved without him appearing to be labor's mouthpiece, a balancing act which burnished his political image among liberals and most Democrats.

Having spent much time and energy mastering the arcane field of labor law, Kennedy also pursued his ongoing interest in foreign affairs. In 1957 he was chosen by his majority leader, Lyndon Johnson (whom Joe Kennedy had lobbied personally), to serve on the Senate Committee on Foreign Relations, a prestigious assignment. Kennedy's sense of the importance of the

U.S. rivalry with the Soviet Union in the late 1950s was as strong as ever. Where he was beginning to depart from traditional American thinking on the Cold War concerned U.S. relations with the emerging nations of the world. From his seat on the Foreign Relations Committee, Kennedy criticized U.S. foreign policy as slow to recognize the nationalist aspirations of peoples in the Third World. He argued that the United States focused too much on military aid to the newly independent nations of Asia and Africa and not enough on encouraging their economic and social development. In a similar fashion, he chastised France for its refusal to grant greater freedom to its colony of Algeria.

The cause of freedom at home had a similar theme, one that Kennedy and many others in the political establishment were not willing to fully acknowledge. The Senate did take up civil rights legislation in 1957, its supporters hoping to enact the first law of that kind since Reconstruction. His national ambitions now clear, Kennedy faced a dilemma, as the Democratic Party he sought to lead was divided on civil rights. Majority Leader Lyndon Johnson, with his own designs on the presidency, sought to craft a measure acceptable to both northerners and southerners in his party. The devil was in the details, as it usually is in legislation of this importance. Seeking to find a middle ground as the Senate voted, Kennedy sided with liberals and northerners on most substantive matters but with the South on procedural votes.[28] The latter raised eyebrows among civil rights supporters. On a key provision, Kennedy voted with his southern colleagues in support of allowing jury trials for those charged with violating civil rights. Civil rights proponents strenuously opposed this, claiming it would damage the pending law by allowing white juries to acquit the accused. Kennedy expressed some sympathy for this position and lauded the bill itself as "a turning point in American social and political thought" in confronting a racial problem too long ignored.[29] But he also maintained that trial by jury was a cornerstone of the American legal system and that southern juries, even all-white ones, would not necessarily consist of unrepentant racists.

Although he voted for final passage of the bill, some civil rights activists believed that he had helped to weaken it. His supporters in the South, however, appreciated what they regarded as his efforts on their behalf, with one overly enthusiastic Alabama newspaper columnist claiming that Kennedy was emerging as the "living antithesis of Earl Warren," the Chief Justice of the Supreme Court who authored the Brown decision.[30] John F. Kennedy's views on civil rights in the late 1950s were like those of many Americans, ambiguous and not fully defined.

In 1958, Kennedy published his third book, a slim volume entitled *A Nation of Immigrants*. He was asked to write it by the B'nai B'rith Anti-Defamation League, a Jewish organization. While it did not attract nearly as much attention as had *Profiles in Courage,* the subject was also rooted in American history. Unlike his earlier Pulitzer Prize-winning effort, the heroes of *A Nation of Immigrants* were the ordinary people who had long come to America to start new lives. Kennedy's immigrants were predominantly European. He gave brief sketches of the stories of various ethnic groups, giving healthy attention to his own, the Irish, and told of the discrimination they and others faced in coming to a new land. In the 1950s, American culture was largely centered on unifying forces and the celebration of a shared past and present; Kennedy in *A Nation of Immigrants* argued otherwise, highlighting differences and conflict in American history.[31] Even so, the question of race was not Kennedy's concern here, although he did mention how various incarnations of the Ku Klux Klan had targeted African-Americans, along with Jews and Catholics, for discrimination.

Kennedy also brought the story up to the present in his review of immigration law. While still in the House, in 1952, he had strongly opposed those laws which discriminated against people not of northern European birth, and in *A Nation of Immigrants* he urged reform. He wrote this pamphlet-sized book with an eye on the 1960 campaign, of course. His father speculated prophetically in the 1950s about who might be part of Jack's coalition in a presidential bid:

> [T]his country is not a private preserve for Protestants, there is a whole new generation out there and it's filled with the sons and daughters of immigrants from all over the world and those people are going to be mighty proud that one of their own is running for President. And that pride will be your spur, it will give your campaign an intensity we've never seen in public life.[32]

While some of this was overstated, Jack himself knew from Massachusetts the great numbers and growing political weight of those of recent immigrant stock. Across the United States, most were in the Democratic Party and many were Catholic. Kennedy understood that he would need their support in order to win in 1960. His connection to his own immigrant heritage gave him an underappreciated advantage over others aspiring to the White House.

By the late 1950s, Kennedy was already accepting some of the many speaking invitations that came his way from all over the country after the 1956 convention and his winning of the Pulitzer Prize. Before he could completely turn to running for president, he knew he had to leave no doubt about his political standing in Massachusetts. Jack's Republican opponent in 1958, when he ran for re-election to the Senate, was Vince Celeste, who had already lost to Kennedy once before, in his final House race in 1950. Celeste fell back on the now old line that he was "running against that millionaire,

Jack Kennedy."[33] The people of Massachusetts, of course, had been aware of the Kennedys' money for some time. Jack's strong record of constituency service, his broad appeal, and his rising national profile overwhelmed any message intended to weaken him.

The results on Election Day were beyond even what the Kennedy camp had thought possible: a massive victory, with Jack winning 73 percent of the total, good for a margin of well over 800,000 votes. In a state with a strong Republican Party, he had won every county. This was an impressive result, unprecedented in Massachusetts' history. Kennedy could now focus entirely on winning the Democratic presidential nomination in 1960. Through his appearance at events around the country, a series of flattering portraits in popular magazines, and articles in more serious publications on a wide range of issues, Kennedy was positioning himself for a national campaign. As in his first efforts for the House and Senate, he concluded that he would have to start earlier and work harder than his opponents. He was not assuming anything, aware as he was of both his strengths heading into 1960, and his potential handicaps.

CHAPTER 4

"The Torch is Passed"

John F. Kennedy announced his candidacy for the presidency on January 2, 1960. Surrounded by his family in the Senate Caucus room on Capitol Hill, Kennedy spoke of the potential of the presidency to promote "a more vital life for our people."[1] Emphasizing the kind of leadership he intended to offer the country, Kennedy voiced his determination to "give direction to our traditional moral purpose, awakening every American to the dangers and opportunities that confront us."[2] Although he mentioned domestic issues such as urban decay and a weakening farm economy, the Cold War was front and center. Kennedy warned that recent Soviet gains in the arms race "threaten our very existence."[3] He said that in his travels around the United States and the world—"from Leningrad to Saigon"—he had developed a vision for the United States. It was both inspiring and grandiose: Kennedy declared that the United States was charged with "fulfilling a noble and historic role as the defender of freedom in a time of maximum peril—and of the American people as confident, courageous and persevering."[4] He offered a highly personal style of leadership, reminiscent of the British statesmen of old he so admired, such as William Pitt, who famously declared in 1756: "I am sure I can save this country, and no one else can."

Why would a promising politician, so young (and paradoxically one whose health was often fragile), seek the presidency at the height of the Cold War? Barely into his forties when he began seeking his party's nomination, Kennedy risked being dismissed as too inexperienced. Every president elected since 46-year-old Teddy Roosevelt's victory in 1904 had been over 50. To get out in front of such charges, Kennedy pointed, at his campaign launch, to his 18 years of service to the United States, in both war and peacetime. But Kennedy had begun to feel the same frustrations and restlessness in the Senate that he had in the House: being one of many and unable to maximize his talents as he wished.[5] Barring the collapse of his health or a major scandal, a long career in the Senate awaited him. Given his interest in history he was on his way to becoming a scholar-statesman, as Daniel Patrick Moynihan later did. He might have become chairman of the Senate Foreign Relations Committee, an important post in its own right. Or he could have remained in the Senate for the time being, building his leadership and legislative credentials for a run at the White House in 1964 or 1968. Even in 1972 he would only be 55. However, Kennedy believed in 1960 that his time had come; he feared that if he sat back and waited, others would come along and he would be forgotten.

Kennedy's ambitious opening rhetoric and early groundwork notwithstanding, his rivals were not prepared to cede him the nomination. Perhaps the most serious obstacle facing his fledgling campaign was that the established leaders of the party were skeptical of this junior Massachusetts senator becoming the Democratic presidential nominee in 1960. The avowed Democratic contenders in 1960, all white men and senators, were in general agreement on the Cold War, their differences arising over domestic issues. Despite his apparent role as an underdog, Jack Kennedy was not campaigning as an insurgent in the ideological sense. He had begun to position himself to win the support of liberal Democrats, as the party and its liberal wing had a strong year in the elections of 1958. He endorsed a program of increased domestic spending and expanded government activism to combat social ills. With an eye on the Catholic question, in 1958 he jettisoned his previous support for federal aid to religious schools. He also went on record as opposing the appointment of a U.S. ambassador to the Vatican, a seemingly minor issue but one of great concern to those who emphasized separation of church and state. And some liberal intellectuals, most notably historian Arthur Schlesinger Jr., began to move toward Kennedy. Schlesinger, although still a great admirer of Adlai Stevenson, was captured by Kennedy's rhetoric and personality, concluding that he could win the presidency, and as a liberal.

Among the other contenders, Hubert Humphrey of Minnesota, the most outspokenly liberal of the candidates, was a strong advocate of civil rights, had a base of support among organized labor and farmers, and presumably enjoyed a geographical advantage in the Midwest. When the Kennedy campaign looked southward, to states the delegates of which had supported him in his bid for the vice presidency in 1956, it faced the looming presence of Senate Majority Leader Lyndon Johnson of Texas. He was the strong favorite to win a majority of delegates from the South. Johnson's stature and achievements in the Senate afforded him other advantages: the weight of seniority and obvious leadership credentials, in striking contrast to the other candidates. This was especially true with regard to Kennedy, whose accomplishments in Congress were not overwhelming. The fourth candidate was Stuart Symington of Missouri, a favorite of former President Harry Truman, well regarded in the Senate for his expertise on defense matters but with a limited following outside his home state. Like Humphrey, Symington had limited financial resources, a problem the Kennedy campaign would not face. A wild card in 1960 was two-time nominee (and twice defeated) Adlai Stevenson. Still very well regarded by many liberal intellectuals and some of the rank and file, he was coy about stating whether he would seek a third presidential nomination.

Since his performance at the 1956 convention, Kennedy had accepted as many as he could of the thousands of invitations he received to speak at Democratic events across the country. As with his campaigns in Massachusetts, Kennedy organized early, this time traveling all over, meeting Democrats and compiling lists of those who might be able to help him win the nomination. Where necessary, the Kennedy team built political organizations outside of the formal party structures, under the umbrella title "Citizens for Kennedy." Campaign aide Lawrence O'Brien was surprised to find "we had the field entirely to ourselves. As I moved from state to state making friends, nailing down support, I kept waiting for the opposition to show up, but it never did."[6] As with earlier Kennedy campaigns, this one was not without some hitches. Jack and aide Ted Sorensen joked that before they hired a professional scheduler, their speaking tour of New England "consisted of Vermont, New Hampshire, Connecticut, and Nevada."[7]

The campaign decided to go the route of the primaries, competing wherever Kennedy was viable. Although most Democrats in Washington saw Kennedy as an underdog, one Gallup Poll showed him a clear favorite among likely primary voters. Lyndon Johnson, among others, assumed that the political bosses who still had some sway over the Democratic Party would ultimately oppose such a young, unproven figure as Jack Kennedy. As it happened, most of them were Irish-Americans, and Joe Kennedy knew nearly all of them and courted their support for his son, typically sweetening the pot with a generous contribution to the local Democratic Party.[8] Thus, while Kennedy may well have been underestimated by his opponents at the start of the campaign, his position was stronger than it looked. Given his youth, however, it was widely assumed that Kennedy was angling for the vice presidency. He denied that emphatically, saying he would not accept the number two spot on the ticket under any circumstances.

The one matter that remained beyond anyone's ability to predict the impact of was Kennedy's Catholicism. Indeed, the ghost of Al Smith hovered over John F. Kennedy's campaign. Smith, a Democrat and the first Catholic to run for president, had been soundly defeated in 1928, his campaign marred by ugly outbreaks of anti-Catholicism fueled by the Ku Klux Klan and others. Thirty years later, that attitude persisted, deeply rooted in the American past; according to a survey taken in 1959, nearly a quarter of the nation was unwilling to vote for a Catholic for president.[9] Other signs were more promising. The horrors of World War Two had made racial, ethnic, and religious prejudices less acceptable, at least in public, in most parts of the United States. Catholics had served in great numbers in the armed services and many war movies reflected that. Movies significantly shaped public culture in the middle of the twentieth century and—for example—*Going My Way* (1944), *The Bells of St. Mary's* (1945), and *On the Waterfront* (1954) portrayed Catholic clergy in a positive light.[10] The Catholic Church's unqualified opposition to communism and its understanding of marriage and the family were essentially aligned with the cultural and political assumptions of most Americans in the postwar era. Millions of American Catholics during those years, helped by the G.I. bill, gained greater access to higher education, home ownership, and the expanding economy. Entering the middle class and moving to the suburbs, they also started to assimilate into the wider culture and society.

Even so, most Catholics in 1960 were still part of a distinctive subculture that many other Americans found mysterious and potentially divisive. Numerous mid-century American Catholics spent their entire lives within a vibrant institutional framework, from birth in a Catholic hospital to burial in a Catholic cemetery. It was also true that, in its official pronouncements, the Catholic Church had not shown itself reconciled to democracy and religious pluralism. European upheavals and revolutions in the eighteenth and nineteenth centuries had alarmed it, strengthening its support of conservative politics. Catholics in the United States, however, had in practice long adapted to the democratic and republican ethos of America.[11] As Catholics in Kennedy's Boston put it, "we get our religion from Rome, but our politics at home." And John F. Kennedy as a cultural figure was very different from Al Smith, or for that matter millions of his fellow Catholics in the working and middle classes of 1960. A wealthy Harvard graduate and decorated military veteran with a manner more polished than Smith's, Kennedy was a Catholic who could potentially appeal to a much wider audience. As he traveled the nation in the lead-up to 1960, he became aware that his religion could be beneficial as well as harmful. In Carroll, Iowa, a farming community that was heavily Catholic and Democratic and had given most of its votes to Al Smith in 1928, he showed the importance of his family to the campaign by saying, in his opening remarks, that his mother Rose—who had spoken there two years earlier—sent her regards. And even in rural Iowa, Kennedy could not escape the reach of the Cold War. He noted that, just two months earlier, Soviet leader Nikita Khrushchev had visited a farm in nearby Coon Rapids on *his* U.S. tour.

As the primary elections began, Kennedy's goal was not only to win delegates but also to prove his popularity with the voters, build up momentum, and create a sense of inevitability heading into the convention. Most of the others, Johnson, Symington, and possibly Stevenson, took a different approach. They planned to hold back and work for a deadlocked convention, out of which they each hoped to emerge the nominee. As only about a third of the convention delegates would be selected through the primaries, this strategy seemed plausible. Kennedy and Hubert Humphrey thus had the field to themselves, aside from favorite-son candidates. The first primary was scheduled for New Hampshire, which Humphrey passed up as it was next to Massachusetts. Next on the calendar was Wisconsin, which shared a border with Humphrey's Minnesota. Kennedy did not dodge this opportunity; to do so would have undermined his own strategy. Wisconsin's political heritage was rich and contentious; it included the famed LaFollette family, most of whom were champions of progressive politics, as well as Joseph McCarthy, three years dead in 1960.

In Hubert Humphrey, Kennedy faced an energetic and ebullient campaigner, one well versed on the issues. Humphrey was especially popular with the state's large farming population, so much so that he was sometimes referred to as "Wisconsin's Third Senator." The Minnesotan also rarely missed an opportunity, especially in rural Wisconsin, to remind his audiences that Senator Kennedy was from the east coast. Jack was not in his element in relation to farm policy and knew it, but could not afford to entirely ignore the rural Wisconsin vote. He concentrated most of his efforts, however, on the largely ethnic and Catholic voters of Milwaukee, Green Bay, and other cities. Not particularly well known in Wisconsin initially, Kennedy was snubbed by more than a few voters as the campaign opened in the dead of winter. But through perseverance, organization, money, and his unique appeal, he began to catch on as the weather warmed and the primary approached. And Wisconsin was where Jack unveiled the full force of his family, with his brothers, sisters, and in-laws exuding energy, vitality, and youth on the campaign trail. It was a new thing in American presidential politics to see so many surrogates for the candidate in their thirties and younger; Ted Kennedy was only 28 in 1960. Jackie Kennedy was not as taken by the swirl of politics, but she too came to the Midwest to help. She later recalled that she found not only the weather but the people of Wisconsin cold and unforgiving.[12] Still, the family's overall impact was quite remarkable. Hubert Humphrey complained of the Kennedys that "They're all over the state and they look alike and sound alike [. . .] I get reports that Jack is appearing in three or four places at the same time."[13]

Jack's campaign rallies often included music, such as "High Hopes" by Frank Sinatra, updated with Kennedy-themed lyrics, and a welcome for the candidate that often seemed more appropriate for a movie star. The candidate himself, looking both pleasantly confident and a bit bemused by all the fuss, waited to be introduced.[14] Kennedy usually opened his remarks with some self-deprecating humor and a historical reference, for instance to the origins of the Wisconsin primary itself, before warming to the main subject. Once begun, he lost much of his usual reserve and in a quite serious tone argued that the United States was at risk of falling into a dangerous complacency, one that might cost the nation dearly in the Cold War. The sober nature of Kennedy's message was sometimes in jarring contrast to the joviality and hoopla that surrounds American campaigns, his own included, and his growing status as a political celebrity.

As the campaign drew to an end, Humphrey bemoaned the Kennedys' wealth and their willingness to spend it on Jack's behalf. The Kennedy camp did have more money, a more effective organization, and closer relations with major national newspapers, and pressed these and other advantages to the full; they had many more offices around the state and a private campaign plane (named after Kennedy daughter Caroline). Humphrey was also outraged, and justifiably so, when a Kennedy campaign worker was found to have mailed some anti-Catholic literature in order to drive up the vote for Jack among Wisconsin's large Catholic population.[15] Most significantly, Humphrey questioned Kennedy's commitment to liberalism, charging that Jack's domestic program in particular was motivated by political expediency rather than long-held principles. Even so, Kennedy triumphed over Humphrey, with 56 percent of the vote, carrying six of Wisconsin's ten congressional districts. Despite losing in his neighboring state, Humphrey, straining to keep his candidacy viable, claimed that Catholic Republicans had entered the Democratic primary, giving Kennedy his margin of victory.[16] He decided impulsively to continue on to the next primary state, West Virginia, a decision that angered the Kennedy camp, who now saw Humphrey as a spoiler. The other contenders, including Stevenson and Johnson, were prepared to support Humphrey financially in hopes of slowing the Kennedy bandwagon. And the religious issue, which had been mostly below the surface in Wisconsin, promised to emerge fully in overwhelmingly Protestant West Virginia.

A small state, geographically isolated and very poor, West Virginia had a culture in which county sheriffs and other local officials expected what amounted to bribes for supporting a candidate. Kennedy's pollster Lou Harris (employing him was another of the campaign's innovations) found that Kennedy was far ahead of Humphrey among West Virginia voters. Once Kennedy's Catholicism became widely known in West Virginia, however, his support plummeted. This shook Jack and his team, to the point of abandoning any hope of winning the state. One potential strategy was to plan on a defeat and afterward have Jack portray himself as the underdog Catholic who had done well enough in a heavily Protestant state.[17] This sort of thing was not a sustainable approach to winning the presidency of the United States, though, and the Kennedy campaign ultimately rejected it and committed itself to winning an outright victory in West Virginia.

Thus, somewhat unexpectedly, Kennedy was forced to gamble that West Virginians were not complete religious bigots. There was some reason for optimism: Al Smith had won the Democratic primary there in 1928 and, more immediately, the Kennedy campaign had already invested substantial resources and effort during the previous year in anticipation of the primary. Still, there was great risk; a defeat there by Humphrey, especially if attributed to the religious issue, might do great harm to Kennedy's hopes of winning the nomination. Humphrey did not directly raise the religious issue in West Virginia, but his campaign featured the hymn "Give Me That Old Time Religion," traditionally sung in Protestant churches. Kennedy decided to meet the question head on. At his first rally in the state he appealed to his audience's patriotism and sense of fairness, declaring that no one asked about his or his late brother's religion before they entered combat on behalf of the United States during World War Two. In West Virginia, a state founded during the Civil War, Kennedy stressed his military service and loyalty to the nation. His campaign brought in Franklin Roosevelt Jr., whose father was revered in West Virginia for the New Deal. Roosevelt, like Jack a decorated naval veteran, was encouraged by the campaign to imply that Humphrey had deliberately avoided military service in World War Two. Humphrey had had legitimate medical reasons for not fighting and deeply resented the charge. Although Jack distanced himself from the allegation, the damage had been done. Relations between the two camps deteriorated, with Humphrey repeating that the Kennedys, with their great expenditure of money, were in effect buying votes. There was certainly a lot of money floating around West Virginia courthouses that spring and the Kennedys spent their share and then some. But complaining about one's opponents' advantages is not generally a path to victory in American politics, and it was not for Humphrey in West Virginia. In addition, Kennedy was telling West Virginians why he was in their state, he was meeting them, hearing their concerns, learning their problems; Johnson, Symington, and others were not. Both he and Jackie found West Virginian people friendly and polite, with quiet dignity amidst material want; in that respect they reminded Jack of those he met visiting Ireland.

Kennedy was genuinely moved by the scenes of profound poverty and dire working conditions in the hollows and coal mines of West Virginia. Not all the state's people were living in abject poverty, but Kennedy met people aged far beyond their years by poor nutrition and health care and whose standard of living was significantly lower than the middle-class ideal the United States had prided itself on since World War Two. In a competition with the Soviet Union that was in part economic, this poverty weakened the American claim that a free enterprise system best met the material needs of human beings. What he witnessed in Appalachia was so different from his own circumstances and background that it became part of his education as a politician. Kennedy's commitment to a domestic liberal program to alleviate such conditions was strengthened by his experience in West Virginia. Jack boosted his chance of victory with an election-eve television appearance in which he quietly repeated some of his earlier themes, including his unequivocal support for the separation of church and state and his declaration that there is not, and nor should there be, a religious test for office in the United States under the Constitution. His victory in West Virginia was 60 percent to 39 percent over Humphrey, larger than his margin in Wisconsin, knocking his rival out of the race.

Kennedy next moved to consolidate his position as the Democratic front-runner. Bobby Kennedy pressured party leaders who were not yet on board with his brother. Although only in his mid-thirties, he could be aggressive and single-minded to the point of harshness, subjecting powerful men many years his senior to withering tongue-lashings. Hardened political pros were shocked at his behavior. In Bobby, Jack had a highly motivated and effective campaign manager, and beyond that, someone he could trust completely. Kennedy's family was united in its efforts to get Jack elected president. Younger sister Eunice Kennedy Shriver, a woman of great talent and energy, was so devoted to her brother and his ambitions that she flung a glass of champagne across the room at a man who made a mildly critical remark about the campaign.[18] As the convention opened, some of the leading old-line party bosses came over to the Kennedy camp, most notably Mayor Richard Daley of Chicago and Governor David Lawrence of Pennsylvania. Both of them were Catholics—Lawrence, haunted by the agony of Al Smith's 1928 campaign which he had witnessed as a young man, had been worried that Kennedy's Catholicism would doom him as well.

With the bulk of the large Illinois and Pennsylvania delegations now with him, Kennedy was moving toward a first ballot nomination. His team feared that without such a victory his support would weaken and the convention would turn to another contender, most likely Lyndon Johnson or Adlai Stevenson. Johnson had nursed an ambition to be president even longer than Kennedy. His strategy in 1960, however, was puzzling. His massive ambition carried with it a dread of failure, so much so that he kept his candidacy under wraps, in ways that confounded and frustrated his supporters. Given their starkly different standings and accomplishments in the Senate, he found it difficult to take Kennedy seriously as a candidate.

Senators tend to see each other as either "work horses" who undertake the unglamorous tasks of building coalitions, crafting legislation, and mastering an often arcane area of public policy, or "show horses" who are primarily interested in publicity and boosting their profile. Johnson, while respecting Kennedy's intellect, clearly saw him as among the latter. He and Jack were amiable enough when together, but in private Johnson derisively referred to Kennedy as "the boy" or "Johnny Boy" and repeatedly remarked, despite Kennedy's accumulation of delegates, that "the boy can't win."[19] Kennedy was impressed by Johnson's dominance of the Senate but considered the Texan to be deceitful and manipulative. The two were not friends.[20] Complicating matters was the terrible relationship between Johnson and Bobby Kennedy, who had taken an instant loathing to each other at their first meeting in the early 1950s, with the animosity only deepening over time.[21]

As the 1960 convention opened, however, Lyndon Johnson finally entered the race officially. His strategy was to win enough support among southern and western delegates to deny Kennedy a first ballot victory and eventually prevail. Aware that the hour had grown extremely late, Johnson launched a blistering attack on Kennedy, bringing in Jack's father and his missteps in London and Jack's reticence on the McCarthy issue in a clear effort to dislodge liberals from the Kennedy camp. Johnson's lieutenant John Connally also raised the sensitive question of Jack's health, alleging that he suffered from Addison's disease. These last-minute charges angered the Kennedy camp, especially Bobby, but Johnson had to tread carefully with regard to health matters, for he had suffered a serious heart attack just a few years earlier. And although Jack Kennedy's sexual peccadilloes were an open secret among political insiders, Johnson was also vulnerable on that score. Both men, and others, were protected by the consensus among politicians and the press that such matters were not to be publicized. Johnson tried one last gambit to shake things up by inviting Kennedy to a joint session of the Texas and Massachusetts delegations. Jack accepted, but left his home-state delegates behind; after listening to Johnson lash into him, he stepped to the podium and used his poise and humor to defuse the situation. He told the Texans that he had "come here today full of admiration for Senator Johnson, full of affection for him, and strongly in support of him—for Majority Leader."[22] Even Johnson laughed and Kennedy had impressed the roomful of Texans that the rich man's son from the East had his own tough streak.

Kennedy was seeking victory in Los Angeles, a city selected by the Democratic Party as a way of looking to the future, a nod to California's astonishing growth (only New York then carried more weight in the electoral college) and its robust economy and modern way of life.[23] Kennedy hoped to combine his own optimism with the aura of the golden state and he was able to tap into the sprawling city's most visible industry, entertainment, in a way that no previous Democrat had done. The Kennedy family's connections in Hollywood dated to Joe's work there in the 1920s and his son had become quite taken with its celebrity culture. For example, Jack and Frank Sinatra's "Rat Pack" genuinely enjoyed each other's company. Kennedy's younger sister Pat was married to Peter Lawford, a British-born actor, giving him another entrée into show business circles. He spoke at a fundraiser with many of Hollywood's most familiar faces, tapping a new source of funds for himself and his party.

But these were pleasant diversions for Kennedy. There remained serious opposition to his candidacy among leading Democrats as the party gathered. Harry Truman, Eleanor Roosevelt, longtime Speaker of the House Sam Rayburn of Texas, and Adlai Stevenson remained immune to Kennedy charm and pressure. Truman described the convention as fixed and left town before it officially began. The Kennedy team focused on rounding up final delegates and making sure their commitments held firm. A raucous demonstration for Adlai Stevenson could not shake Kennedy's lead; it was confined largely to the balcony, while the delegates were on the convention floor. Ironically, the greatest show of emotion at the convention was for Stevenson, the older intellectual; the Kennedy camp had its own youthful enthusiasm, but it also kept a cool eye on what counted most—support among the voting delegates. Leaving nothing to chance after communication breakdowns during Jack's brief run at the vice presidency at the 1956 convention, the campaign kept in close contact with delegates and party leaders through a sophisticated electronic system.[24] In the end it was the Kennedys' long-range planning and detailed organization that paid off. It was, fittingly, Wyoming, a rural western state that might well have gone for Johnson, which put Kennedy over the top and gave him the nomination toward the end of the first ballot. To maximize his time on national television, Kennedy appeared in person at the Los Angeles sports arena, flanked by his mother and sister Pat, to acknowledge the nomination. Meanwhile, in seclusion 3,000 miles back east, Joe Kennedy watched on television as his son claimed victory, his family's capture of the Democratic Party now complete.

Focused completely as he was on the nomination, Jack Kennedy had not yet thought through his vice-presidential selection. Much to the shock and even dismay of many of his supporters, he announced in Los Angeles that Lyndon Johnson was his choice. Johnson's record on organized labor was at odds with most Democrats; he had supported the Taft-Hartley bill, for example. And although he had shepherded civil rights legislation through the Senate in 1957 and again in 1959, Johnson was a southerner and the consensus among the party's liberals was that he could not be trusted on that issue. At Kennedy's urging, the Democratic platform of 1960 included language strongly supportive of civil rights, albeit at the end of a lengthy document. This, along with Kennedy being a Catholic from the Northeast, made firming up southern support critical. Democrats had lost Texas twice in a row and were determined to win it in 1960. The last candidate the Democrats had nominated for president from the Northeast, Franklin Roosevelt, had also chosen a Texan, John Nance Garner, for vice president. Lyndon Johnson had strong support from Democratic politicians across the region, as his showing on the first ballot of the convention demonstrated. Some of them, including Johnson's mentor Sam Rayburn, had serious reservations about Johnson throwing in his lot with Kennedy. Despite some strong dissent too within the Kennedy camp, especially from Bobby and among labor and civil rights leaders, Kennedy-Johnson emerged from Los Angeles as the Democratic ticket in 1960.

Television was generally a great asset to John Kennedy's presidential campaign. In his nationally televised acceptance speech, held at an unusual outdoor venue, the Los Angeles Coliseum, it was not. Kennedy appeared tired, there were problems with the light and sound, and in the vastness of the huge stadium he appeared small. The speech too was not one of his best. After acknowledging the risk the Democratic Party had taken in nominating a Catholic, he repeated his earlier declarations in favor of separation of church and state. He then turned to his opponent, Vice President Richard Nixon; to defuse the youth question, Kennedy referred to him as "also a young man." But Kennedy also belittled Nixon personally; he knew that if any one thing united the Democratic Party's leadership and much of its rank and file, it was their intense dislike of Richard Nixon. They saw him as hyper-partisan, an opportunist of the first order, and only barely more acceptable than Joseph McCarthy. Still, Kennedy came across as petty and shrill in this regard.

Kennedy did not hit his stride until later in the speech, when he challenged Americans to shake off their complacency. In this way he introduced what he called the New Frontier, speaking as he did on the California coast, with the continental United States to his back. Kennedy did not define his metaphor in specific terms, describing it instead as "a frontier of unknown opportunities and perils—a frontier of unfilled hopes and threats."[25] After placing himself and the New Frontier in the liberal tradition of Woodrow Wilson's New Freedom and Franklin Roosevelt's New Deal and, though not naming it, Harry Truman's Fair Deal, Kennedy boldly declared that what he meant was

> not a set of promises—it is a set of challenges. It sums up not what I intend to offer the American people, but what I intend to ask of them. It appeals to their pride, not their pocketbook—it holds out the promise of more sacrifice instead of more security.[26]

Underlying the rhetoric was Kennedy's claim that the United States was falling dangerously behind the Soviet Union, and that a new commitment to national excellence was needed across a wide range of areas—combating poverty, fighting prejudice, and exploring space, in addition to keeping pace with the Soviet military. On matters less momentous than war and peace things did not seem to be moving in the right direction. John F. Kennedy promised to "get this country moving again," a phrase that caught on during the subsequent fall campaign. He also raised the possibility that the United States might not be able to "compete with the single-minded advance of the communist system" and asked: "are we willing to match the Russian sacrifice of the present for the future?"[27] Not everyone was on board, however; Eleanor Roosevelt, still doubtful that her party's nominee was a trusted liberal, left quite distraught at Kennedy's success.

Two weeks later, Richard Nixon, seeking to become the first incumbent vice president to be elected president since Martin Van Buren in 1836, accepted the Republican nomination in Chicago. Although critical of the Democratic Party, he left Kennedy himself largely out of his remarks. He did remind the nation that Kennedy had suggested that President Eisenhower consider apologizing to the Soviet Union when an American U-2 pilot was shot down over Russia a few months earlier. The U-2 incident had done serious damage to U.S-Soviet relations and Kennedy's remarks brought him considerable criticism at the time. Nixon and Kennedy had been friendly as young congressmen, each recognizing the talent and ambition of the other. During the 1950s, Kennedy's Senate office was across the hall from Nixon's vice-presidential quarters, and Nixon had been genuinely concerned about Jack when his health problems were at their worst. Still, as Kennedy said to friends throughout his career, politics can be a tough business and opponents in campaigns almost naturally come to loathe each other.

The two contenders for the presidency agreed on the justness of the American cause in the Cold War and were not very far apart on most other issues. Urged on by New York Governor Nelson Rockefeller, the Republicans in their platform also expressed strong support for civil rights. They used the word "Negro" (then in common use) several times, while the Democrats made no mention of any particular race in their platform, so as not to offend southern sensibilities. Richard Nixon in his own right could point to a strong record on civil rights. His selection for vice president, former Senator Henry Cabot Lodge of Massachusetts, shared his views on matters of racial justice. The reason that he was no longer in the U.S. Senate, of course, was that he had been defeated for re-election by Congressman John F. Kennedy eight years earlier, making him a curious choice on domestic political grounds. Nixon chose Lodge to strengthen his ties with the party's eastern establishment and to emphasize the Republican record on foreign policy. The public generally approved of the Eisenhower administration's handling of the Cold War and Lodge had contributed to that success, serving as U.S. ambassador to the United Nations with distinction since his defeat by Kennedy. Lodge proved to be a poor choice, however, as he was not a very energetic campaigner and did little to help the Republican ticket, in Massachusetts or anywhere else.

Kennedy opened his fall campaign with a traditional rally at Cadillac Square in Detroit on Labor Day, appealing to a core Democratic constituency as he began the frenetic two-month push to Election Day. A half-dozen or more times a day, Kennedy gave his standard stump speech, exhorting his audiences, interlacing his remarks with his wry, understated sense of humor, which helped to put him and his audience at ease. But, above all, he emphasized the seriousness of what was at hand. As one close observer of Kennedy, who heard him speak many times that fall, the central theme of his basic speech went something like this: "*America cannot stand still; her prestige fails in the world; this is a time of burdens and sacrifice; we must move.*"[28] He also rarely missed an opportunity to educate his audiences about the American past, telling a crowd at the state capitol in Albany, N.Y. that Thomas Jefferson and James Madison had come to their city in the 1790s as they built what eventually became the Democratic Party.[29] One reporter who followed the campaign experienced it as a moving lesson in American history. Kennedy liked to quote from a wide range of historical figures, and generally without regard to party or ideology. They included not only Abraham Lincoln but also lesser known writers such as Tom Paine and T. S. Eliot.

Early that fall, the campaign turned its attention to the Catholic question in the hope of keeping it from dominating the news coverage. It looked as if it might already be too late for that. The National Conference of Citizens for Religious Freedom, led by Norman Vincent Peale, a prominent Protestant minister, declared emphatically that no Catholic could serve as president without being dominated by the Vatican.[30] Richard Nixon, for his part, was on record as saying that Kennedy's loyalty to the United States was beyond question. Leading Democrats, Harry Truman especially, nonetheless tried to hold Nixon accountable for the enormous amount of anti-Catholic literature being circulated around the country, though these charges were not sustained by evidence. But with the nation enjoying general prosperity and a bipartisan agreement on a Cold War that at that time was not hot, Kennedy's religion became more of a focus. James Michener, a best-selling author who campaigned for Kennedy, was not particularly interested, one way or another, in his Catholicism. He was struck, however, by how many Americans he met on the campaign trail were. One woman, in Bucks County, Pennsylvania, an educated and affluent Philadelphia suburb, exclaimed, "My minister told us if we voted for John Kennedy we would live to see the day when Protestants were crucified in Levittown shopping center."[31] This bizarre mixing of ancient imagery with a symbol of twentieth-century America showed how deeply the unease was rooted. To Kennedy (and most Americans, presumably) this was preposterous, but as a pragmatic politician he could not ignore such sentiment. The fear at its root—and it was impossible to know how widespread it was—was that if a Catholic became president, the Catholic Church would emerge full force from its relative quiescence and extend a tyranny over America.

Kennedy accepted an invitation in early September from the Houston Ministerial Association, an organization of Baptist ministers, to speak directly to the religious question. Texas was an ideal venue for such an address; the state was home to millions of Protestant Democrats and, by putting Johnson on the ticket, the campaign had clearly made Texas a priority. It was also the home of some of the most open anti-Catholic activity aimed at Kennedy anywhere in the country. He was understandably trepidatious about his appearance, knowing that if things went badly, his campaign might be damaged beyond repair. Kennedy walked into the hall in Houston, took his seat on the podium, and waited his turn to speak. The Baptist ministers stared impassively back at him. When he addressed his audience, both those in the hall and Texans watching on statewide television, Kennedy was at his most poised. He began by asserting that the religious issue was not the most important question facing the nation, taking the opportunity to summarize the main themes of his campaign. He spoke of

the spread of communist influence, until it now festers 90 miles off the coast of Florida—the humiliating treatment of our President and Vice President by those who no longer respect our power—the hungry children I saw in West Virginia, the old people who cannot pay their doctor bills, the families forced to give up their farms—an America with too many slums, with too few schools, and too late to the moon and outer space.[32]

Kennedy then turned to the topic in hand. He came to the Baptist ministers not to refight the Protestant Reformation or argue theology, but to neutralize the Catholic question as best he could and calm the deeply rooted, almost atavistic fears of millions of Americans. In the face of a 400-year-old rift in Western culture, this was not easily done. Kennedy stated boldly that if his faith and his obligations to his office ever came into conflict, he would resign the presidency, thus giving more precedence to the obligations to his Church than those to his nation. He did little to educate his audience about Catholicism as a religion but did point to Catholic countries, such as Ireland and France, where religious liberty was universal, as well as "the independence of such [Catholic] statesmen as de Gaulle and Adenauer."[33] Declaring his own autonomy from any religious authority and affirming his commitment to the separation of church and state, he said he would expect no less from a president of any religion: "This is the kind of America I believe in—and this is the kind I fought for in the South Pacific, and the kind my brother died for in Europe."[34]

What Kennedy left unsaid in Houston was the possibility that the teachings of his Church and his political judgment might coincide. At that moment, John F. Kennedy was part of a long tradition of in the United States of Catholics insisting that it was possible to be both devout in their faith and loyal Americans. Al Smith made that case in a 1927 *Atlantic* magazine article entitled simply "Catholic and Patriot." And as early as 1806, Catholics in New York argued that their allegiance to Rome was purely religious, and that their political and military loyalties were firmly with the United States.

Kennedy tried to deflect some of the focus away from the Catholic Church itself. Denouncing religious bigotry as antithetical to the nation's best traditions, he reminded Baptist ministers that their Church had once been persecuted for its beliefs, necessitating Thomas Jefferson's Statute of Religious Freedom in Virginia. He also nimbly told his listeners that there were no religious tests among defenders of the Alamo, the iconic event in Texas history. Kennedy then answered questions from his audience and, when the formal program ended, some of the ministers, won over, came forward to greet him warmly.

In the estimation of Theodore White, who closely followed many presidential campaigns and wrote about them to great acclaim, Kennedy's performance in Houston was the best of that kind of presentation he ever witnessed. He had defused the Catholic issue for those who would be open to voting for him, regardless of his religion. The campaign circulated tapes of Kennedy's performance across the country, especially to Democratic and Catholic audiences. With Democrats outnumbering Republicans by a significant margin in 1960, Kennedy's first and most important task was to solidify support within his own party. His appeal for religious tolerance across the board was also meant for Jewish Americans, most of whom were Democrats but who might have had some lingering concerns about Joe Kennedy.[35] And Jack Kennedy himself was relieved about and energized by his performance in Houston and, later on, was even able to laugh about the religious question. He told the audience at an Alfred E. Smith dinner in New York about a long-ago defeated presidential candidate, who suffered much and even lost his home state, ending with, "you all know his name and religion: Alfred M. Landon, *Protestant.*"[36]

After his less than stellar performance in Los Angeles that summer, Kennedy had mastered television once again. Richard Nixon, had his own successes with the medium, including a highly regarded acceptance speech at the 1960 Republican convention, and had taken note of Kennedy's uneven performance in his nomination speech. Encouraged by a recent Congressional resolution, his campaign and Kennedy's agreed to four televised debates, the first of their kind in American history. Nixon's campaign had gotten off to a slow start in the fall. The candidate had to endure two weeks in hospital due to an infected knee and his schedule before and after that was weighed down by his pledge to visit all 50 states (Alaska and Hawaii having just joined the Union) *after* the summer Republican convention. President Eisenhower had warned Nixon against debating with Kennedy, fearing that the most significant outcome would be more exposure for the lesser-known challenger.

The first debate was held in late September at a television studio in Chicago. Kennedy arrived at the studio intellectually prepared, tanned, and rested. One of his campaign's technological innovations was an expensive videotape recorder that allowed him to review all his speeches and work on improving his performance.[37] Nixon admitted he had never seen any recordings of his own public appearances. Once the debate began (in the form of a joint news conference), Kennedy took command and was appropriately aggressive, his cool demeanor and telegenic features helping him considerably on camera. As the challenger he had the advantage of blaming every shortcoming and ill of the United States on the Eisenhower administration, now in its eighth year of power, thereby placing Vice President Nixon on the defensive. The focus of the first debate was domestic affairs, but Kennedy declared at the outset, "I would not want any implication to be given that this does not involve directly our struggle with Mr. Khrushchev for survival."[38] One of his priorities was not to allow Nixon in any way to tar him as being soft on communism.

Nixon had lost some weight during his recuperation from his knee problem, looked slightly ill at ease, and suffered from a poor makeup job. The bitter irony for Nixon was that he, who had enjoyed a lifetime of good health, looked sickly at this most critical moment, while Kennedy, with his legions of health problems, had never looked better.[39] He also found himself agreeing in principle with Kennedy's main argument that the United States had slipped into complacency during the 1950s. His main disagreement seemed to be over the cost and scope of Kennedy's proposals—those relating, for instance, to federal aid to education, aid to depressed regions, and a greater role for the federal government in the provision of medical insurance. Nixon was so uncharacteristically acquiescent in Chicago that his office was flooded with telegrams and letters from disappointed Republicans all over the country, stunned at his concurring with the thrust of Kennedy's remarks and dismayed by his appearance. Three similar joint appearances followed, with Nixon recovering his self-assurance and displaying his own considerable debating skills, but the largest television audience, some 70 million, was for the first. As President Eisenhower had feared, Kennedy benefitted from holding his own with the sitting vice president and proving to be, in the eyes of most observers, Nixon's equal. His strong performance also blunted Nixon's claim to be the more experienced of the two, rarely the most exciting of campaign themes in any election.[40] Overall, the debates were a boost for the Democratic candidate, as Kennedy's large, enthusiastic rallies and upward movement in public opinion surveys after the first debate demonstrated—even Nixon admitted in his memoirs that "Kennedy had done extremely well."[41]

One of the most important battlegrounds of the 1960 campaign was the South. Republicans hoped that the old Democratic "Solid South" was a thing of the past, Kennedy's selection of Johnson notwithstanding. Nixon drew unexpectedly large crowds on a trip to the region, especially in Birmingham and Atlanta. The latter liked to think of itself as the city "too busy to hate," one that had epitomized since the Civil War the New South of business and commerce. Meanwhile, the Democrats pro-civil rights language in the platform was something of a risk in that it might alienate white southern Democrats, and Kennedy was unlikely to be elected without winning at least some southern states. He managed to not mention civil rights in his acceptance speech and also gave private assurances to leaders in the South that, among other things, would move slowly on school desegregation.[42] Even so, Governor Ross Barnett of Mississippi organized a strategy that stirred memories of the Dixiecrats of 1948. The goal was for his and other southern states to vote for Democratic electors who would not support the national ticket in the Electoral College. These independent electors would hold great leverage if neither Kennedy nor Nixon won an Electoral College majority and it fell to the House of Representatives to select the next president.[43] An unlikely scenario, but one that contributed to the Kennedy campaign's worries that, one way or another, much of the South might be lost.

Lyndon Johnson campaigned with Kennedy early in the fall, then they went their separate ways, with Johnson concentrating on the South. In October he embarked on a whistle-stop rail tour from Washington to New Orleans, his accent becoming more southern as he went. In contrast with Nixon's forays into the bustling, urban New South, Johnson's train took him to the Old South, to smaller cities and old railroad towns. There he spoke not so much of John F. Kennedy and the New Frontier but appealed rather to traditional southern loyalty to the Democratic Party, asking his listeners plaintively, "what excuse have you got for not voting with the party of your fathers?"[44] He also deployed a certain populism, at one stop in rural Virginia asking, "What has Dick Nixon ever done for Culpepper?"[45] When he did mention his running mate, he emphasized Kennedy's military service and the wartime death of Joseph P. Kennedy Jr. In speaking to crowds that sometimes included African-Americans, he alluded, although not too specifically, to the concept of equal rights for all. Johnson also galvanized, flattered, threatened, and cajoled hundreds of local Democratic leaders into supporting the national ticket.[46] His campaigning through Dixie and his native Texas (where a crowd of overzealous Nixon supporters harassed Johnson and wife Lady Bird at a Dallas hotel, an incident which Johnson played up for all it was worth) was a rousing success, one overlooked at the time by the national press corps.

The challenge for the Kennedy-Johnson campaign was to hold onto as many white southern Democrats as possible and at the same time boost the significant African-American vote in the northern cities, which had been trending Democratic since the New Deal. In 1960 the latter was not necessarily a monolith for the Democrats, however. Some leading African-American leaders were for Nixon; these included Jackie Robinson, who had integrated major league baseball and was a hero to black Americans. Robinson insisted that Kennedy was not to be trusted on civil rights. Martin Luther King Jr. had been generous in his public comments on Nixon and, as a native southerner, had an instinctive wariness of Democrats. Race became part of the campaign when Kennedy placed a phone call to King's wife Corretta, pregnant at the time, expressing his concern after her husband had been arrested on a minor traffic charge and sentenced to six months hard labor at a remote Georgia prison. Kennedy did so at the urging of his civil rights advisors; his political aides were furious, however, thinking that the South had been unduly jeopardized. Richard Nixon, on the other hand, said it would be inappropriate for him as vice president to interfere in a local legal matter. Rev. Martin Luther King Sr. announced that he had been planning to vote for Nixon because of Kennedy's religion, but because of the phone call to his daughter-in-law and Bobby Kennedy's work in getting his son released from prison he was going to take a "suitcase full of votes and put them into Senator Kennedy's lap." Kennedy noted the irony of the senior King being motivated by religious bias, adding, "we all have our fathers, don't we?"

Kennedy also endorsed sit-ins by African-American college students at segregated lunch counters in the South. Looking for more ways to tap into the energies and idealism of the nation's large and growing number of young people, at two in the morning he asked a boisterous crowd of students at the University of Michigan in Ann Arbor, "How many of you would be willing to spend your days working—as teachers, doctors and engineers—in Ghana?"[47] Hubert Humphrey had introduced legislation in

Congress along these lines and Kennedy had read a report by a college professor about the prospect of young Americans going overseas to help the
poor.[48] That question of his in Michigan, that later gave rise to the Peace
Corps, was spontaneous, however, and Kennedy was heartened when the
students roared their approval at his proposal.

The idea of a Peace Corps aside, Kennedy knew that he had to present himself as Nixon's equal as a traditional Cold Warrior or face defeat.
He maintained throughout the campaign, and in a published collection of
speeches entitled *The Strategy of Peace* (1960), that "a missile gap" had developed between the United States and the Soviet Union, with the latter
in the lead. This in part was designed to inoculate him from criticism by
Nixon and had clear echoes of his strategy in the 1952 Senate race, where he
came at Lodge from the left on domestic issues and the right on foreign policy.[49] Kennedy pointed to leading generals who shared his concern at a time
when the Soviet Union had taken a clear lead in space and its leaders were
speaking of an inevitable victory over the capitalist West. And there was a
general sense that, at the least, the Soviet Union was catching up with the
United States in many areas. In the summer Olympics of 1960, for example,
for the first time the Soviet Union won more medals than the United States
While his anti-communist rhetoric on Cuba may have been motivated in
part by his desire for votes in nearby Florida, his statements on the rivalry
with the Soviet Union carried a greater ring of conviction.[50]

In the closing weeks of the campaign, Kennedy's lead in the public opinion polls began to shrink. Nixon had been understandably eager, after eight
years as vice president, to get out from under the shadow of President Eisenhower and kept him at arm's length for most of the campaign. Desperate
to close the gap, however, the GOP featured Eisenhower in its final week
television "blitz" in which the party bought national airtime to broadcast
its message. In one such appearance, Eisenhower went after Kennedy quite
hard, denouncing the Democratic nominee's "phony schemes" and declaring that the "young genius" was not ready to become president.[51] Sent out
on the campaign trail, Eisenhower, still a widely popular figure (he was
greeted by more than a few good-natured signs reading, "We Like Ike But
We Back Jack), drew big crowds in the closing days.[52] Nixon's remarks about
Kennedy also became more biting, painting Kennedy as a big spender who
wanted to concentrate power in Washington, D.C. And some voters may
have had second thoughts connected to Kennedy's age, experience, and religion. Both candidates were under enormous strain as they traveled the
huge country by plane, rail, and car, meeting the nearly impossible expectations of appearing refreshed, upbeat, and commanding at every stop. Kennedy was buoyed along the way by his ability to relax and even nap between
appearances. Even so, beneath his sun tan and big smile, careful observers

could occasionally glimpse utter exhaustion. Although he maintained his generally sunny disposition throughout the ordeal of the campaign, toward its end he erupted in fury behind the scenes when a scheduling mistake put him in New York City instead of California, where he thought he could do more good. But Kennedy's spirits were lifted the final weekend of the campaign on a visit to Waterbury, Connecticut. In one of the nation's most Catholic cities, thousands lined the motorcade route from the airport and, when Kennedy finally appeared at three in the morning, he was greeted by a wildly enthusiastic crowd of around 40 thousand, most of whom had been huddled in their cars for hours, some in nightclothes, as they awaited their candidate's arrival.[53]

On Election Day, November 8, 1960, Kennedy voted at his polling place in Boston, the city where his immigrant ancestors had arrived more than a century earlier. He then flew on the *Caroline* to Cape Cod to await returns at the family home. The percentage of his fellow Americans who also voted in the election, in a time before widespread negative advertising, was the highest since 1908 and has not been surpassed since. The televised debates, the closeness of the race, the Kennedy campaign's quiet efforts to register and mobilize new voters, and the nation's growing fascination with Kennedy himself all contributed to the turnout. Most of the final public opinion polling showed a very tight race and early returns were inconclusive. Kennedy edged into a slight lead but, when Nixon went on national television after three in the morning east coast time, the final outcome was still unclear. He somewhat awkwardly announced that Kennedy was leading but did not concede defeat. Kennedy declined to make a similar appearance and, although seemingly on the verge of a majority in the Electoral College, simply went to bed.

When Kennedy awoke the next morning, several states, most notably Illinois and Michigan, had fallen into his column, making him president-elect of the United States. The race was one of the closest in American history. The popular vote was especially tight, with Kennedy receiving just under 50 percent, just over 100,000 votes more than Nixon, which amounted to less than a half-vote per precinct. Under the Constitution, however, what mattered was not the popular vote but the Electoral College, and there Kennedy's lead was clearer, at 303 to 219. He had won four of the five most populous states, only losing Nixon's home state of California, where, as he suspected, he was trailing as the campaign ended. Lyndon Johnson had contributed enormously to the Democratic victory. In addition to narrowly winning Texas, the Kennedy-Johnson ticket captured five other southern states; North Carolina, South Carolina, Georgia, Louisiana, and Arkansas; their winning margin in Georgia was topped only by that in heavily Catholic Rhode Island. The Republican effort in much of the Deep South was hampered by a lack of party organization. But Ross Barnett's plan eventually resulted in 15 electoral votes—8 from Mississippi, 6 from Alabama, and 1 from Oklahoma—being cast for segregationist Democrat Harry Byrd of Virginia. The solid Democratic South was not restored, but Nixon's 43 Electoral College votes were more than matched there by Kennedy's 114.

An important part of Kennedy's coalition was the overwhelming support he received from Catholics, which proved crucial in heavily populated states such as New York, Pennsylvania, Michigan, Illinois, the three southern New England states, New Jersey, and New Mexico, one of the few western states Kennedy won. An estimated 80 percent of American Catholics had voted for Kennedy, many with great enthusiasm, four years after a majority of them had supported Eisenhower. Although Joe Kennedy complained bitterly of what he considered the betrayal by leading Catholic clergy (family friend Cardinal Cushing of Boston a prominent exception) in not supporting his son, Catholic voters had done so in overwhelming numbers.[54] Wealthier and more educated Catholics were slightly more likely to vote for Nixon. Although it is not possible to know exactly how much Kennedy's Catholicism influenced the decision of individual voters (few will admit to pollsters that they are motivated by prejudice), the best studies indicate that, on the whole, his religion cost him more popular votes than it gained him. In the Electoral College, however, losses in border and southern states such as Kentucky, Tennessee, Virginia, and Florida were more than offset by wins in the Northeast and Midwest, where his Catholicism was more to his advantage. As one Republican lamented, 'the bigots were mal-distributed.'[55] According to one study, Jewish voters, traditionally Democratic and also seeing Kennedy as a fellow cultural outsider bent on tearing down an important barrier, supported him even more than had Catholics.[56]

Many of Kennedy's Catholic voters were in the cities of the nation's industrial core, in the Northeast and Midwest. In most of those same cities African-American voters turned out for Kennedy in greater numbers than they had for Stevenson in 1952 and 1956. And in the South, where many black Americans were denied the right to vote, most of those able to do so cast their votes for Kennedy, providing crucial support in the Carolinas and Texas.[57] In general, however, Kennedy's appeal was limited in much of rural America. He did little to weaken the Republican grip in the predominantly Protestant countryside stretching from New England to the Mississippi Valley. Nor did he mount much of a challenge to Nixon in the Great Plains or Mountain West. One traditional Republican stronghold in which he did manage to make some headway was the suburbs of Chicago and major cities of the east coast, where his call for national improvement—including in education—appealed to the growing number of families new to the middle class.[58]

On the heels of the election there were complaints of election fraud from Republican and conservative ranks—unsurprisingly, given the close race. A few of the state totals were absurdly close, with Kennedy eventually declared the winner in Hawaii by a margin of 115 votes out of some 180,000 cast. Most of the allegations centered on Illinois and Texas, states that had a reputation for such things. In Texas, effectively a one-party state, Republicans had essentially no way to substantiate their charges. Illinois was a different story, divided as it was between Democratic Chicago and Republican control in most of the rest of the state. Each party alleged that the other was guilty of malfeasance, and Chicago Mayor Richard Daley, convinced of Republican improprieties, offered to pay half the cost of a statewide recount. That never happened, but unofficial investigations indicated that Chicago's tradition of Election Day irregularities continued in 1960. Even if Kennedy had lost Illinois, he still would have had enough electoral votes to win the presidency. Both Eisenhower and Nixon sent Kennedy telegrams of congratulations, and Nixon, seeking to preserve national unity during the Cold War and also thinking of his political future, declined to press the matter of voter fraud. Yet allegations surrounding the vote in Texas and Illinois, however unproven, raised longstanding questions about Kennedy's victory. And the slightness of the margin of victory over an opponent they considered Jack's inferior disquieted Kennedy and his closest aides.

But those were concerns for another time. At 43 the youngest elected president in American history, Kennedy had been underestimated by his opponents ever since he launched what seemed to doubters a quixotic presidential bid. If nothing else, John Fitzgerald Kennedy had overcome the religious prejudice that the first English colonists brought to America in the early 1600s. Drawing on the old politics but also innovating where he could, Kennedy developed a new standard for the successful American politician. The victory also belonged his family, his talented and dedicated campaign team, the political pros who supported him, and countless others who had labored on his behalf. Before heading off to a victory rally on the day after the election, the Kennedy family posed for photographs in Joe and Rose's home. In one of the pictures, everyone is looking at Jack. The eyes of the nation and much of the world were also to be riveted on him for the rest of his days.

CHAPTER 5

"THOUGH EMBATTLED WE ARE"

Just after the inauguration ceremony on January 20, 1961, Jacqueline Kennedy caught up with her husband inside the Capitol, for their first moments together since the swearing in and speech. As Jackie reached out to touch her husband's face, she noticed tears in his eyes.[1] The moment was captured on film, one of the more private photographs of the day. The couple then led the parade that followed (which featured the surviving crew from Kennedy's PT 109) down Pennsylvania Avenue in an open-air limousine. As they approached the viewing stand where his parents were, the new president he rose up out of the car and in a poignant gesture doffed his hat to his father out of gratitude and respect.[2] It was the only time that day he did such a thing. For Joseph Kennedy, a long-held dream had been realized, albeit not by the son he had originally imagined as a future president but by his second son, whom he confessed he never fully understood. Rose Kennedy had shared her husband's ambition for their children, but her mind was on the next world as well. She was especially heartened to look up from her pew that morning at Holy Trinity Church in Georgetown and see that her son had slipped quietly around the corner from his home for Mass.[3] Her son and daughter-in-law, despite their troubles, had another reason to look to the future with happiness. Between the election and inauguration, on November 25, 1960, they welcomed their second child into the world, naming him John Fitzgerald Kennedy Jr.

After his narrow victory in November, Kennedy had a prolonged period of recovery from the rigors of the campaign at his parents' home in Florida. As he regained his energy and began to put together his administration, foreign policy became the priority. Kennedy's first choice for Secretary of State was William Fullbright of Arkansas, chairman of the Senate Foreign

Relations Committee. The southerner was politically committed to racial segregation, which could have presented awkwardness in dealings with the emerging nations of Africa and Asia. Adlai Stevenson expressed interest in the position, but Kennedy did not want such a prominent figure, a former rival with whom he had had an uneven relationship, heading the State Department. Eventually he persuaded Stevenson to accept his offer of ambassador to the United Nations. Kennedy then named Dean Rusk, a mild-mannered former college professor and diplomat whom he did not know, to that important post. He was in effect signaling that he had decided to act as his own Secretary of State.

Aware of his narrow margin of victory, he took bi-partisanship into account when nominating Douglas Dillon, a Republican, to be Secretary of the Treasury, a position that Kennedy, like all modern presidents, valued highly. One of the more surprising selections Kennedy made was Robert McNamara, a leading executive in the automobile industry. As with Rusk, Kennedy was not personally acquainted with McNamara, who was only 44 but already had a reputation as a quantitative and managerial wizard. He was also a Republican who had supported Kennedy in his election campaign. Only after being assured that McNamara, with an Irish surname that many Catholics shared, was in fact a Protestant did he nominate him to be Secretary of Defense.[4] Kennedy was concerned about having an administration that might be considered too "Catholic," especially with regard to the most important positions.

One member of Kennedy's cabinet whose Catholicism was not an issue was his brother Bobby, whom he nominated for attorney general. Joe Kennedy had insisted on the appointment, which, given the familial relationship and Bobby's age and limited legal experience, was not universally acclaimed. The new president's personal members of staff, most of them young men in their thirties and forties, reflected his path to the presidency, including as they did veterans of Boston politics, his days on Capitol Hill, and the presidential campaign. One difference from most previous presidential staffs was that Kennedy decided it would have no chief. Sherman Adams had served President Eisenhower in that role and some observers thought he had gathered too much authority into his hands and kept Ike unduly isolated. Kennedy, whose executive and managerial experience was limited, preferred to see himself as the center of a wheel, with its spokes connecting to him.

Since entering politics 15 years earlier, Kennedy had been most impressive as a candidate. Now, one observer of the new administration described Kennedy and his New Frontiersmen as "the junior officers of the Second World War come to responsibility."[5] The burdens were enormous and the decisions that Kennedy made would have great consequences. His first crisis as president came early. He had staked out strongly anti-communist positions during the campaign, among them denouncing the "festering" of communism 90 miles from the Florida coast, in Cuba, and voicing his support for anti-Castro "freedom fighters." His inaugural address could be read as moving away from Cold War orthodoxies, but it also re-affirmed his commitment to the struggle against tyranny. Senator Kennedy, among others, had initially lauded the coming to power of Fidel Castro and his revolutionaries in 1958. Kennedy compared the young Cuban revolutionary, nearly a decade his junior, as acting in the Latin American tradition of Simon Bolivar, liberator ("and sometime Dictator," he added).[6]

Once in power, however, Castro began to emulate the Soviet ideal of thoroughgoing revolution, with its complete transformation of society, culture, and economics, rather than the American political and anti-colonial model of which Kennedy had spoken in his inaugural address. Cuba had been closely tied to the United States since the Spanish-American War of 1898. The prospect of it aligning with the Soviets seemed to violate the spirit of the Monroe Doctrine, in which the United States had declared that European powers should not intervene in affairs of the Western Hemisphere. Castro's move toward Moscow also contradicted the principle of containing communism, the goal of U.S. foreign policy since the start of the Cold War. Relations between the United States and Cuba deteriorated in the final year of the Eisenhower presidency, as Havana signed a trade treaty with Moscow, prompting Washington to end diplomatic relations with Cuba. In 1960, the U.S. government also embarked upon, in secret, a strategy to drive Castro from power. A key part of this plan, put together by the Central Intelligence Agency (CIA), involved an American-sponsored invasion of their homeland by Cuban exiles. Soviet leader Khrushchev raised the stakes shortly before Kennedy took office with his declaration that the Soviet Union would actively support "wars of national liberation" around the world. This raised the specter of Cuba becoming a springboard for communist revolutions in Central and South America.

The Cuba plan, already in motion, was presented to Kennedy during his first week in office, awaiting only his final approval. The military and intelligence experts who briefed him on it were confident of its success, seeing the Cuban people as trapped behind their own iron curtain and waiting only for the opportunity to rebel. Kennedy was also caught in the tension between wanting to overturn what increasingly seemed like a communist dictatorship in the making, and respecting the right of self-determination of small nations.[7] It would have been difficult for him at that early point in his presidency to overrule the leadership of the military and the CIA and stop the clock on the operation. The plan had originated under Eisenhower, whose credibility on military issues was enormous. And if Kennedy was not intimidated by the senior generals and intelligence chiefs, some of whom were old enough to be his father, he was well aware of how skeptical they were of him. It is also true that the generals did not know quite what to make of the charismatic young president.[8] For whatever reasons, Kennedy failed to ask the hard questions, which was unlike him, of the Joint Chiefs of Staff and the CIA. If he canceled the mission, hundreds of men trained and armed by the United States, already gathered in Guatemala and awaiting the signal to go, would have been angry and convinced they had been betrayed, potentially causing problems for Kennedy at home and in Latin America. Kennedy did not want to be tarred at home, especially so early in his term, as weak in the face of communism. At the same time, if the U.S. military did become directly involved in Cuba, the risk of the Soviets and their allies retaliating in Europe and Asia would increase.

As the day for the landing on the southern coast of Cuba approached, Kennedy maintained his insistence that the U.S. military keep its distance from the invasion. Some of the planners had assumed from the start that if the landing of the small contingent of 1,400 Cuban exiles met heavy resistance from Castro's forces (numbering about 200,000 men), the United States would intervene, at a minimum, with air support. Kennedy had some qualms about letting things go forward. However, after reading a highly positive report from a Marine colonel who was with the Cubans in Guatemala and convinced of their readiness, he gave the go ahead.[9] The operation was launched on April 17, 1961. What followed was what one historian rightly called a "Perfect Failure."[10] Castro's government had gotten wind of the plan, met the invaders on the beach, and crushed them. Nearly all of them were killed, wounded, or captured (most surrendering on the beach); a few escaped with the aid of U.S. ships. The popular uprising never occurred. The U.S. military remained offshore after Kennedy rejected pleas for direct intervention one final time and canceled a second air strike by the Cuban exiles.

Overlooked in the chaos were the deaths of four member of the Air National Guard of Alabama, who flew over Cuba hoping to provide air cover for the exiles on the beach, even though this had not been officially approved. They expected to be protected by U.S. fighter planes from a nearby aircraft carrier. Due to confusion regarding different time zones, they did not get this cover and their plane was shot down. Their fate exemplified the bungled nature of the U.S. role at the Bay of Pigs. It also was a reflection of Kennedy's own ambivalence about the entire operation. Had the United States, which had a military base on the island of Cuba at Guantanamo Bay, set out to destroy the Castro government, it could have done so easily. Instead, Castro remained in power, the Communist bloc enjoyed a propaganda windfall, and the United States and its new president were humiliated.

President Kennedy admitted publicly that the United States had been behind the debacle and that "he was the responsible officer" of the government. At a news conference he was not vigorously challenged by the media, who were influenced by the deferential attitude toward authority that prevailed in the early 1960s. Kennedy's forthright admission of responsibility, the traditional rallying around the president at times of crisis (especially true for that era in the Cold War), and the widespread view that communism ought not to be permitted to make headway in the Americas all worked in his favor. His public approval rating reached new heights after Cuba—83 percent in the Gallup Poll. That was small consolation to Kennedy, who said bitterly in private: "It's just like Eisenhower; the worse I do, the more popular I get." But on the far left, Kennedy was harshly criticized for his "aggression" by the Fair Play for Cuba Committee, and leading academic C. Wright Mills charged that, "Kennedy and Company have returned us to barbarism."[11] To those critics, he now looked like an old-fashioned imperialist, and a ham-fisted one at that. Conversely, those who saw Kennedy as not going far enough believed he had displayed a lack of nerve and courage; one U.S. officer involved in the operation mocked Kennedy's manhood.[12]

John F. Kennedy was not used to the sting of defeat; that, and his grief over the loss of life and the plight of the captured Cuban exiles, whose courage and patriotism he admired, left him devastated. A key part of Kennedy's success had been his quiet self-confidence; that had now been shaken. In their private White House quarters, a tearful Kennedy shared his anguish with Jackie.[13] The pain of the bitter experience stayed with Kennedy for quite a while; well into the summer, a visitor to the Oval Office said meeting Kennedy was "like talking to a statue." But he took proactive steps as well, asking for and receiving the resignations of CIA director Allen Dulles and his deputy Richard Bissell. Kennedy told them bluntly that in a parliamentary system of government, he himself would have to resign, but in the United States, it was they who must go. Kennedy's government continued to look for ways to change the regime in Cuba, putting an economic embargo on the small nation, getting the Organization of American States to expel Cuba, and planning more covert operations, although the latter never amounted to much. Kennedy preferred working informally with trusted advisors than through bureaucratic structures. He therefore determined that the two men in Washington he knew best and trusted most, Bobby Kennedy and Ted Sorensen, both essentially out of the loop on Cuba, would in the future be brought in on future critical major foreign policy discussions.

Presidential historian and Kennedy aide Arthur M. Schlesinger once said that politics is in essence a learning profession. Kennedy hoped to profit from his mistakes and indecision at the Bay of Pigs. He was fortunate that he made such a blunder early on and that the damage arising from

Cuba in retrospect was relatively minor. Soviet leader Nikita Khrushchev, who said he found "constructive things" in Kennedy's inaugural speech and ordered it printed in Soviet newspapers, was stunned at the reports of the Bay of Pigs.[14] He said privately, "I don't understand Kennedy, what's wrong with him? Can he really be that indecisive?" [15] It was in this climate of both increased tension and potential for peaceful conflict resolution that John F. Kennedy and Nikita Khrushchev agreed to meet in Vienna (Austria being neutral in the Cold War) in June of 1961.

Before he left for Europe, Kennedy injured his back while planting a tree at a ceremony in Ottawa, Canada. In order for him to function properly, he had to take increased doses of painkillers. For the first time since his back surgery in 1954 he was forced to use crutches to walk when he was out of the public eye, although while in it he managed without them. Kennedy lived with near-constant pain, not only from his back but also from the effects of Addison's disease, fevers, and continued troubles with his digestive system, among other ailments. To combat all this he enlisted a variety of doctors to treat him with cortisone and a variety of medicines, in addition to the painkillers. No one doctor was in charge of his overall treatment in the first year of his presidency and at least one physician, Max Jacobson, known as "Dr. Feelgood," who treated the president and Mrs. Kennedy with amphetamines, had a dubious reputation in medical circles.[16] Kennedy was determined to present himself as a young, healthy, active man. There was no doubting his overall vitality and zest for life, nor the fortitude he showed in overcoming his pain and illnesses. However, the extent and variety of his conditions and the massive amount of medical treatment he required raises questions of how prudent it was for a president to serve under those circumstances, especially in the nuclear age.

On their way to Vienna, the Kennedys stopped in Paris, where the president met with Charles de Gaulle, the leader of France, and Jacqueline impressed her hosts with her ease in speaking French. Her ability to speak languages other than English, one her husband never developed, was a great asset to Kennedy in their travels. The Kennedys' generally pleasant visit to the French capital was not matched by their time in Vienna. John F. Kennedy and Nikita Khrushchev cut very different figures. Khrushchev came from peasant stock, lacked much in the way of formal education, and was both a survivor of, and implicit in, Stalin's brutal system. In his late sixties, he had a son older than President Kennedy. Kennedy at six foot one was a full foot taller than his Soviet counterpart. The two men had met once before, a brief introduction during Khrushchev's 1959 visit to the United States. Now they were anxious to take the measure of each other, especially in light of the tensions between their two nations over Cuba, Southeast Asia, and Berlin.

The Soviets were particularly keen to resolve the Berlin situation. Twice in the twentieth century the Soviet Union (i.e. Russia in 1914) had endured invasions from German armies; its leaders was acutely aware of that history. Khrushchev referred to West Berlin—which although deep inside communist East Germany, was divided into sectors by the Allies after World War Two and had an American military presence—as a "bone in my throat."[17] He was eager to sign a separate peace treaty with East Germany, which would have potentially resulted in West Berlin being absorbed into the communist state. Khrushchev knew his Marxist-Leninism and Kennedy, either forgetting or ignoring advice not to get into a theoretical debate, allowed himself to be diverted from a discussion of specific contemporary issues into philosophical ruminations on socialism. It was the Harvard-educated Kennedy, who despite his interest in history was, like most American politicians, not a political philosopher or theoretician, who found himself out of his depth. His Soviet adversary could be extraordinarily forceful and Kennedy was taken aback. "Is he always like this?" he asked the U.S. ambassador to the Soviet Union. Kennedy's personal skills, usually so effective with American politicians, simply did not work with the feisty and belligerent Soviet leader, much as Roosevelt's had failed with Stalin. As Kennedy himself candidly said afterwards, Khrushchev "just beat the hell out of me."

Trying to manage the news coverage of the summit, Kennedy's press team put out an anecdote portraying their man as witty and sharp. Apparently he had pointed to two medals on Khrushchev's jacket at the end of the summit and asked what they were; Lenin Peace Prizes, came the reply; "I hope you get to keep them," said Kennedy, and even Khrushchev joined in the laughter. Despite that, the two men did not establish much of a constructive rapport. And while Kennedy's men later disputed that their boss had been harassed and bullied by his counterpart, Soviet officials stated afterwards that Khrushchev left Vienna seeing Kennedy as an inexperienced, even immature politician, one who could be pushed around. Kennedy himself sensed that was Khrushchev's conclusion, leading to a somewhat gloomy state of mind as he and the Soviet leader said their goodbyes. "It's going to be a long winter," Kennedy said as the two parted.

The question of Berlin remained unresolved. Kennedy returned to the United States vowing to show the Soviet Union a strong face, to disabuse it of the dangerous notion that he could be taken advantage of and intimidated. He repeated his determination that the United States and its allies would defend West Berlin, although not necessarily *East* Berlin. In private, he recognized the oddity of the Berlin situation, a relic of the wartime alliance between the West and the Soviet Union. But to jettison all of Berlin would potentially throw the Western alliance into chaos and tempt the Soviets further; Kennedy concluded that the United States had no choice but to stand its ground. A month after meeting with Khrushchev, he called for another comprehensive defense buildup, which included a new role for the federal government in building fallout shelters, to which tens of millions of Americans would presumably retreat in the event of an all-out nuclear war.[18] Khrushchev reacted in anger, terming Kennedy's action a "preliminary declaration of war" and ordered the resumption of nuclear testing, which he had promised in Vienna he would not do.

The Soviet leader, and more immediately his comrades in East Germany, had another major problem. Thousands of East Germans, many of them well educated, were fleeing into West Berlin and thus leaving the Soviet bloc. In response, on August 13, 1961, the East German government began work on a barrier sealing off East from West Berlin. It was built in stages, so as to gauge the Western reaction. Its official name was the Anti-Fascist Defense Wall, but its construction was an admission of defeat for the Soviet Union and its allies. President Kennedy did take a few steps signaling his disapproval of this provocative move. He beefed up army divisions already stationed in Germany and sent U.S. troops through communist East Germany's autobahn in a high-profile show of ongoing support for the embattled West Berliners. He also dispatched Vice President Johnson and General Lucius Clay, hero of the Berlin airlift of the late 1940s, to demonstrate the ongoing American commitment to West Berlin. But privately, despite criticism that he should have ordered U.S. forces to physically prevent the wall from being built, Kennedy was relieved when it happened. It had been longstanding U.S. policy under both Presidents Truman and Eisenhower to recognize East Berlin as within the Soviet sphere of influence, as agreed by treaty at Yalta in 1945.

It was Khrushchev's impatience that helped to spark the crisis in 1961. A U.S. military response to the construction of the wall would have almost certainly triggered massive conflict between the two heavily armed camps, which could have quickly escalated. The Soviet Union and its allies in the Warsaw Pact had a considerable advantage in troops and conventional weaponry. They might have used that to thrust into central and even western Europe, forcing the United States and NATO to consider seriously the use of nuclear weapons to stem the advance of communist forces. In light of those possibilities, Kennedy's private musing, "better a wall than a war," had its wisdom, even as millions of East Germans and others were now denied an avenue of escape.[19] Not long afterwards, Khrushchev announced that the Soviet Union would not seek to sign a separate peace treaty with East Germany, which for the moment brought the crisis to an end. In contrast to the Bay of Pigs, Kennedy could at least take a measure of satisfaction from his own performance in managing the Cold War in Berlin.

One of the advantages that the United States had in its rivalry with the Soviet Union was a decided lead in nuclear weaponry, especially long-range intercontinental missiles. Never far from Kennedy, as commander-in-chief, was the military officer carrying the "football," a special briefcase which contained the codes by which the U.S. nuclear arsenal could be unleashed. Overall, the United States had about three times as many such weapons as did the Soviet Union. And Khrushchev kept a close eye on Cuba, angered by reports of continuing efforts by the CIA, pressured by President Kennedy and his brother, to undermine Castro and remove him from power. Despite the defusing of tension in Berlin, both the United States and the Soviet Union continued to view their Cold War rivalry as a zero sum game, and the crises of 1961 had dashed any hopes that the new president and his counterpart in the Kremlin might find a way out of the 15-year standoff.

The year 1962 became the most dangerous of all in the long history of the Cold War. Senators Kenneth Keating, Homer Capeheart, and Strom Thurmond, none a Kennedy ally, alleged that the Soviets were up to something in the Caribbean and that the administration was slow to recognize what was happening. In July, U.S. intelligence services did notice something startling: the Soviet Union had indeed commenced a military buildup on the island of Cuba. Khrushchev had promised Kennedy that the Soviet Union would not place offensive nuclear weapons in that country. Kennedy, responding to his domestic critics and also warning Khrushchev, said publicly in early September that the "gravest issues" would arise if the Soviets deployed offensive weapons in Cuba. On October 16, as he prepared for the day in his private quarters, National Security Advisor McGeorge Bundy showed Kennedy photographs taken two days earlier by U-2 spy planes, flying 70,000 feet above Cuba. They indicated that the Soviets were well on their way to installing two bases with at least 40 surface-to-surface medium and intermediate missiles. These sites were on the north coast of Cuba, aimed directly at the United States. The Soviets had also landed combat and support troops on the island, estimated by the United States at the time to be 4,000 in number, revised a week later to 10,000. It was only many years later that it became known that the actual number exceeded 40,000. The offensive missiles had the capacity to destroy major American cities, including Washington, New York, and Chicago. In fact, Seattle was the only U.S. city of significant population that was clearly outside their potential range. And Soviet field commanders were authorized, without prior permission from Moscow, to use short-range nuclear weapons in the event of a U.S. invasion of Cuba.

What motivated the Soviets to take this most provocative of steps? Nikita Khrushchev himself was the architect of the plan. The project was his from the start—rather than Fidel Castro's or anyone else's. "What if we throw a hedgehog down Uncle Sam's pants?" was how he broached the subject to his Soviet colleagues.[20] The initial U.S. reaction was that the move was somehow linked to Berlin. However, the Soviets largely considered the Berlin crisis settled when they erected the wall in 1961, even though the situation remained a source of frustration to Khrushchev. It was Cuba itself that was at the center of Khrushchev's thinking. As early as June of 1960 he said publicly that the Soviets considered Cuba to be under their nuclear protection.[21] Cuba was not Eastern Europe, considered by the Soviet government to have been liberated from Nazi Germany by the Red Army during World War Two at enormous cost in lives. But Fidel Castro had captured Khrushchev's imagination as a Third World revolutionary, courageously holding forth on the very doorstep of the American imperialists.

After the Bay of Pigs, Khrushchev concluded, and not without reason, that a second invasion of Cuba, this one led by the U.S. military and much more formidable, was only a matter of time. In the spring of 1962, the U.S. military conducted a mock invasion of a "Caribbean nation." And Khrushchev was also feeling pressure from another corner: Mao Zedong and Communist China had begun to denounce the Soviets as bowing to the imperialists. Forcefully defending the revolution in Cuba (and Castro agreed to accept the missiles) would be one way to counter that argument. The Soviet Union had limited capacity in intercontinental missiles and its defense experts were quite aware of how badly they lagged behind the United States in this crucial area. The deficiency increased the value of placing missiles close to the United States, allowing some redressing of the strategic and nuclear balance of power. The United States had deployed nuclear missiles, known as Jupiters, in Turkey, pointed directly at the Soviet Union, and these added to the Soviet leader's anger and anxiety.

Khrushchev was also looking to bolster his flagging political fortunes at home. Despite his bold predictions that the performance of the Soviet economy would allow the U.S.S.R. to become a truly socialist nation by 1980, growth was in fact sluggish. Khrushchev was personally identified with the agricultural sector, especially his highly publicized efforts to boost Soviet grain production. His trip to Iowa notwithstanding, Khrushchev's expensive projects to grow cereal crops in the wastes of Siberia and the Russian north had yielded little, other than making himself the subject of mockery. A bold stroke in Cuba, however, one that forced Kennedy and the United States to recognize Soviet power, would help to silence Khrushchev's critics at home and abroad. His plan was for the missiles to be made operational as quickly as possible under the cover of total secrecy. After the fall U.S. elections, he would then inform Kennedy about them in person, either in Washington or at the United Nations. In his earthy way, Khrushchev predicted that Kennedy's reaction to the missiles would be—to paraphrase—that of "the peasant who has to bring his goat into the hut for the winter. He does not like the smell, but he will get used to it."[22] And Khrushchev believed that Kennedy would ultimately accept the missiles in Cuba, just as he had the wall in Berlin and indeed the very presence of Castro's revolutionary state. He had not seen much in Kennedy's performance in office that led him to think otherwise.

During their meeting in Vienna, Khrushchev had exploded in anger at Kennedy's use of the word "miscalculation." It was in Cuba, however, that the Soviet leader made the biggest miscalculation of the entire Cold War. A dissenting voice or two within the Soviet leadership had told him that placing offensive missiles in Cuba would trigger a dangerous crisis, and they were right. Within hours of learning of the missiles in Cuba, Kennedy had created what was officially established a week later as the Executive Committee of the National Security Council. Known as the ExComm, it was made up of leading members of Kennedy's cabinet, military, and intelligence chiefs, and Vice President Johnson, among others. In the Bay of Pigs episode he did not have a decision-making process best suited to his personality. Favoring personnel over formal structure, he now knew exactly who he wanted in the room to discuss what became known among Kennedy intimates as the "Second Cuba." And that meant Bobby Kennedy and Ted Sorensen. It also included General Maxwell Taylor, an ally of Kennedy who he had appointed Chairman of the Joint Chiefs just two weeks before the crisis in Cuba broke. The ExComm met in secret at the White House to focus solely on the situation at hand. Learning from that painful "First Cuba"—the Bay of Pigs—Kennedy placed his trust in a group of men with a variety of perspectives and experiences who could analyze the situation and craft serious recommendations about what should be done. He had recently read historian Barbara Tuchman's new book, *The Guns of August,* on how European leaders had blundered into World War One, a sobering lesson indeed. During the deliberations of the ExComm, Kennedy frequently absented himself from the proceedings, initially to maintain some of his public schedule, but more importantly to give its members the freedom and latitude to discuss all possible options without him there to unduly influence their thinking. In this he demonstrated trust in the judgment of his advisors and himself at this critical hour.

Soon after it began its deliberations, the ExComm reached an important decision. One way or another, the Soviet missiles could not and would not remain in Cuba, and there would be no negotiating on that central point. An emboldened Khrushchev might well next make a decisive move on Berlin or elsewhere, triggering a world war. Kennedy was also acutely aware of the perception among his conservative critics that he had not been sufficiently decisive vis-à-vis the Soviet Union. With the fall elections approaching, he had to be concerned about appearing weak and giving the Republicans evidence to support such allegations. Kennedy said to his closest aides, "If I don't do anything about removing those missiles from Cuba, I ought to be impeached."[23] But how to remove the missiles without triggering a general war, one that would almost certainly involve the use of nuclear weapons by both sides? One option the ExComm discussed initially was quietly seeking their withdrawal through a negotiated settlement. That option was rejected, as Kennedy now knew that Khrushchev had been lying about Soviet intentions in Cuba for some time and a protracted dialogue between Washington and Moscow would only give the Soviets more time to make all the missiles fully operational, thus weakening any U.S. negotiating position.

The option initially favored by most on the ExComm at the outset, especially the military, was a series of airstrikes, followed by an invasion of Cuba. After the Bay of Pigs and in view of the magnitude of what was now before him, Kennedy would not be rushed into making a decision. In the defining moment of his presidency, Kennedy, now 45 years old, held firm against enormous pressure. His ability to detach himself from his surroundings and look at matters objectively was surely of great use to him in October 1962. So was the confidence his parents and upbringing had instilled in him and that he further developed on his own. He could also draw on the benefits of his travel, education, reading and writing, and his own experience of war. Kennedy was also fortified by his resilient buoyancy as he struggled against giving in to a horror that was beginning to seem inevitable.

Kennedy was determined that U.S. knowledge of the missiles be kept secret until he had decided on a course of action. The members of the ExComm maintained that embargo, as did Kennedy himself in one of the strangest high-level meetings of the entire Cold War. Soviet Foreign Minister Andrei Gromyko kept his previously scheduled appointment with Kennedy, with neither man acknowledging the gravity of what was happening between their two nations, even as Kennedy had the U-2 photographs of the missiles in his desk. When he did participate in meetings of the ExComm, Kennedy, unlike during the Bay of Pigs deliberations, asked hard and detailed questions. He demanded to know the specifics of the missiles, what could be known about the Soviets' intentions, and the implications of various courses of action the United States might take. Another possibility that began to emerge during the ExComm's deliberations was a blockade of Cuba, first suggested by Secretary of Defense McNamara, for whose judgment Kennedy had high regard. Kennedy, after nearly a week of deliberations and meetings, chose the blockade, seeing it as the best way to both ensure removal of the missiles and prevent war. The ExComm supported this decision, but congressional leaders of both parties were not convinced, seeing it as a weak response, and during a tense and difficult meeting with Kennedy, urged him to invade Cuba.[24] President Kennedy also sent Khrushchev a terse letter expressing the determination of the United States to remove the missiles, but also urging him to work to find a peaceful resolution to the situation.

John F. Kennedy made many television appearances during his presidency, but none more dramatic than that on Monday night, October 22, 1962. He had asked for network airtime to speak on a matter of the "highest national urgency." With about a hundred million Americans listening in, Kennedy looked fatigued but also very much in command of himself. He had many different audiences in mind. He denied the criticism that his administration had been slow to realize what was happening in the Caribbean. "As promised, this government has maintained the closest surveillance of the Soviet military buildup on the island of Cuba."[25] To the whole United States, Kennedy outlined his strategy to "quarantine" Cuba and remove the Soviet missiles, which he described as "weapons of sudden mass destruction."[26] The use of "quarantine" was significant because, under international law, a blockade could be considered an act of war. In the most chilling words of an extraordinarily sober speech, Kennedy, speaking plainly so that Moscow would make no mistake, declared that "it shall be the policy of this nation to regard any nuclear missile launched from Cuba against any nation in the Western Hemisphere as an attack by the Soviet Union upon the United States, requiring a full retaliatory response upon the Soviet Union."[27]

Kennedy placed the crisis in a broad geographical context, invoking the Rio Pact of 1947, by which the United States and most Latin American nations pledged to view an attack on one signatory as an attack on all. Kennedy pointed out that the missiles were capable of reaching Mexico City and other targets in Central and South America. In traditional Cold War rhetoric, he spoke to the Cuban people "on that imprisoned island," as a friend, and denounced Castro and his cohorts as "puppets and agents of an international conspiracy." Further, he declared that the United States would enlist the Organization of American States in this effort. And he pledged that the United States would also take its case directly to the Security Council of the United Nations, asking for a resolution demanding immediate withdrawal of the missiles, under the supervision of U.N. observers. Looking toward U.S. allies in Europe, Kennedy also made sure to remind the Soviet Union that "in particular the brave people of West Berlin" were among those whose freedom and safety the United States remained committed to protecting. He ended by stating the U.S. goal as "peace and freedom, here in this hemisphere, and we hope, around the world."[28]

But in the meantime, the United States of America prepared for World War Three. Around the world, U.S. forces went to Defensive Condition (Def Con) 2, the highest state of readiness short of war itself. Backing up Kennedy's diplomatic initiatives was the strength, range, and versatility of the U.S. military. The Navy moved ships into position to set up the blockade line, sending nearly 200 of them to the Caribbean and reinforcing its base at Guantanamo Bay in Cuba. The CIA increased its overflights of Cuba and the Air Force sent its B-52 bombers into the air, loaded with nuclear bombs, awaiting orders to drop their payloads on Soviet cities and military targets. The Army massed divisions in southeastern United States, ready to invade Cuba if the blockade failed. U.S. missiles in Europe were up and ready, aimed directly at the Soviet Union. In Washington, Kennedy struggled with some of the nation's military chiefs, who saw the missiles in Cuba as a grave and immediate threat to the United States and their duty to be to remove them by armed force. Kennedy resisted that course, and one of the contentious moments of those deliberations involved Air Force Chief of Staff, General Curtis LeMay, an aggressive, burly veteran of World War Two bombing campaigns. The general told Kennedy that the blockade and diplomatic route was a display of weakness along the lines of appeasement at Munich and would lead to war. He further insulted Kennedy by saying, "you're in a pretty bad fix at the present time." "You're in there with me," Kennedy answered back.[29]

In his inaugural address, John F. Kennedy had proclaimed that he embraced "the role of defending freedom in its hour of maximum danger. I do not shrink from this responsibility—I welcome it." That hour had now come, and Kennedy and those around him were under enormous strain as they tried to avert a cataclysmic and unprecedented war with consequences beyond calculation. A war in 1962 involving dozens of nuclear weapons, each with many times the firepower of the atomic bombs the United States dropped on Japan in 1945, would have an existential quality about it, "mankind's final war," as Kennedy himself said in his inaugural address. Very rough estimates had it that at least 100 million people would die in the United States and Soviet Union in a full-scale nuclear exchange. Soon after being briefed on the missiles, Kennedy and his friend and aide Dave Powers dropped into Washington's St. Matthew's Cathedral during the day to say a quiet prayer.[30] Jackie Kennedy had been away at one point during the crisis. When her husband called her to ask her to return to Washington, she noticed "there was just something funny in his voice."[31] Once back, she told Kennedy that, if the worst came to pass, she wanted to be there with him and their children at the White House. When the president and his ExComm were awaiting word from the blockade line, Bobby Kennedy looked at his brother and saw that "his hand went up to his face and covered his mouth. He opened and closed his fist. His face seemed drawn, his eyes pained, almost grey".[32] Out in the country, millions of Americans began to stock up on water and food and think seriously about where they might take shelter if war came. Others, refusing to accept that war was imminent, demonstrated in major cities and college towns across the nation for a peaceful resolution to the crisis.[33]

Khrushchev initially denounced the quarantine as an "act of aggression which pushes mankind toward the abyss of a world-nuclear missile war."[34] He said flatly that Soviet ships would not honor it. The enormous armed forces of the Soviet Union and its Warsaw Pact allies also moved to combat readiness. What Washington did not know was that Fidel Castro, fearing a U.S. invasion of his country, frantically urged the Soviets to launch a nuclear first strike. Kennedy, not trusting the chief of naval operations to carry out his orders, ordered Secretary of Defense McNamara to personally direct the blockade, and also saw to it that every U.S. ship that might encounter Soviet forces had Russian-speaking officers on board.[35] There was great trepidation as to what would happen when Soviet ships approached the blockade, for which the United States had secured approval by the Organization of American States. If Soviet ships tried to run the blockade line, shooting would almost certainly commence in the Caribbean and would most likely escalate into a general war. There was consequently enormous relief when the first Soviet ships stopped on the high seas, turned around, and headed home. Their directives from Moscow had changed. "We're eyeball to eyeball, and the other fellow just blinked," said Secretary of State Dean Rusk, when the ExComm learned the news. However, that oft-quoted statement, which implies that American and Soviet ships came within sight of each other at the decisive moment of the crisis, is misleading. Careful research of the positioning of the Soviet and American vessels in the Caribbean has demonstrated that the lead Soviet vessels never got closer than several hundred miles from the quarantine line.[36] Still, the crisis was not over. To ensure that it did not deepen, Kennedy ordered the Navy not to harass Soviet civilian ships and to let one oil tanker pass through unmolested.

In the midst of all this, back-channel negotiations took place, involving, among others, Bobby Kennedy, senior Soviet diplomats, and even American journalists. This avenue of communication, which the Soviets favored during the Cold War, allowed for certain issues to be raised first and then brought to Kennedy and Khrushchev. On Friday, October 26, Khrushchev, still fearing the worst, sent Kennedy a long rambling letter in which he pleaded for them both to loosen their grip on the "knot of war."[37] In so many words he proposed that in exchange for a U.S. promise not to invade Cuba, the Soviets would remove their missiles from Cuba. This is what Kennedy and his ExComm had been waiting for. A second communication from Moscow, however, the following day (Saturday, October 27), was couched in much less personal and conciliatory language. The Soviets now demanded that the United States remove its own nuclear weapons from the Soviet doorstep, these being the Jupiter missiles in Turkey. This was a blow to the hopes for peace, and members of the ExComm long remembered that Saturday as the lowest point in the crisis, when it looked as if war might come after all. With military forces on high alert around the world, it was not surprising that there some dangerous moments. One U-2 pilot flew into airspace near Alaska, apparently by mistake, causing brief but intense anxiety throughout the Soviet military and civilian leadership. Another U-2 pilot, Major Rudolf Anderson Jr., died after being shot down over Cuba. Standard military procedure called for an airstrike on the site from which that surface-to-air missile had been launched. Kennedy canceled any such strike immediately. Most seriously, a Soviet submarine commander, his vessel bombarded by U.S. depth charges and his crew urging him to fire a nuclear-tipped torpedo in response, thought better of it.[38]

President Kennedy took the advice of his brother, the attorney general, and Secretary McNamara by responding directly to Khrushchev's first, more promising letter, and essentially ignoring the second, more bellicose one. The back-channel negotiations involving the attorney general were critical in defusing the crisis. The Soviet government announced over Radio Moscow that it had "given a new order to dismantle the arms which you describe as offensive, and to crate and return them to the U.S.S.R."[39] A relieved Kennedy said that he welcomed Khrushchev's "statesman-like decision." For its part, the United States had agreed not to invade Cuba (nothing of that magnitude was being planned before the crisis) and, under a promise of secrecy, to remove the Jupiter missiles from Turkey. Detailed, difficult and highly technical negotiations followed, facilitated in part by U Thant, the General Secretary of the United Nations. But the immediate threat of war had now ended.

With Soviet ships retreating back across the Atlantic Ocean, with U.S. Air Force planes flying above them (Castro's government in the end rejected U.N. supervision of the removal of the missiles), it was easy to view the Cuban Missile Crisis as a victory for the United States and a defeat for the Soviet Union. In the wake of the Soviet withdrawal of the missiles, Khrushchev's star began to fall in the Soviet Union, the Cuban adventure derided within the nation's leadership circles as a "crackpot scheme." Two years later he was unceremoniously removed from power. Yet Khrushchev's efforts, however reckless, had still benefitted his cause. He insisted to his dying day that the missiles, whatever their technical capacities, were at bottom *defensive*, in that their true purpose was to deter U.S. aggression against socialist Cuba. In that sense, he had been successful in protecting what he considered a fraternal revolutionary state, living in the shadow of the world's leading imperialist power, even though the missiles themselves were only on Cuban soil for a short time. A Marxist-Leninist to the end, Khrushchev wrote in his memoirs: "the American imperialist beast was forced to swallow a hedgehog, quills and all. And that hedgehog is still in his stomach, undigested."[40] The hedgehog, as it turned out, was not the missiles but a long-lasting socialist Cuba. The Soviets themselves maintained a small military presence on Cuba for decades after 1962, in the eyes of some a violation of the Monroe Doctrine. Fidel Castro's government remained in power in Cuba for 50 years after the crisis, with Castro himself still alive in 2013. And the Soviet Union did achieve the removal of the Jupiter missiles from Turkey, a NATO ally of the United States. Although they had been made militarily obsolete by submarine-based missiles soon after their installation in April of 1962, the United States insisted that their removal, symbolic as it was, be kept secret in order to avoid the appearance of a tradeoff. The Soviet political and military leadership, dismayed at what it considered a military defeat of sorts in Cuba, vowed to close the significant U.S. advantage in nuclear weapons. Within a decade, they had largely reached that goal, with significant implications for the Cold War.

Despite all this, John F. Kennedy's prestige as commander in chief was enhanced greatly at home; his approval ratings rose and his Democratic Party won seats in the midterm elections, a rarity in American political history. There remained critics in the military who saw the end result as a kind of American defeat. Although he forbade members of his administration from gloating in public over Cuba, in private he did so himself. The United States had achieved the goal, set by Kennedy and the ExComm, of removing the Soviet missiles from Cuba without triggering a war. The nation suffered only a single casualty from enemy fire in doing so. He had established an informal but effective managerial style that suited his personality. The crisis in Cuba had taxed every bit of his energy, judgment, and courage. Most observers outside the United States were duly impressed, and Khrushchev himself admitted to an aide that any doubts he had had about Kennedy's strength and intelligence were now gone.[41] As the crisis eased, Kennedy briefed former President Eisenhower, whose support and advice he found helpful throughout the crisis, on its apparent resolution. However dramatic it may have been, he saw it as "one more chapter in a long story" of Cuba, and the wider Cold War.[42] In looking forward to how historians might judge his performance in October 1962, Kennedy hearkened back to another president from Massachusetts. John Adams had successfully avoided a war with France in the 1790s, and Kennedy told his closest aides, "All I want them to say about me is what they said about John Adams, he kept the peace."[43]

After pulling back from war, both the United States and the Soviet Union began to look for opportunities to reduce tensions and ensure that any future crises would be easier to manage. Khrushchev announced in late

1962 that the Soviet Union would focus on its domestic economy and de-emphasize wars of national liberation. Kennedy, for his part, indicated that the United States might be willing to negotiate with the Soviets on a nuclear test ban treaty. Progress on such matters and on the overall U.S.-Soviet relationship was halting, however, as both sides needed time to ponder the lessons of Cuba. Kennedy was dismayed at the macabre absurdity of two men, sitting on opposite sides of the world, having it in their power to destroy much of civilization.

The following year, Kennedy sought to move things forward when he delivered one of the most important speeches of his presidency. The setting was American University's commencement in Washington, D.C. on June 10, 1963. In giving what his aides referred to as the "peace speech," Kennedy was "really at home with himself" (in the words of one of his leading ambassadors) as he challenged the nation to rethink the Cold War.[44] He was purposeful but less exuberant in this speech than in his inaugural address, tempered as he now was after narrowly avoiding a catastrophic war. The peace that Kennedy envisioned that June day was not "a Pax Americana enforced on the world by Americans weapons of war," "nor the peace of the grave or the security of the slave," as he reaffirmed U.S. commitments to its allies around the world.[45] Comprehensive war, he reminded his audience, must be understood as obsolete in an age when "a single nuclear weapon contains almost ten times the explosive force delivered by all the allied air forces in the Second World War." As in the missile crisis several months earlier, Kennedy refused to accept war as inevitable. Thus, more than at any time in human history, the "necessary rational end of rational men" must be the pursuit of peace. In a clear challenge to conventional U.S. thinking on foreign policy following the end of World War Two, he asked every American to re-examine their attitude toward the Soviet Union and the Cold War. Despite ongoing differences with the communist system, Kennedy declared: "we can still hail the Russian people for their many achievements—in science and space, in economic and industrial growth, in culture and in acts of courage." Kennedy also took the unprecedented step of highlighting the enormity of Soviet losses during World War Two, which he argued, with good reason, surpassed anything else in the long history of warfare. "At least 20 million lost their lives. Countless millions of homes and farms were burned or sacked. A third of the nation's territory, including two-thirds of its industrial base, was turned into a wasteland—a loss equivalent to the devastation of this country east of Chicago."[46] As Nikita Khrushchev knew, to his great bitterness, the United States had never experienced anything remotely similar. It was thus quite difficult for Americans to comprehend the Soviet experience of World War Two, but Kennedy placed this history and geography in terms Americans could understand. At the same time he was sending a message to Moscow that he recognized that the Soviet Union had its own deep interest in avoiding another war.[47]

Kennedy sought to find commonalities between the Soviet and American peoples, accustomed as they were to think of each other as adversaries. He pointed out that as the world's two leading nations, the United States and the Soviet Union "[bore] the heaviest burdens" of the Cold War. Both would endure horrendous losses on the first day of a nuclear war, he pointed out, and both nations felt compelled to divert "massive sums of money to weapons that could be better devoted to combating ignorance, poverty and disease." Emphasizing a shared humanity that might transcend their differences, Kennedy—a father of two—said, "we all inhabit this planet. We all breathe the same air. We all cherish our children's future." And finally, "we are all mortal."[48]

Kennedy then moved on to details of policy, announcing that the United States, the US.S.R., and the United Kingdom had agreed to commence negotiations, in Moscow, on a treaty banning nuclear tests. This news drew spirited applause from his audience. He further pledged that the United States would not be the first to resume nuclear testing in the atmosphere. Kennedy saw such a test ban treaty as the first step in a long march toward stopping the arms race, reversing the spread of nuclear arms, and even a general disarmament and a new era of peace. In 1961 he had overseen the creation of the Arms Control and Disarmament Agency, an independent body charged with pursuing such matters. There was a grand vision, and Kennedy thought the beginnings of realizing it were at hand. Pointing to progress in one area, Kennedy said that the U.S. and Soviet governments were working on establishing a "direct line between Moscow and Washington, to avoid on each side the dangerous delays, misunderstandings, and misreadings of the other's action which might occur at a time of crisis." Soon after Kennedy's address, which Khrushchev hailed as the "best speech by any president since Roosevelt," he permitted the Voice of America to broadcast it in the Soviet Union, and the "hotline" between the two capitals was put into effect.[49]

The speech garnered more attention overseas than at home. One liberal British newspaper, the *Manchester Guardian,* called it "one of the great state papers of American history."[50] Immediate reaction in the United States was muted, however, with little coverage in the newspapers. Some conservatives thought Kennedy had gone much too far in overlooking the evils of the Soviet system, one Republican Congressman calling it a "soft line which can accomplish nothing," and Senator Barry Goldwater of Arizona, emerging as the leader of a new conservatism within the Republican Party, denouncing it as a "dreadful mistake." [51] Just two weeks later, however, it was Kennedy himself who threatened to jeopardize the diplomatic opening his speech helped create. His second trip to Europe as president featured a visit to West Germany, as he sought to solidify that country's ties to NATO. It included a dramatic stopover in the beleaguered city of West Berlin. At the very heart of the Cold War divide, Kennedy was carried away by the enthusiasm of the massive crowds and the courage of West Berliners and, reverting to some blunt Cold War rhetoric, declared the two camps as separated by a huge and seemingly impassable divide. Speaking only 50 yards from the Berlin Wall and improvising much of his speech, Kennedy denounced the Communist system, saying, "freedom has many difficulties and democracy is not perfect, but we have never had to put a wall up to keep our people in." Indeed. He chided unnamed others who claimed that communism was the future, allowing economic progress, and that the West might be able to work with Communists after all; as he made each point, Kennedy shouted first in imperfect German and then in English: "Let them come to Berlin!" Identifying himself with West Berliners, he placed them in the long tradition of the West striving to achieve and maintain freedom. The crowd responded to him with almost fierce roars of approval; it could not have been a comfort to the Kremlin to see a political leader inspire such passion in a German audience, albeit one tucked within the Soviet orbit only by an accident of history.

Later that day in the city, Kennedy, aware of the potential damage he might have done to the sensitive test ban treaty negotiations, gave a more restrained speech, in which he reiterated his belief "in the great powers working together to preserve the human race."[52] Khrushchev, in a manner reminiscent of Kennedy's decision during the Cuban crisis to overlook the combative letter from Moscow and reply to the more practical one, disregarded Kennedy's emotional remarks and proceeded with the treaty negotiations. Despite that potential misjudgment, Kennedy was elated as he left the city: "We'll never have another day like this one, as long as we live," he said to his closest aides on Air Force One as it flew westward.

The matter of nuclear testing had become of great importance to Kennedy. Every time the United States, the Soviet Union, or another country "tested" a nuclear device, they were in effect exploding a bomb of unimaginable power. The fallout from such events seeped into the planet's air and water and threatened the health and wellbeing of the world's peoples. Kennedy was no scientist, but he grasped this essential fact. In the first two years of his presidency he had directed the resumption of nuclear testing, over the protests of some peace groups, after the Soviets had done so unilaterally. The weapons now being made ready were thousands of times more powerful than those dropped on Japan in 1945. After the Cuban Missile Crisis, Kennedy began to pursue a test ban treaty with great zeal. Such an agreement had been a goal of liberals such as Adlai Stevenson and Hubert

Humphrey and science and peace groups for some time. Kennedy sent Averell Harriman, former U.S. ambassador to the U.S.S.R. and known and respected by the Soviet leadership, to Moscow to negotiate the treaty and kept in close contact with him during the talks. Those negotiations were difficult and at one point Kennedy considered abandoning them. But he was encouraged to keep trying by British Prime Minister Harold Macmillan, whom he greatly respected, and he persevered. Finally, the three nations—the United States, the U.S.S.R. and the U.K.—agreed in principle on a treaty that would ban any further nuclear tests in the atmosphere, underwater, or in outer space, only permitting them to be conducted underground. The two Western nations were not able to reach agreement with the Soviets on a comprehensive ban.

Learning from Woodrow Wilson's mistake at the Versailles Conference that chartered the League of Nations after World War One, Kennedy made sure to include Republicans in the Senate delegation he sent to Moscow to witness the signing of the treaty.[53] Only ratification of the treaty by the full Senate remained. To build support for that battle, Kennedy went on a tour of the western United States. He was surprised and heartened to find strong support for the treaty, even in conservative Utah. As Kennedy explained to his country what the treaty meant, the Gallup Poll showed a clear majority in favor of it. He even persuaded former Presidents Truman and Eisenhower to come out in its support. Kennedy lobbied the Senate hard, eventually overcoming the reluctance of Minority Leader Everett Dirksen, an Illinois Republican, and Democrat Henry Jackson of Washington, an ally of Kennedy but a fierce critic of the Soviet Union. In late September 1963, the Senate overwhelmingly approved the treaty, by a vote of 80 to 19. Among those voting "yes" was the president's younger brother Ted Kennedy, serving his first year in the Senate after surviving a bruising Democratic primary in Massachusetts and winning election in 1962. The White House issued a statement praising senators of both parties for their support and hailing the treaty as a step along "the path of peace." Those who remained unconvinced were primarily Republicans from the emerging Sun Belt, including Barry Goldwater, and John Tower of Texas, who had won a special election to replace Lyndon Johnson, becoming the first Republican to represent Texas in the Senate since Reconstruction. Some southern Democrats also voted "no". They concluded that the Soviet Union could not be trusted to uphold the agreement and, when breaking it, would gain a strategic advantage over the United States. Around the world, however, the treaty proved to be enormously popular and a hundred nations rushed to add their names to it. Within the communist world, China, however, hoping to develop its own nuclear weapons, denounced the treaty as yet another Soviet capitulation to the imperialists.[54]

The Partial Test Ban Treaty of 1963 was a major victory for John F. Kennedy, but more significantly, it represented a move away from what had become the most dangerous of rivalries and a step toward a future where peaceful coexistence, however unsatisfying it might be to some on both sides, would prevail over conflict. In the context of the challenges of war and peace that Kennedy faced, the test ban treaty was surpassed in importance only by his vital role the previous year in ensuring that, unlike the guns of August, the missiles of October remained unfired.

CHAPTER **6**

"ACROSS THE GLOBE"

The developing nations of the world became a priority for President Kennedy. Representatives of those countries, many of which had won their political independence in the years just before Kennedy became president, had met in Bandung, Indonesia, in 1955 to create a potential "third way" as an alternative to the two established camps of the Cold War. As they threw off the yoke of colonialism, Kennedy's goal was that the United States thwart any efforts by the Communist bloc to bring those nations into its orbit. To the newly independent states of Africa and Asia, he declared at his inaugural: "we pledge our word that one form of colonial control shall not have passed away merely to be replaced by a far more iron tyranny." He further promised: "To those peoples in the huts and villages across the globe struggling to break the bonds of mass misery, we pledge our best efforts to help them help themselves." The reason for doing so, Kennedy claimed, was "not because the communists might be doing it, not because we seek their votes, but because it is right."

As the world's leading economic power, the United States had an interest in reducing global poverty and raising living standards. In 1954 it had established a program under which it would send food surpluses overseas to poorer nations, and by 1960, liberals such as Hubert Humphrey were encouraging its expansion. In his second executive order as president, Kennedy renamed the program "Food for Peace," gave it a higher profile, and made George McGovern of South Dakota, a farming state, its first director. McGovern was a well-regarded, one-time college history professor and former congressman who lost a bid for the U.S. Senate in 1960. By 1963, the program was feeding over 90 million people a day around the world.[1]

One of Kennedy's ideas for how the United States might engage the Third World outside traditional diplomacy, military alliances, and economic investment involved a volunteer organization, the Peace Corps, which he had first proposed during the 1960 campaign. This was formally created by executive order on March 1, 1961, its mission being: "to help foreign countries meet their urgent needs for skilled manpower." It was also a goal of the Peace Corps that Americans would have the opportunity to learn about other peoples and cultures. In making this appeal to the nation, Kennedy emphasized the virtues of courage and sacrifice: "Life in the Peace Corps will not be easy. There will be no salary and allowances will be at a level sufficient only to maintain health and meet basic needs."[2] When Congress passed legislation later that year putting it on a permanent basis, Kennedy happily signed it into law. The Peace Corps fitted in well with the ethos of Kennedy's challenge to citizens of the United States: "ask what you can do for your country." He appointed his talented, energetic brother-in-law, R. Sargeant Shriver, to be its first director. Sarge, as he was known, was an ideal choice for the post. He was a man of genuine idealism and a creative and imaginative administrator. The Peace Corps met with broad support from the public and thousands of volunteers, primarily young people, most of them just graduated from college, enlisted. It had its critics, especially among those who opposed foreign aid. One denounced the enterprise as "Kennedy's Kiddie Corps, a lot of kids bouncing around the world in Bermuda shorts."[3] Richard Nixon saw it as a potential haven for draft dodgers. The Soviet Union was also critical, convinced that it was a front for the CIA.[4] At Shriver's insistence, however, a firm barrier was put up between the CIA and the Peace Corps.

Kennedy saw the Peace Corps as an effective way to counter Soviet claims that the United States was a selfish, capitalist nation, interested only in profit and exploitation. It was not wholly altruistic, designed as it was to encourage the world's newly independent nations to look to the United States—rather than the Soviet Union—as their model. The first Peace Corps volunteers, after meeting with Kennedy on the White House lawn, left for their assignments in Ghana and Tanganyika. They and others like them served in Africa, Asia, India, and Latin America as teachers and in health care, economic and community development, and agriculture.

The Peace Corps did not eliminate or even significantly reduce poverty around the world. There were some not unexpected cultural clashes between Americans and their hosts, and a few of the volunteers were guilty of a certain ugly Americanism. But within a few years of its creation, the Peace Corps became something of a rarity: an iconic government program with wide public and bipartisan support. Over the decades it expanded exponentially and became an established part of the federal government, without ever losing its independent character. Many of its veterans returned home to make significant contributions in a variety of fields. The Peace Corps in Kennedy's mind was always a U.S. foreign policy sideline, but he was proud of the young Americans who were serving overseas at his urging. He would frequently ask diplomats, "How are Sarge's kids doing over there?" At its best, the Peace Corps demonstrated that the United States could be a beneficial partner of the world's emerging peoples. With its optimism, energy, and ambitious global mission, the Peace Corps became over time the government program most identified at home and abroad with John F. Kennedy himself.[5]

In his inaugural address, Kennedy spoke directly to the nations of Latin America. "To our sister republics south of our border, we offer a special pledge—to convert our good words into good deeds—in a new alliance for progress—to assist free men and free governments in casting off the chains of poverty." He and his foreign policy team concluded that it was not enough to bottle up Castro and keep him from spreading his revolution throughout the Western Hemisphere. Cuba was not the only nation in the region with an active communist movement. Relations between the United States and Latin America had their troubled moments in the 1950s, most publicly the near disastrous visit by Vice President Nixon to Venezuela. An angry mob, furious at U.S. support for a recently deposed dictator, attacked his car, threatening his life. Indeed, during the five years before Kennedy became president, as many as ten Latin American dictators fell from power. Kennedy's advisors pointed to recent U.S. policy toward Latin American, which emphasized the interests of American business while neglecting opportunities to encourage broad social, political, and economic reform. U.S. ambassadors had too often been closely tied to undemocratic governments. The Eisenhower administration had intervened militarily and politically in Latin America, its foreign policy largely driven by the anti-communist logic of the Cold War, although there had been some U.S. policy efforts in the late 1950s designed to generate economic development in that part of the world.

Kennedy took office in 1961 believing that Latin America was potentially the most dangerous area of the world. He had no special expertise in Latin America, but planned to develop a comprehensive strategy to strengthen it in ways that would also ultimately benefit the United States. It was the consensus of Kennedy's advisors that proactive efforts were needed to encourage and build a peaceful and prosperous Latin America, with representative governments and market economies. He said to an aide privately: "There is a revolution going on down there, and I want to be on the right side of it."[6] Kennedy thus intended to establish a new direction for U.S. relations with Latin America, the historical precedent for which was Franklin Roosevelt's Good Neighbor Policy of the 1930s and 1940s.[7] On March 13, 1961, at a White House reception for members of the Latin America diplomatic corps, he formally introduced the Alliance for Progress (Alianza para el Progreso), calling it a "a vast cooperative effort, unparalleled in magnitude and nobility of purpose, to satisfy the basic needs of the American people for homes, work and land, health and schools."[8] This project of enormous scope was driven by belief in the power of government to drive social and economic change. Kennedy spoke of the common history of the United States and the nations of Latin America, sharing as they did an anti-colonial heritage. He quoted Thomas Paine on the democratic legacy of the American Revolution and hailed George Washington and Thomas Jefferson as examples of what free men can accomplish. But he also quoted Benito Juárez of Mexico on democracy, José Figueres of Costa Rica on his people's striving for a better life, and Simon Bolivar on the great potential of the Western Hemisphere if its nations acted in concert to solve their common problems.

Kennedy was not oblivious to the historical record in which the United States, from the Mexican War of 1846–1848 onward, had all too often not been a good neighbor in the Western Hemisphere. In his remarks that day, broadcast throughout the hemisphere over the Voice of America in English, Spanish, French, and Portuguese, he admitted: "we North Americans have not always grasped the significance of this common mission." Beyond that, European colonialism had prevailed in Latin America for centuries. He added that the nations of Latin America have for their part "not fully understood the urgency of the need to lift people from poverty and ignorance and despair." Recognizing that rhetoric, good intentions, and a well-developed plan would not be enough, he asserted:

> This political freedom must be accompanied by social change. For unless necessary social reforms, including land and tax reform, are freely made, unless we broaden the opportunity for all of our people, unless the great mass of Americans share in increasing prosperity, then our alliance, our revolution, our dream, and our freedom will fail.

In this rendering of the Latin American future, the United States would act as a guiding partner of the nations of the Western Hemisphere, promoting economic growth and peaceful change. The mission of the Alliance, as Kennedy envisioned it, was nothing less than having the "American Republics begin on a vast new Ten Year Plan for the Americas, a plan to transform the 1960s into a historic decade of democratic progress." Teodoro Moscoso, the director of the Alliance for Progress, was no less effusive: "Within a decade the direction and results of centuries of Latin American history are to be changed."[9] If successful, the Alliance would make the siren song of communism less appealing. Congress appropriated $500 million for its initial funding. Among its specific goals was the elimination of adult illiteracy by 1970 and generation of significant economic growth. The Alliance was designed with the Marshall Plan in Europe, and parallel U.S. efforts to help rebuild postwar Japan—both successful—in mind.[10] At a hemispheric conference in Uruguay later in 1961, the United States announced its goal of making more than $20 billion dollars available in public and private loans to the most impoverished nations of Latin America over the next decade, using the Alliance and the Agency for International Development—also established in 1961.

During his presidency, John F. Kennedy invested much attention and energy in the hemisphere, as he often referred to it. He made three trips to Latin America and was planning a fourth, to Brazil, in 1964.[11] In terms of creating interest, the effort was fairly successful. An enthusiastic crowd of over a million people greeted the Kennedys in Mexico City, roaring their approval at Jackie's fluent Spanish and shouting "Viva Kennedy."[12] The Kennedys' youth, glamour, and Catholicism only added to their appeal. Kennedy made a point of welcoming leaders from Latin America to Washington and got along quite well with many of them, especially Adolfo López Mateos of Mexico and Alberto Lleras Camargo of Columbia, both of whom embraced the spirit and ambitions of the Alliance.[13]

Not every Latin America leader shared Kennedy's vision. On the left, Fidel Castro denounced it as an anti-Cuban plot, which in a sense it was; his comrade, Che Guevara, thought that the reforms would inevitably raise expectations and lead to socialist revolutions. Right-wing dictators in Haiti and the Dominican Republic were silent or belittled the Alliance. Conservatives in Chile denounced Kennedy as "naïve" and "an unwitting ally of the communists."[14] Between those two extremes, however, the reaction was positive, even enthusiastic. Brazil's leading newspaper hailed the proposal as "an American Marshall Plan . . . destined to transform the 1960s into an historical period of democratic progress."[15]

Through the Alliance for Progress, Kennedy was trying to encourage, or even create, a broad, prosperous, democratic center in Latin America, one that would supplant the dictatorships and oligarchies of the past. While in Columbia, Kennedy repeated, even more forcefully than when launching the Alliance, the need for land and tax reforms, without which he feared violent uprisings.[16] Behind the high-minded rhetoric and economic commitments of the Alliance for Progress there continued to lurk the specter of Cuba and the Cold War. And its idealism was hampered by private U.S. investors more interested in profit than reform and the wealthy of Latin America's determination to protect what they had. As Kennedy had warned in his inaugural address, "those who make peaceful revolution impossible make violent revolution inevitable."

The ten-year plan to "transform Latin America" yielded mixed results. A few countries did enjoy economic growth, especially Venezuela. The Alliance, however, in contrast to the Peace Corps, suffered from mediocre leadership and bureaucratic inertia. And Latin America had historically rooted problems of economic inequality, political instability, and racial discrimination that could not easily be swept away. The Dominican Republic provided one example of the seemingly intractable sort of difficulties that Kennedy and the Alliance faced. A brutal military dictator, Rafael Trujillo, whom Kennedy purposefully excluded from all Alliance programs, had been assassinated in 1961. The U.S. military intervened to keep his family from returning to power. The difficulty of replacing dictatorships with what Kennedy privately called "decent democratic regimes" was not a problem confined to Latin America. The United States was often forced into accommodating less than ideal governments; six Latin American nations witnessed military coups during the Kennedy years, none of them opposed by the United States.[17] Some of the Alliance funding was used for military training, to try and thwart guerilla movements with possible links to Castro and communism. The promises made by Kennedy and the Alliance for Progress in early 1961 were far from realized in late 1963. Kennedy himself admitted that the task of the Alliance was "staggering;" as he conceded later in his presidency: "The Alliance for Progress . . . has failed to some degree because the problems are insuperable, and for years the United States has ignored them . . . and so did some of the groups in Latin America."[18] Kennedy liked to quote Edmund Burke, who counseled the politics of gradual change and respect for the limitations imposed by history. The struggles of his policy in Latin America and the challenges of getting government, society, and business to collaborate in such a far-flung and diverse part of the world were a painful reminder of that. Even so, Kennedy said on November 18, 1963: "despite dangers and difficulties, I support and believe in the Alliance for Progress more strongly than ever before."[19] Disappointments aside, Kennedy had encouraged legitimate hopes and expectations across Latin America for peaceful change and a rising standard of living for all. Before such promises can be realized, they must after all first be spoken.

Kennedy's efforts for a new departure in Africa were not burdened by the legacy of U.S. intervention and economic exploitation as they had been in Latin America. In fact, the United States had not historically concerned itself with Africa much at all. Kennedy's challenge here, as it turned out, was balancing support for the rising nations of Africa with the interests of the European allies of the United States in Africa. Africa was further evidence of the global nature of Kennedy's presidency. He had chaired the Foreign Relations Subcommittee on Africa while in the Senate. In the late 1950s he had made something of a name for himself with his outspoken criticism of French colonialism in Algeria. As in Latin America the previous century, many African nations were emerging from European colonization. Presidents Truman and Eisenhower were reluctant to encourage nationalism in Africa, largely out of concern for the colonial enterprises of the European allies of the United States. When African nations began to win their independence in the late 1950s, the United States became more open to a new Africa—as well it should have, for between 1957 and 1961, 19 African nations won their independence from European empires and were admitted to the United Nations. In 1961, the Non-Aligned Movement was formally established, the newly independent nations seeking a neutral path between the two Cold War blocs. Kennedy recognized this change. He and his advisors also concluded that Khrushchev's wars of national liberation might find fertile ground in Africa if the West did not place itself squarely on the side of these rising nations. Kennedy also began to understand that the growing civil rights movement in the United States was ultimately linked to the fate of sub-Saharan Africa.

Viewing the continent as a priority, Kennedy named former Michigan governor G. Mennen "Soapy" Williams, a supporter of civil rights at home, to be Under Secretary of State for African Affairs. Williams created a stir while in Kenya early in 1961 when he said: "What we want is what the Africans want for themselves." Misreported as: "Africa should be for the Africans," this caused consternation among South Africa's apartheid regime, the Portuguese government (which still claimed a colony in Angola), the U.S. Department of State (historically oriented toward Europe), and others invested in the status quo on the continent. When asked about it at a press conference, Kennedy defended Williams, saying, "I don't know who else Africa should be for."[20] He was determined, of course, that it *not* become for the Soviet Union. Aware of traditional State Department attitudes toward Africa, Kennedy appointed ambassadors like Williams, who could speak the languages of Africa and were broadly concerned with the wellbeing of its people. Since the start of the Cold War, the United States was widely seen as a de facto reactionary force, supporting colonialism and entrenched inequities around the globe. Kennedy, as diplomat George Ball asserted, sought to place the United States on the side of the rising nations of Africa, encouraging them in their efforts to break free of European rule and shape their own destinies.

Kennedy, from the start of his presidency, wooed African leaders, in part to prevent their turning toward Moscow.[21] He welcomed nearly 30 of them to Washington, showing unprecedented interest in the hopes and aspirations of African nations for a U.S. president, and directing the Voice of America to significantly increase its presence in Africa.[22] Kennedy sent Vice President Johnson to the continent, as well as several members of his family, and many of the first Peace Corps volunteers served there.

As with the Alliance for Progress, however, Kennedy's good intentions and the re-orientation of U.S. policy collided with some difficult realities, most dramatically in the Congo. Belgium had abruptly granted the Congo independence in 1960, leaving behind a society with few resources for self-governance. Chaos and division ensued, which the Soviet Union looked to exploit by sending military advisors and arms to their allies there. Just three days before Kennedy became president, Patrice Lumumba, the first Congolese Prime Minister, with ties to Moscow, was brutally murdered by the Belgian military, apparently with assistance from the CIA. Kennedy backed neither Lumumba's supporters nor the far right in the Congo, favoring instead U.N.-sponsored efforts to bring about order and unity and avoid a U.S.-Soviet conflict in central Africa.[23] After some hesitation, the Kennedy administration finally settled on a moderate figure, Cyrille Adoula.[24] As things deteriorated, there were calls for the United States to send in troops to prevent factions backed by Moscow from seizing power. Kennedy refused to respond to this, but kept open the option of sending the U.S. Air Force to assist the U.N. mission as a last resort. Ultimately, this was unnecessary, as the United Nations—which Kennedy took seriously as an institution capable of such work—brought an end to the conflict, at least for the moment.

Kennedy faced a similar predicament in Angola, where a nationalist movement sought independence from Portugal, a NATO ally of the United States. Breaking with previous U.S. policy in Africa, the Kennedy administration, through the offices of U.N. ambassador Adlai Stevenson, initially supported the rebels, some of whom were Marxist. The Soviet Union also voted against Portugal in the U.N. This course was strongly opposed by those in Washington who feared Kennedy was running the risk of weakening NATO for a peripheral cause. Making matters worse, the authoritarian Portuguese government, determined to keep its overseas possessions, threatened not to renew the U.S. lease on its airbase on the Azores Islands in the North Atlantic. The Azores were a Portuguese territory and the U.S. military deemed it strategically important. At the prodding of the United States, the United Nations agreed to change its stated goal for Angola from "independence" to "self-determination."[25] By 1963, the centrality of the NATO alliance to U.S. foreign policy began to win out within the Kennedy administration; the bases on the Azores had proved crucial in tracking the movements of Soviet submarines during the Cuban Missile Crisis.[26] Kennedy, concerned too that a dramatic step in this matter might weaken support in the Senate for the test ban treaty, now ordered Stevenson to abstain on motions before the U.N. on the Angola crisis.[27] Civil war in Angola continued and the United States retained its bases in the Azores. Concerns over the Western alliance and Cold War military priorities ultimately prevailed, in this instance, over Kennedy's anti-colonial impulses. However, his administration continued to press Portugal to adopt a more liberal attitude toward its colonies and did not abandon its general principle of encouraging the self-determination and independence of African states.

In the early 1960s, South Africa was the only country on the continent with which the United States had a significant economic relationship. It possessed rare minerals, including gold, that were of great value to the United States. In addition, the South African government had granted the United States military privileges. As anti-colonialism arose in much of sub-Saharan Africa in the late 1950s, the South African government re-committed itself to racial apartheid (by which whites of European ancestry dominated native Africans), a reaction that included police killing or wounding nearly 300 anti-apartheid demonstrators.[28] The Kennedy administration denounced apartheid, as both Truman and Eisenhower had, but even more forcefully, urging South Africa to accept what British Prime Minister Harold Macmillan called the "Winds of Change" blowing through the continent.[29] What South African leaders found especially disturbing, however, was that Kennedy in his inaugural address seemed to link the anti-colonial movement in contemporary Africa to the American Revolution, although one white South African later tried to convince Soapy Williams that the founders of the United States never meant their principles to apply to African-Americans.[30] When President Kennedy took part in the White House celebration of "African Freedom Day" in 1961, more alarm bells went off in South Africa's capital, Pretoria, where the government was so concerned about the new attitude in Washington that it banned Williams from entering the country.[31]

Washington and Pretoria found common ground, however, in their view of the African National Congress, an organization both governments viewed as influenced by communists—a judgment that hampered some of the Kennedy administration's criticism of the South African government. Despite this significant misgiving, the United States placed a limited arms embargo on South Africa in 1963, angering Pretoria, which viewed this as a betrayal of the international fight against communism.[32] Segregationists in the U.S. Congress opposed efforts by Kennedy to isolate South Africa, as they too saw a connection between the civil rights movement at home and the democratic aspirations of Africans. What the Kennedy administration would not enact, to the dismay of Martin Luther King Jr. and other American civil rights leaders, were sweeping economic sanctions that might have forced significant change in South Africa. The changes Kennedy made to U.S. policy toward South Africa were largely rhetorical and symbolic, as Cold War priorities were given precedence.

John F. Kennedy hoped to travel to Africa, where he would almost certainly have been as warmly received as he was on his trips to Latin America and his brother Bobby was on his visit to South Africa in 1966. Kennedy's personal diplomacy in courting black African leaders, his support of increased U.S. foreign aid to Africa, the presence of Peace Corps volunteers, and his sustained interest in the politics of the continent was unprecedented for a U.S. president. His youth was also an asset, as Africa's population and most of its emerging leadership were also young. He had set in motion a new direction for U.S. foreign policy in Africa, even if at times his policies did not match the expectations he raised. Kennedy's overtures to Africa, although simultaneous with the civil rights movement at home, were not primarily driven by domestic political concerns. Something else may have been at work. Explaining to Indian leader Jawaharlal Nehru his own opposition to colonialism, Kennedy observed that his Irish ancestors had suffered under the domination of the same foreign power that had exercised authority in India, albeit less brutally than in Ireland.[33] Perhaps he was seeking to identify with his Indian counterpart. But in the summer of 1963, Kennedy visited Ireland, despite the objection of some his advisors who saw no strategic value in it and in the face of criticism that the trip was a personal indulgence. Ireland, both the Republic and the six northern counties still under British rule, was then in a rare moment of quietude in terms of political and sectarian violence. Kennedy highly valued the U.S. alliance with Great Britain, as well as his close relationship with Prime Minister Harold Macmillan, and had long admired the public-minded members of the English aristocracy. This did not prevent him, however, from attending a ceremony in Dublin dedicated to the memory of Irish nationalist leaders executed by the British after the Easter Rising of 1916 and placing a wreath on their graves. He was the first foreign head of state to so honor the Irish nation.[34]

In May 1963, U.S. astronaut Gordon Cooper spoke from his spacecraft orbiting the earth a hundred miles above ground, extending the good wishes of the United States via a special transmission to African leaders meeting in Ethiopia.[35] The available technology permitted only a one-way conversation, something Kennedy tried hard to avoid in his courting of African leaders, but it did demonstrate his government's eagerness to engage the new Africa. The communication also highlighted the Cold War context in which the U.S. space program was accelerated during the early 1960s. Two years earlier, Kennedy had taken the unusual step of giving a second State of the Union address, one devoted entirely to the international scene. The previous month, Soviet cosmonaut Yuri Gagarin had become the first man in space. This marked the second time in four years that the Soviet Union had leaped ahead—Kennedy's suggestion that they explore outer space together having been rejected. As with Sputnik a few years earlier, it was a major breakthrough, one the Soviet Union trumpeted loudly. Kennedy recognized it as such, sending Khrushchev a letter of congratulations. But he also saw it as a defeat of sorts for the U.S., and immediately began to ask his science advisors how the United States might surge ahead of the Soviet Union in space. A few weeks later, U.S. astronaut Alan Shepard matched Gagarin's feat when he piloted the Freedom 7 spacecraft, becoming the first American in space. Now, in May of 1961, Kennedy, after intense discussions with space experts about what might be possible, challenged the country to go even further: "I believe that this nation should commit itself to achieving the goal, before this decade is out, of landing a man on the moon and returning him safely to the earth."[36]

Reaching the moon had been a long-term ambition for NASA, the National Aeronautics and Space Administration; it was not clear whether or not the Soviet Union was seriously planning such an effort. President Kennedy, however, made it the overriding goal of the space program, recognizing that such a grandiose project would "carry very heavy costs" and place a "heavy burden" on the nation's resources.[37] He persuaded Congress to triple the budget for NASA, which did not have a particularly distinguished reputation when Kennedy took office. He appointed James Webb to lead it, and Webb proved to be an extraordinarily capable administrator of this unprecedented endeavor. Researchers who favored a moon program were excited about the scientific benefits it might yield; Vice President Johnson, whom Kennedy appointed to oversee the space program, saw it from a Cold War perspective. Whichever nation took the lead in outer space, Johnson argued, would "determine which system of society and government [would] dominate the future . . . in the eyes of the world, first in space means first, period; second in space is second in everything."[38] Kennedy agreed wholeheartedly with this assessment, and it was competition with the Soviet Union that drove him to pressure NASA for rapid progress, telling Webb, "This is, whether we like it or not, a race."[39] Even more bluntly, he said, "Everything we do ought to really be tied in to getting onto the moon ahead of the Russians."[40] Kennedy made it clear that, aside from national defense, the race to the moon should be the number one priority of the U.S. government. He was not particularly interested in the science of the project, and Webb and others struggled to make him understand that a successful manned moon landing required a deep understanding of space flight and the moon itself. Kennedy's impatience at times caused friction with his science advisors, but they knew that he took a great interest in their work and was willing to invest his political capital in their work.

By early 1962, the program reached a new milestone, when astronaut John Glenn became the first American to orbit the earth. Kennedy was especially taken with the courage and skill of Glenn and his colleagues; for him, they embodied what the United States needed to prevail. Later that year, during a speech at Rice University in Houston, Texas, home to NASA's new Manned Spacecraft Center, Kennedy said that the decision to commit to reaching the moon was one of the most important of his presidency. In order to build the support of a public which was not yet particularly enthused about going to space, he emphasized the economic and educational benefits of the quest for the moon. The greatest profits might well be intangible but worthy of a great nation, as he suggested in closing his speech at Rice:

> Many years ago the great British explorer George Mallory, who was to die on Mount Everest, was asked why did he want to climb it. He said, "Because it is there." Well, space is there, and we're going to climb it, and the moon and the planets are there, and new hopes for knowledge and peace are there.[41]

After the Cuban missile crisis, Kennedy once again spoke of U.S.-Soviet cooperation in space, but his main focus remained making sure that the first person to set foot on the moon was an American. On November 21, 1963, in a speech in Florida, he said that the United States was like the boys in the Irish writer Frank O'Connor's story who threw their hats over a high wall and then went after them. "This nation has tossed its cap across the wall of space and we have no choice but to follow it." At the decade's end, in the summer of 1969, Neil Armstrong of Apollo 13 landed on the moon, the first human being to do so. He and his crew were returned safely to the earth.

Secretary of State Dean Rusk said that the Middle East was "not a matter of deep concern" for John F. Kennedy.[42] This was in large part because the region was, by its standards, relatively quiet in the early 1960s. Kennedy's policy in relation to the Middle East was of course shaped by the Cold War. Kennedy had spoken in favor of Algerian independence when a senator, and as president he emphasized—as he did in Latin America and Africa—the anti-colonial roots of the United States and encouraged U.S. policymakers to look at Arab nationalism with fresh eyes.[43] He did not want to see the Arab states of the region tilt too far toward Moscow, nor did he want the United States to be perceived as concerned only with Israel's interests. Despite his father's reputation for anti-Semitism, Kennedy had done particularly well among Jewish voters in 1960.

During the 1950s, Egypt's charismatic leader, Gamal Abdel Nasser, had had a poor relationship with the United States. Kennedy was determined that the ambitious Nasser, who sought to unite the Arab Middle East under Egyptian (i.e. his) leadership, would not become a close ally of the Soviet Union. His campaign to woo Nasser included personal diplomacy (the two leaders conducted a lengthy correspondence), aid through the Food for Peace program, and a pledge that the United States would seek to remain as neutral as possible in the Arab-Israeli dispute.[44] Kennedy was able to establish a relationship of trust and mutual respect with Nasser, especially in the first two years of his presidency; this proved to be especially helpful when Kennedy made sure to inform Nasser personally before the United States announced any policies which Egypt might find troubling.[45] Chief among those was Kennedy's decision to sell surface-to-air missiles to Israel, thus breaking with the longstanding U.S. policy of not selling major weapon systems to Middle Eastern nations.[46] He and Robert McNamara overruled the State Department on this matter. Both believed that the Arab states had gained a strategic advantage over Israel through the purchase of arms from West Germany and the Soviet Union, and the defensive Hawk missiles would redress that imbalance and reduce the likelihood of war. The United States also offered the missiles as incentive to get Israel to agree in principle to a U.N. plan designed to end the Palestinian refugee problem.

By 1963, however, Kennedy moved the United States even closer to Israel, declaring American support for its right to exist and pledging military assistance in case of an Arab attack.[47] Nasser's ambitions began to threaten more conservative Arab states, including Saudi Arabia, on whose oil U.S. allies in Europe were dependent and in which American oil companies were invested. The United States had begun to quietly press those Arab governments to introduce reforms, but Kennedy's ambitions for the United States to play the role of a neutral broker in the region's disputes foundered on a civil war in Yemen divided the Arab Middle East.[48] The most significant result of Kennedy's foreign policy in the Middle East was a strengthening of the U.S.-Israeli relationship, which had not necessarily been a goal at the outset of his presidency.

U.S. policy toward China was not marked by any great changes during the Kennedy years. In July of 1961, both houses of Congress voted unanimously that the United States continue to oppose the People's Republic of China's admission into the United Nations and blocked the establishment of diplomatic relations with Bejing.[49] These policies had been in place since the Communists took power in China in 1949. The United States continued to support the Republic of China, situated on the island of Taiwan. Nevertheless, looming behind Kennedy's foreign policy in Southeast Asia was Communist China. He took office less than a decade after the end of the Korean War, in which soldiers from both countries were engaged in combat for nearly three years. The United States did recognize that, by the early 1960s, the world's two leading communist powers were increasingly at odds; talk of a monolithic "Sino-Soviet bloc" was becoming outdated.[50] Part of what was at work was Bejing's disgust at what it considered Moscow's series of "capitulations" to imperialist America. As U.S. relations with the Soviet Union began to improve in 1963, opportunities to normalize ties with Bejing faded. Kennedy briefly considered, but then abandoned, including China in the Food for Peace program. He was also concerned about China developing nuclear weapons and hoped to curb any progress it was making through the test ban treaty. However, the Chinese declined to sign the agreement, seeing it at bottom as a joint American-Soviet effort to restrict their ambitions in this direction. Little was accomplished, then, during Kennedy's presidency to thaw this frozen but potentially important relationship.

Competing with Cuba for Kennedy's attention in the first months of his presidency was Laos, a small nation in Southeast Asia unfamiliar to nearly all Americans. It was Laos, however, that dominated discussions when Kennedy met with Eisenhower as president-elect. As with Cuba, the outgoing president strongly urged the incoming one to take a hard line. Laos was in the middle of a civil war involving the communist group, Pathet Lao, aided by the Soviet Union, China, and North Vietnam, an embattled neutral government, and a third faction friendly to the United States and supported by the CIA. Before the Bay of Pigs, Kennedy said privately to a reporter that he would go to war to defend Laotian independence, even if it cost him a second term.[51] His thinking at this point was influenced by the classic domino theory of the Cold War: he feared that if the Communists won in Laos, they would use the landlocked nation as a staging post for attacks elsewhere in Asia.

At a press conference in March of 1961, Kennedy appeared with three easels, each showing the advance of communist forces in Laos, and asserted that the United States supported a "neutral and independent Laos . . . and not a Cold War pawn."[52] Kennedy declared that the United States reserved the right to intervene in Laos militarily if neighboring communist states continued to arm and assist the Pathet Lao. In a show of strength, he sent 500 marines to Thailand, with which the United States had a security commitment through the Southeast Asia Treaty Organization, along its border with Laos. He also ordered U.S. aircraft carriers into the South China Sea. But eventually he came to see Laos as a losing proposition. The Laotians, despite their current troubles, were more peaceful than militaristic and Kennedy increasingly viewed the pro-Western forces in Laos as unreliable. Laotian culture certainly did not lend itself to warfare; one observer noted that in the midst of battle, the opposing sides left to attend a local festival.[53] Even so, when it looked as if the communist forces were close to victory in May 1961, U.S. military leaders urged Kennedy to send 140,000 troops to Laos and guaranteed victory if he authorized the use of nuclear weapons. Kennedy wanted no part of such a strategy, nor did congressional leaders of both parties. Not wanting to risk a defeat or even the appearance of one in the wake of the Bay of Pigs, Kennedy was prepared to make a deal with the Soviets over Laos, something Eisenhower had rejected out of hand as a "compromise with evil."

In fact, the timing of the failure in Cuba was fortunate for Kennedy in that he could hardly commit U.S. troops thousands of miles away in an unknown country to fight communism after refusing to do so right off the U.S. coast.[54] One of the few positive outcomes of the Vienna summit was movement toward a ceasefire and neutral government in Laos. In the summer of 1962, the United States, skillfully represented by Averell Harriman, the Soviet Union, and other nations agreed on a coalition government in a neutral Laos. The principals agreed that this small nation was not the place for military conflict. For a variety of reasons, then, Laos would not be the country where Kennedy and the United States would make a military stand against communism in Southeast Asia.

No newly independent nation ultimately loomed so large in John F. Kennedy's presidency and its aftermath than the ancient one of Vietnam. For centuries the Vietnamese had struggled to maintain its independence from China, its massive neighbor to the north. Then, in the nineteenth century, it was colonized by France, which did not hesitate to bring its religion and culture to Vietnam. In 1940, proclaiming "Asia for the Asians," forces of Imperial Japan effectively replaced France as the dominant power. During World War Two, resistance to the Japanese was led by Ho Chi Minh and the Vietminh. A Vietnamese nationalist, Ho was also a communist, a mixture of identities that proved crucial to Vietnam's relationship with the United States over the next 30 years. When the war ended, Ho, before a crowd of 400,000 in Hanoi, proclaimed the birth of the Democratic Republic of Vietnam. In doing so, he quoted Thomas Jefferson's Declaration of Independence: "all men are created equal; they are endowed by their Creator with certain unalienable rights, among these are Life, Liberty and the Pursuit of Happiness." The Vietnamese leader had visited the United States as a young man and took seriously the anti-colonial legacy of the United States, so much so that he tried to meet with U.S. President Woodrow Wilson at the Versailles Conference of 1919 in order to raise the question of Vietnamese independence. He was rebuffed. Twenty-five years later he wrote to President Harry S. Truman on the same subject; he received no answer.

The war against Japan was followed by eight more years of warfare against France, which sought to re-impose its colonial rule over Vietnam. President Franklin Roosevelt, no great champion of Charles de Gaulle or French ambitions, was initially hostile to these efforts. Roosevelt's successor, Harry Truman, emphasized the Cold War alliance in Europe. Having just fought the Japanese in a brutal war, one involving a considerable amount of racial and ethnic hostility, the United States was not prepared to support the Vietminh against the French. This Cold War view was only amplified by North Korea's invasion, with Soviet and Chinese support, of South Korea in 1950. The first U.S. military advisors arrived in Vietnam that year. As France struggled to defeat the Vietminh, the United States, now seeing this conflict as part of the wider Cold War, financed the lion's share of the French war costs in Vietnam. Although they mostly controlled the cities, the French had little support in the countryside. After their catastrophic defeat in 1954 at Dien Bien Phu, they withdrew, and Vietnam once again asserted its independence. The Cold War powers, meeting in Geneva to decide the fate of Vietnam, divided it at the seventeenth parallel, leaving to its north a communist state, the Democratic Republic of Vietnam, and a noncommunist state, the Republic of Vietnam, to its south, with its capital in Saigon.

From the start, the Democratic Republic of Vietnam, known in the United States as North Vietnam, denounced the Saigon government as a "puppet state" and worked to establish itself as the government of the whole of Vietnam. Few Vietnamese living south of the seventeenth parallel in 1954 chose to move north, however. For its part, the United States, as early as 1954, pledged itself to support the Saigon government, and in 1960 sent military advisors. The then-senator, John F. Kennedy, said that such aid should be directed toward building independence and "indigenous strength that would stop communism and move toward democracy."[55]

The fledgling nation of the Republic of Vietnam (generally termed South Vietnam) struggled to establish its legitimacy. From 1956 it was led by the aristocratic and strongly Catholic Ngo family. The United States supported their decision to violate the Geneva Agreement by foregoing nationwide elections on the grounds that Ho and his supporters would win and then establish a communist dictatorship. Kennedy's trip to Vietnam in 1951 had left him highly skeptical of French efforts to defeat the Vietminh. Maintaining his interest in Vietnam after the climactic events of 1954, he shifted his emphasis from anti-colonialism to anti-communism. Speaking at a meeting of the American Friends of Vietnam in 1956, Kennedy said, "Vietnam represents the cornerstone of the free world in Southeast Asia, the keystone to the arch, the finger in the dike."[56] Vietnam, Kennedy claimed, represented "the alternative to communist dictatorship. . . . If we are not the parents of little Vietnam, then surely we are its godparents who presided at its birth. . . . it is our offspring—we cannot abandon it, we cannot ignore its needs."[57] He praised the Saigon government for its success in resettling close to a million refugees from the north, most of them Catholics fleeing communism; its economic, social, and political progress; the increased professionalism of its army. Finally, Kennedy said that what the United States must offer the nation he called "Free Vietnam" was "a revolution—a political, economic and social revolution far superior to anything the communists can offer."[58] This ambitious vision was in keeping with Kennedy's thinking vis-à-vis the Third World, that the United States must not simply be a reactionary power, but one that would work with the emerging nations of the world to help them create, along American lines, a better life for their people.

In his inaugural address, John F. Kennedy proclaimed that under his leadership the United States should "pay any price, bear any burden, meet any hardship, support any friend, oppose any foe, to assure the survival and success of liberty." He inherited a policy of U.S. involvement in Vietnam that had been in place, in one form or another, for more than a decade. In 1961, Kennedy found a situation that had deteriorated since his optimistic speech five years earlier. Just a month before his inauguration, Hanoi and its allies south of the seventeenth parallel, frustrated by Saigon's refusal to participate in national elections, formally established the National Liberation Front (NLF) for South Vietnam. Its goal (announced two weeks before Khrushchev proclaimed Soviet support for such wars of national liberation) was the overthrow of the South Vietnamese government and unification of all Vietnam under the leadership of Ho Chi Minh. For the NLF and Hanoi, the United States was the successor to the colonial French, the latest in a long line of foreign powers seeking to dominate the Vietnamese people. For his part, President Ngo Dinh Diem of South Vietnam derided the NLF as "Viet Cong" (Vietnamese Communists). Its operations included a campaign of terror in the countryside, marked by the assassination of local officials who were working with the government in Saigon and the seizing of villages and towns for the communist cause.

To combat such tactics, Kennedy turned to the idea of "flexible response," a phrase coined by his military advisor, General Maxwell Taylor, by which the United States would train its allies to match the guerilla-led insurgencies of their common foes. It was also understood to be a reasonable alternative to Eisenhower's strategy of massive nuclear retaliation to deter aggression. Vietnam seemed the ideal place for such tactics, its long coastline being more accessible to the U.S. military than landlocked Laos. One piece of this strategy was the Special Forces, or "Green Berets," who intrigued and greatly impressed Kennedy by their dedication and talent. In May of 1961 he authorized them to conduct clandestine warfare in Vietnam in response to the influx of NLF guerrillas into the country. Even so, the NLF continued to make strong headway in the countryside, where the Saigon government's power was weakening. Although Laos was a more pressing concern to him for most of 1961, Kennedy actively sought out advice and information on Vietnam from his first year in office, sending some of those he most trusted to be his eyes and ears to the country. In addition to General Taylor, Walter Rostow of the National Security Council, Bobby Kennedy, and Vice President Lyndon Johnson, among others, made the long journey to Vietnam. Despite his triumphant visits to Latin America and his plans for going to Africa, Kennedy himself did not return to Southeast Asia.

Late in 1961, Kennedy rejected a recommendation by General Taylor and Secretary McNamara to introduce combat troops into Vietnam to support the increasingly beleaguered Diem government. But in a somewhat weakened political position in late 1961, in the wake of Laos, Cuba, Vienna, and Berlin, he also refused to pursue a negotiated settlement to the conflict there. Instead he chose a middle path, continuing to increase the number of U.S. advisors, many now engaged (and some dying) in combat through Operation Beef-up, in which the United States used helicopter gunships to attack NLF guerrillas. Early in 1962, the U.S. military presence was given a bureaucratic upgrade, to Military Assistance Command Vietnam (MACV) status. The number of U.S. advisors was increased over the next two years, totaling about 16,500 by late 1963. The United States also launched the Strategic Hamlet program in early 1962, aiding Saigon create safe villages, to be governed by the peasants themselves and protected from harassment by NLF guerrillas. The reports back to Washington over the first year of the program claimed it was meeting and even surpassing expectations. The reality on the ground, however, was quite different. The Diem government had little success in getting peasants to volunteer for the experiment, so they coerced them into the hamlets, creating even more resentment against Saigon.[59]

By late spring 1963, the crux of the matter for the Kennedy administration had become the Saigon government itself. Was it building support and legitimacy, was it winning the "hearts and minds" of the Vietnamese people, and was its army capable of defeating its foes? The U.S. government had very few experts in Vietnamese history and culture to put these questions into a meaningful context. Increasingly, it was the military that was driving U.S. policy in Vietnam. In the late spring, another crisis arose in the country. Buddhist monks, frustrated at what they saw as a lack of religious equality in South Vietnam and the government's deadly reaction to their peaceful protests, reacted most dramatically. They began to voluntarily burn themselves to death on busy Saigon streets. Photographs of the horror were published widely; looking at one of these, Kennedy said, "No news picture in history has generated as much emotion around the world as that one has."[60] In Washington, President Diem, his brother Ngo Dinh Nhu—who ran the secret police—and his brother's controversial wife Madame Nhu were increasingly seen as detrimental to the cause of fighting communism in Southeast Asia. Madame Nhu openly mocked the Buddhists' self-immolations, calling them a "barbeque." There had been tensions and violence between the Catholic and Buddhist communities in Vietnam since the nineteenth century, and the Diem government, its leadership heavily Catholic, failed to reach anything resembling an accommodation with its religious rivals.

Doubts were also being raised about the wisdom and effectiveness of the U.S. mission in Vietnam. The criticism by David Halberstam, a young, aggressive reporter with the *New York Times,* highly annoyed Kennedy. Yet he had told a friend early in 1962, "Diem is Diem, and the best we've got."[61]

Mike Mansfield of Montana, the new Senate Majority Leader and a former college professor of Asian History, supported U.S. efforts to bolster the Diem government. He visited Vietnam in late 1962 at Kennedy's request. Mansfield reported that Diem's government was plagued by corruption and inefficiency, that the substantial commitment by the United States of military personnel and equipment was not winning the war, and that the United States should begin to disengage from Vietnam.[62] His findings stunned Kennedy, who told his aides afterwards that he was initially angry at Mansfield's dissent, and then, "I got angry at myself for agreeing with him."[63] Several months later Mansfield further irked Kennedy when he repeated his deep misgivings about the U.S. military role in Vietnam at a breakfast of Congressional leaders, with the president in the room.

Kennedy's Vietnam policy crumbled further in the summer of 1963. The Diem government had raided a series of Buddhist pagodas as part of its campaign to crack down on dissent. Diem and his brother were increasingly isolated, having alienated wide swathes of South Vietnamese society. When two more of his emissaries to Vietnam reported back to Washington in September with profoundly different interpretations of what they had seen, an exasperated Kennedy asked them if they had visited the same country.[64] The United States began to get wind of a possible coup against Diem and his brother by their own generals. Continuing his search to find the right personnel in Vietnam, Kennedy appointed a new ambassador to Saigon, his old rival, Henry Cabot Lodge Jr., in part to shield himself from Republican opposition to his policies there. Lodge's predecessor, Frederick Nolting, was a supporter of Diem. Lodge was not, and he immediately began to reshape U.S. policy. A turning point occurred on a Saturday afternoon in late August, when the White House sent a telegram to Ambassador Lodge, expressing the view that the United States was open to supporting a military coup against Diem if he did not make significant changes in government, including dismissal of his brother and sister-in-law from power. President Kennedy, who understood how a politician might value having members of his own family in high places in government, was out of town that summer weekend, as were Secretaries McNamara and Rusk. He was, however, consulted from Cape Cod on the substance of the telegram.

By the early fall of 1963, Kennedy himself was giving mixed signals on Vietnam. On Labor Day, during the first half-hour news broadcast by CBS, he told anchorman Walter Cronkite:

> In the final analysis, it is their war. They are the ones who have to win it or lose it. We can help them, we can give them equipment, we can send our men out there as advisors, but they have to win it, the people of Vietnam, against the Communists.[65]

He was now apparently less fully committed to protecting South Vietnam's independence than he had been in the 1950s, and his views now represented something of a step back from the ringing defense of liberty in his inaugural address. Repeating that the United States had no plans to abandon Vietnam, he framed the matter as part of the "desperate struggle against communism in Asia."[66] He also hinted broadly that the United States wanted to see new leadership in Saigon. The Diem government over the previous two months had "gotten out of touch with the people. . . . With changes in policy and perhaps with personnel I think it can [win the war]."[67] A week later, in another television interview, his emphasis was different, as he reiterated his belief in the domino theory and the threat of increasing influence by Communist China in Southeast Asia. He concluded, "we should use our influence in as effective a way as we can, but we should not withdraw."[68] Kennedy and his top advisors were clearly not of one mind on Vietnam as events there moved toward a climax.

On November 2, 1963, President Ngo Dinh Diem and his brother Ngo Dinh Nhu, having fled the presidential palace when the coup against them began, were abducted coming out of a Catholic church in Saigon and shot to death by the military. President Kennedy was in a meeting with some of his own generals when he got the news. He put his hand to his face in shock and rushed out of the room. "What did he expect?" asked General Maxwell Taylor, his most trusted military advisor.[69] Kennedy had no wish to see Diem and his brother killed; he had sent one of his oldest friends in politics, Congressman Torbert Macdonald of Massachusetts, to Vietnam to warn Diem that he was in grave danger and should leave the country.[70] Even so, the Diem coup was the most serious mistake of Kennedy's foreign policy since the Bay of Pigs. The latter was a faulty plan he inherited; the coup in Saigon was something his own government had helped set in motion. Kennedy immediately expressed deep regret over the killings, admitting that he had lost some control over his own policy in Vietnam with the sending of the cable to Lodge: "[It was] badly drafted. . . . I never should have given my consent to it without a roundtable conference."[71] Although there were some high-level staff meetings during Kennedy's presidency on Vietnam, he never convened an ExComm on the subject. Despite his differences with Diem, Kennedy admired how "over a ten-year period he held his country together to maintain its independence under very adverse conditions."[72] He expressed some cautious hope that the generals who had seized power might bring a measure of stability and progress to South Vietnam. They did not, and for several years one military coup followed another. Finally, in 1967, Nguyen Van Thieu established his authority, holding on to power until Saigon fell to the Communists in 1975, 12 long agonizing years after the death of the Diems.

It is right, of course, that John F. Kennedy should be evaluated on the basis of his policies in Vietnam while in office. Given the tragedy that eventually unfolded there, however, there has also been much contentious debate over what he would have done had he remained president into 1964 and then served a second term. One side of the argument holds that he increased the level of commitment to South Vietnam that he inherited in 1961. This meant a substantially higher number of advisors—many engaged in combat—and sophisticated U.S. military hardware brought to the war on Kennedy's watch. In some of his final public comments on Vietnam, he re-affirmed the U.S. commitment there as part of the global fight against communism. His own Secretary of State, Dean Rusk, said Kennedy never mentioned the possibility of pulling out of Vietnam, and perhaps his closest confidante, Bobby Kennedy, said in 1964 that his brother never wavered from the goal of winning the war. The officials who advised President Johnson to dramatically escalate U.S. involvement in Vietnam in 1965, particularly Secretary of Defense Robert McNamara, were veterans of the Kennedy administration. Kennedy, furthermore, was acutely aware of the criticism he would receive, as a Democrat waging the Cold War ineffectively, if he unilaterally decided to pull out of Vietnam. And U.S. participation in the Diem coup tied the two nations together even more tightly.[73]

There is another speculative case to be made. Toward the end of 1963, Kennedy ordered the withdrawal of 1,000 U.S. military personnel from Vietnam. He also told Senator Mike Mansfield and aide Kenny O'Donnell that, unless things improved dramatically, he planned on a complete U.S. withdrawal in 1965, assuming his re-election in 1964.[74] Given his skepticism of the military after the Bay of Pigs, his confidence in his own judgment on foreign affairs, and the stature he would have had at the start of a second term, this scenario is plausible. Lyndon Johnson, for all his impressive achievements in shepherding domestic legislation through Congress as president, was not as interested or experienced in foreign affairs as Kennedy and more dependent on his advisors. And Charles de Gaulle and Douglas MacArthur, two men with significant experience in such matters, both warned Kennedy to avoid a land war in Asia at all costs. Kennedy was highly competitive, but it was not in his character to support a losing proposition for long. Before the United States had become tragically mired in Vietnam, he may also have explored the possibility of a negotiated settlement, with Laos serving as a recent example of how such an agreement might be reached between the United States and leading communist powers.

John F. Kennedy, more than any of his predecessors, made the nations of Africa, Asia, and Latin America an important part of his foreign policy. He drew the attention of his own nation to the problems of the Third World and inspired some of his fellow citizens to commit themselves to solving those problems. He also established personal connections with the leaders of those nations who wanted peaceful democratic change, and made them feel that they had a friend and partner in the White House. Kennedy's policies were not driven by altruism alone, of course, as he sought desperately to keep communism from sweeping across the Third World. He had concluded that the United States must play a positive role, and not merely a reactive one, in the battle for the hearts and minds of the peoples of those emerging nations. The Cold War was never far from the center of these relationships and at times its priorities won out. Much of the genuine idealism that Kennedy generated was eventually lost in the rice paddies and jungles of Vietnam. But not all of it. The Peace Corps and other international enterprises begun under Kennedy have endured, and his efforts to lend the hand of the United States across the globe, for the common good of humanity, still resonate.

CHAPTER **7**

"AT HOME"

John F. Kennedy, as the financially well-off son of a very wealthy man, had benefitted enormously from the capitalist system of private enterprise and was not inclined to initiate fundamental changes to it. Hence, he was not an economic populist in the tradition of William Jennings Bryan or even Harry Truman. Nor was the United States of January 1961 in the middle of a lengthy systemic economic crisis, as it had been in 1933 during the depths of the Great Depression. Kennedy did believe, however, along with many liberals, that the United States was burdened by social and economic problems that needed to be addressed in a serious way. And in the aftermath of the Great Depression and World War Two, many Americans believed that the national government was crucial to meeting those challenges. Many liberals believed that, at home, the eight-year Eisenhower presidency was a series of missed opportunities. The social and economic burdens of the nation were a drag on its efforts to present itself to the world as the model of a prosperous, harmonious society.

The Soviet Union had a fundamentally different view of what constituted the ideal polity. Such matters thus became an important aspect of the Cold War, as both camps looked to enlist the support of developing nations. Nikita Khrushchev frequently boasted about the Soviet Union's capacity to provide for the material needs of its people, justly and equitably. As a convinced Marxist-Leninist he was sure the Soviet Union was on the right side of history as the world moved inexorably toward communism. Capitalism, in the United States and elsewhere, was accompanied by great economic and social inequities. The postwar economy in the United States was marked by growth but had become sluggish by the late 1950s, with persistent problems of poverty and unemployment.

Despite his promise to "get the country moving again," Kennedy had not swept into office with a mandate to reshape the domestic economy. Campaigning in West Virginia in 1960, however, had brought him face to face with an American poverty he had not previously encountered. His Congressional district in Massachusetts included poor neighborhoods, but nothing comparable to the entrenched scarcities of Appalachia. Kennedy "never forgot West Virginia," according to White House historian Arthur M. Schlesinger Jr.[1] He was also intrigued by the idea of federal action to boost economic growth in regions such as Appalachia, ordering a task force to study the problem and pushing hard for Congress to fund resultant efforts. Looking to Franklin Roosevelt's New Deal, Kennedy had gained the support of conservative southern Democrats by promising that impoverished parts of their region would benefit from such a program. On May 1, 1961, Kennedy signed the Area Redevelopment Act, which provided nearly half a billion dollars in federal aid for chronically depressed sections of the country. He had promised during the West Virginia primary that, if elected, he would do something about poverty in the state, and he took special satisfaction in keeping his word.[2]

As a reader of serious books, Kennedy became aware of Michael Harrington's *The Other America: Poverty in the United States* (1962). Harrington was drawn to Dorothy Day's Catholic Worker movement, which interpreted its Christian mission as serving the poor. He later became a democratic socialist, skeptical of the story that Americans like to tell about their economy in the postwar era. *The Other America* provided a poignant picture of the forgotten American poor, urban and rural, living in the shadows of a generally affluent society. The people Harrington wrote about were found in the nation's urban core, on the Indian reservations of South Dakota, in the cotton belt of the Deep South, and in the hollows of Appalachia. They were young, old, black, white, Hispanic, and American Indian. The problems had deep historical roots and there was no consensus in the early 1960s about what, if anything, the federal government should do about them. That same year, Kennedy's Secretary of the Interior, Stewart Udall, wrote the foreword to Henry Caudill's *Night Comes to the Cumberlands: A Biography of a Depressed Area*, a study of Kentucky, a state rich in natural resources but marked by deep poverty and a range of social problems, including illiteracy, low life expectancy, and poor health care. Udall compared Caudill's book to classics such as Upton Sinclair's *The Jungle* and John Steinbeck's *The Grapes of Wrath*. It brought renewed attention, especially in the circles of Kennedy's Washington, to a largely overlooked section of the country.[3] The following year Kennedy oversaw the creation of an Appalachian Regional Commission, a federal partnership with nine states stretching from northern Alabama and Mississippi to the southern tier of New York.

Kennedy thought that something comprehensive should be done about these deeply entrenched problems. Among his ideas was a domestic "peace corps"; pointing to the successes of the original overseas version, he said of its volunteers, "they are willing to go abroad, I think they'd be more willing to stay at home" to work on Indian reservations and other places suffering from chronic poverty.[4] This came to fruition when President Johnson signed legislation setting up Volunteers in Service to America (VISTA) in 1964. In October 1963, Kennedy told his chief economic advisor, Walter Heller, that he wanted to take a two or three-day trip and call attention on some of the most poverty-stricken areas of the nation. The tour was to include a visit to Kentucky (a traditionally Democratic state he had lost in 1960) to highlight rural poverty.[5] He told his advisors in late 1963 to begin preparations for a broad economic plan, stating, "the time has come to organize a national assault on the causes of poverty, a comprehensive program."[6] In a speech in the final weeks of his presidency, he declared before one audience: "This is generally a prosperous country, but there is a stream of poverty that runs across the United States which is not exposed to the lives of a good many of us and, therefore, we are relatively unaware of it except statistically."[7] The following year, President Johnson unveiled what he styled a "War on Poverty." Kennedy himself was still feeling his way toward such a venture in late 1963.

One early legislative victory for Kennedy came in the spring of 1961, when he signed a bill raising the minimum wage. It had remained at the same level since 1955, despite a rise in the cost of the basic necessities of life. Supporters of a raise regarded it as a moral and humanitarian question; opponents saw it as damaging business and resulting in job losses. Kennedy, though once deriding the importance of the minimum wage, said of opponents of the proposed law: "I find it difficult to understand how anybody could object to paying somebody who works in a business which makes over $1 million a year, by 1963, [a wage of] $50 a week."[8] After some initial setbacks and compromises and with strong backing from organized labor, the bill was passed, raising the federal minimum wage to $1.25 and expanding coverage to more than three and half million workers. It was a modest increase, but it represented the most important change in the minimum wage law since the original Fair Labor Standards Act of 1938.[9] And Kennedy followed up on this achievement the following year when he signed the Manpower Development and Training Act. The purpose of this legislation was to finance retraining and literacy support for workers, especially the unemployed, whose skills had become obsolete. This was at a time when automation was an increasing threat to the jobs of American workers, especially in the manufacturing sector. Kennedy did not see unemployment as a political problem but rather a social ill with potentially dangerous consequences.[10] And in the summer of 1963, as the civil rights movement gathered wide support, Kennedy asked for and received Congressional approval to amend this law by providing targeted aid to African-Americans, especially teenagers.

These domestic problems, important as they were to him, never came close to replacing foreign policy and the Cold War as his chief concerns. And although Kennedy was not known in his Senate days as particularly skilled or interested in building coalitions and counting votes, the demands of the presidency forced him to pay attention to such things. He had not made his political home in either the House or Senate and, though now president, he was considerably younger, with less experience in government, than the well-entrenched figures on Capitol Hill. None of this augured well for persuading Congress to pass his agenda, especially on domestic issues, where legislators tended to be rather territorial in guarding their prerogatives. Kennedy was aided by an energetic, if inexperienced, Congressional liaison team led by Larry O'Brien, who had been with him since his 1952 Senate campaign. O'Brien, like his boss, faced a steep learning curve when it came to shepherding legislation through Congress, but he was considered sufficiently important and effective for *Time* magazine to feature him twice on its cover during Kennedy's presidency. Kennedy's domestic agenda met with much opposition, especially from an *ad hoc* coalition consisting of conservative Democrats, mostly from the South, and a large group of Republicans. This working majority stalled and delayed some of Kennedy's most important legislative proposals.

One area affected was education. A good system of schools, colleges, and universities, Kennedy—and many others—believed, was essential to the strength of the nation in its struggle with communism. There was also a perception in some quarters that too many of the nation's schools were outdated, underfunded, and ill prepared to educate the massive numbers of baby boomers now entering them. Primary and secondary schools in the United States were generally controlled and funded by local communities and governments. Kennedy, educated at some of the country's oldest and most prestigious institutions, made it clear during the 1960 campaign that he supported the concept of federal aid for elementary and secondary education. He saw this as a way to close the gap between wealthy and poor districts and states and to help schools across the country better contribute to the national interest.

In addition to the public schools, there were also a significant number of private and religious schools, many of them Catholic. Leading Catholic clergy announced that they wanted equal federal funding for their schools. This immediately raised questions on constitutional grounds: would such aid result in the establishment of a religion, which the first amendment prohibited? As the nation's first Catholic president, this put John F. Kennedy in a politically awkward situation. Just as he had maintained before the ministers in Houston that he was not the Catholic candidate for president, he was determined once in office not to become the Catholic president. During his trip to Europe in 1963, Kennedy met with Pope Paul VI, newly installed after the death of John XXIII. President Kennedy met him as a head of state, not as a Catholic, shaking hands with the pontiff. His sister Eunice, a devout Catholic, was with him in the papal quarters. She began to fall to her knees, in order to kiss the papal ring. Her brother noticed, grabbed her arm as she descended, and lifted her to her feet.[11]

The role of religion in American public life was beginning to change in the early 1960s. The Supreme Court issued two rulings banning official prayer in public schools. For his part, Kennedy's statement in 1960 that he believed in an absolute separation of church and state limited his options on the matter of funding for religious schools. He remained highly sensitive on this matter and his federal education proposal included direct funding for public schools alone. In consequence of this he met with strong opposition from some of his fellow Catholics, many of whom believed that excluding parochial schools from public funding was discriminatory, forcing them, if they sent their children to Catholic schools, to financially support two parallel education systems. Kennedy, who had spent only one year in a Catholic school, would not be pressured by criticism of the federal aid bill by Catholic prelates such as Cardinal Spellman of New York, who was no friend of the Kennedys. Unfortunately for the president, similarly determined was Congressman James Delaney of New York City, a Democrat and generally a Kennedy loyalist who represented a heavily Catholic district. He parted company with the White House on school aid and, despite intense lobbying efforts by Kennedy himself, he would not yield on a matter of principle. As a member of the powerful Rules Committee, his opposition proved decisive.[12] Southern Democrats also opposed the bill because, in the wake of the *Brown v. Board* decision, it would have prohibited federal funds from going to segregated schools. Two years later and in the midst of historic advances on civil rights, Lyndon Johnson, whose religion was not an issue, oversaw passage of a bill that included a compromise on aid to parochial schools. The situation was less contentious with regard to higher education, for which there was federal government history of support dating back to the Morrill Land Grant College Act of 1862. More recently, the G.I. Bill of 1944, which gave returning veterans financial support for college (permitting veterans to use tuition benefits at public, private, and religious institutions of higher learning) and small businesses, was widely understood to have enabled millions to join the middle class. After Sputnik in 1957, the federal government helped to fund science, math, and foreign languages at university level to meet the Soviet challenge, which could plausibly be conceived of as part of the U.S. mission in the Cold War. In June of 1963, Kennedy made that point, declaring that from the beginnings of the United States it has been broadly recognized that "the national government must play its role in stimulating a [education] system of excellence which can serve the great national purpose of a free society."[13] Part of that vision was realized in the Higher Education Facilities Act of 1963, passed by Congress in the fall of that year and signed by President Johnson in his first month in office. It provided funds for the construction of libraries and graduate schools—especially in mathematics and the sciences (one intended beneficiary of this was the space program)—as well as community colleges across the country. Kennedy himself that fall also signed into law a bill to benefit medical education.

With unprecedented numbers of Americans seeking education at all levels, it was valuable to have a president who appreciated intellectual life and used his office to encourage his fellow citizens in this regard.[14] He asked the venerable Robert Frost to read a poem for his inaugural, the first time a poet had been so invited. The Kennedy White House became a place where artists, including writers and musicians, were welcomed and celebrated. Kennedy's tastes ran more toward books and sports and he was not nearly as interested in the fine arts as was his wife. More than once he was caught snoozing at especially rarefied performances at the White House, but he believed that Americans should be exposed to such things. And he recognized excellence when he could, remarking most famously at a White House dinner for Nobel Award winners that this was the greatest assemblage of intellect gathered there since "Thomas Jefferson dined alone."[15]

A program of national health insurance for the sick and elderly had long been favored by liberals of both parties, dating back to the time of Theodore Roosevelt. It had been a special priority of Harry Truman's, but he was unable to get Congress to approve major changes in the funding of health care. As medical care began to improve after World War Two, so did its costs. And a large part of the public had rising expectations about the kind of medical treatment they would receive. Many U.S. citizens, most of them elderly, were without adequate private insurance and at risk of being denied proper medical treatment when sick. Kennedy, following the Democratic platform of 1960 and the recommendations of a task force he had appointed, proposed in his first weeks of office to increase payroll taxes to finance medical services for social security recipients. In a special message to Congress he asserted that health care was crucial to the nation's "economic vitality, to the morale and efficiency of its citizens, to our success in achieving our own goals and demonstrating to others the benefits of a free society."[16] He later described the bill somewhat defensively as "not a program of socialized medicine" because "every person will choose his own doctor and hospital," but was buoyed up by public opinion polls showing strong support for it.[17]

The American Medical Association's lobbyists, however, had also read the Democratic platform and campaign speeches of 1960 and they denounced Kennedy's proposal as bringing "compulsion, regulation and control into a system of freely practiced medicine."[18] The association unleashed a massive advertising campaign, going so far as to send doctors literature to read and share with their patients.[19] On Capitol Hill, Kennedy's path was blocked by the formidable Wilbur Mills of Arkansas, chairman of the powerful House Committee on Ways and Means, which had jurisdiction on the health care bill.

Kennedy, Vice President Johnson, and leaders of organized labor campaigned hard on behalf of what they now called "Medicare." In May of 1962, Kennedy spoke to a large crowd of older Medicare supporters at Madison Square Garden in New York City and to the nation on the national television networks. Unhappy with his prepared remarks, he spoke largely off the cuff in what became a rambling and disjointed speech. He seemed to forget that he was speaking not just to the thousands of committed in the arena but to the undecided millions around the nation watching on television.[20] An effective and unusually personal moment came, however, when Kennedy explained that he had just come from visiting his ailing father, who had suffered a major stroke at the end of 1961. Joseph P. Kennedy was wealthy enough not to have to worry about paying for his medical costs, but his son observed that millions of other older and ailing Americans were not so fortunate. His version of the bill was defeated in 1962 by the conservative coalition in Congress.

The night before Kennedy gave his Medicare speech, actress Marilyn Monroe sung "Happy Birthday" to him at a fundraiser in the same building, and the images from that event have become part of the cultural memory of the Kennedy presidency. But it was efforts such as Kennedy made the next day, uneven as they were, that put the weight of the presidency behind federal medical insurance, placing it before the American people as part of the "long, long, long labor" of politics in a democracy, as he once put it.[21] After he spoke with Wilbur Mills on a trip to Arkansas in October of 1963, the White House legislative team reached a new understanding with Mills regarding Medicare on the morning of November 22 that same year. Two years later, President Johnson signed Medicare into law at Harry Truman's home in Independence, Missouri.

The early 1960s saw a time of change begin for American women. In 1963, Betty Friedan published *The Feminine Mystique*. In it, she argued that growing numbers of American women, especially those in the suburbs, were growing restive in their roles as mothers and housewives and sought greater opportunities in society at large. The book struck a chord with many American women. John F. Kennedy knew the importance of mobilizing women for his campaigns and his party's platform in 1960 had mentioned the goal of establishing equality for women under the law, including equal pay for equal work. Like nearly all American men he was not particularly interested in challenging the generally accepted postwar roles of the two sexes, which had deep roots in the American past. Kennedy drew criticism from Eleanor Roosevelt and others for not naming a woman to his cabinet, as President Eisenhower had done. He did appoint Esther Peterson, a labor lobbyist he had known since his years in the House, as Assistant Secretary of Labor for Women's Affairs. He was questioned at a press conference toward the end of his first year in office by May Craig, one of the few women in the national press corps, about what he had done to fulfill the promises made to women in the Democratic platform. Using humor, as he often did to deflect questions he did not particularly want to answer, Kennedy said to laughter, "Well, I'm sure we haven't done enough."[22]

A month later, however, after Esther Peterson had impressed upon him its importance, he created the President's Commission on the Status of Women. He had become more open to the view that the talents and abilities of American women were not being fully utilized for the national interest, especially in areas such as teaching, science, and medicine.[23] He spoke of the need to transcend "prejudice and outmoded customs" as a precondition for the "full realization of women's rights."[24] Kennedy named Mrs. Roosevelt, still the most politically influential woman in the nation, as the commission's chair. She died before the commission made its final report to Kennedy in October 1963, with anthropologist Margaret Mead writing the introduction. Esther Peterson then led the commission, which recommended that discrimination based on sex should be challenged through individual law suits to establish equity under the fifth and fourteenth amendments to the Constitution, and not by a separate Equal Rights Amendment (ERA). Advocates of organized labor, including Peterson, thought the proposed ERA would erode protective legislation and hurt women in the workplace. Another of the commission's recommendations was that employers should not pay women less than men for equal work. Supporters of such a bill saw it weakened over the question of comparable worth, a concept by which the law would try to establish how to equalize pay for men and women when they worked at different jobs. The 1963 Equal Pay Act which Kennedy signed was largely symbolic. Still, it was important in strengthening a federal role in promoting fairness to women in the workplace. And Kennedy's Commission on the Status of Women brought attention to this question, leading many states to commence similar studies.[25]

Another matter which Kennedy addressed that did not seem particularly significant in the early 1960s but took on greater importance in the decades that followed, was the plight of mentally disabled Americans. Long dismissed as "retarded" and shunted to the corners of society, they were sadly often a source of shame for their families. One important champion of their cause was Eunice Kennedy Shriver. The Kennedys had their own painful experience in this regard with Rosemary Kennedy, but Eunice Shriver's motivations also came from her experience as a social worker seeing disabled Americans suffering in institutions.[26] She made sure that the family's Joseph P. Kennedy Jr. Foundation, established in 1946, made mentally disabled Americans a focus of its work. When her brother became president, Eunice persuaded him to establish a national panel to study mental retardation, which he did in October of 1961. Eunice quickly emerged as the force behind it and, while she had no official role beyond consultant, she made sure the project had a high profile from the start. Although President Kennedy did not himself necessarily view the issue as a priority, he knew that for his energetic and determined sister it was. He eventually signed two bills in 1963 funding federal efforts to combat mental retardation, handing the first pen to his sister Eunice and marking the most ambitious federal effort to date into this long-ignored and misunderstood area of American life.

Kennedy's relationship with business, especially the larger corporations, was shaped in the main by his being a Democrat. The last two Democratic presidents had had at times a contentious relationship with big business. Most of its leadership, including Wall Street, favored the Republicans as the more predictably pro-business party, seeing the Democrats as beholden to organized labor. John F. Kennedy's direct experience in business was minimal, other than observing his father's flamboyant career, and he was not personally acquainted with very many business leaders. Nor was he particularly interested in re-distributing wealth; his favorite economic metaphor was that "a rising tide lifts all boats." He was especially concerned with industries vital to national defense—in particular, steel—which also had an impact on the economy as a whole.

Working along these lines, Kennedy and Secretary of Labor Arthur Goldberg persuaded, or thought they had, management and labor in the steel industry to agree on maintaining wages and prices at a level that would limit inflation. Kennedy's satisfaction, however, quickly turned to anger when Roger Blough, head of U.S. Steel, the leading firm in that sector, told him at a White House meeting in April of 1962 that he had reconsidered and that his company had just raised prices after all. Kennedy became as publicly furious as his closest aides had ever seen him, heatedly telling Blough: "You have made a terrible mistake, you double-crossed me."[27] He denounced the price increases publicly as unjustifiable, comparing the selfishness of steel executives to the sacrifices of U.S. military personnel—four were killed that week in Vietnam, he pointed out—and coming as they did "in this serious hour in our Nation's history, when we are confronted with grave crises in Berlin and Southeast Asia."[28]

Behind the scenes, the Kennedy administration fought back so vigorously, directing the FBI to interview steel executives about the price increase as a possible violation of collusion laws and even subpoenaing their expense accounts, that its actions drew criticism as an abuse of power. The public, however, mostly sided with Kennedy, and the steel companies, most notably Roger Blough and U.S. Steel, eventually retreated, upholding the original agreement. This was a rare instance in American history of direct confrontation between the head of the national government and a powerful financial institution, echoing the Bank War of the 1830s between Andrew Jackson and Nicholas Biddle, the president of the Bank of the United States. There was lingering resentment on both sides, with Kennedy remarking, "My father always said all businessmen were sons of bitches, but I never believed it until now."[29] Businessmen, proving that humor was not the sole province of witty politicians, began to sport buttons proclaiming themselves members of the "SOB Club."[30] Kennedy was frustrated that many leading executives now considered him "anti-business," even though he did not see himself or his administration in that light.

Kennedy certainly did not want a permanent breach with the business community. To repair some of the damage from the steel crisis, he devoted a speech at Yale University a couple of months later to economics. In this, he attempted to dispel persistent myths regarding economics and business that he believed clouded clear thinking on those subjects. The challenges of the 1960s, he argued, were different from those of the past, and what was needed was not "some grand warfare of rival ideologies which will sweep the country with passion, but the practical management of a modern economy."[31] He referred several times to the need for "administrative and technical solutions" to economic problems, language that did not immediately bring to mind bold crusades such as a war on poverty. Kennedy apparently regarded questions about the basic assumptions of the American economic system as stale, outmoded, and clichéd. Instead, he called for business, labor, and government to "live up to their responsibilities."[32] In this he sounded less Andrew Jackson, defender of the common man against the wealthy classes, than Henry Clay of the antebellum Whig Party. The latter's ideal was for the different economic classes in American society to understand their proper role and live in general harmony with one another, thus producing the greatest national good.

Economics had not been Kennedy's strong suit prior to 1961. He had few preconceived ideas on economic theory; his advisors said that the only things they had to explain more than once had to do with economic issues. He did have an idiosyncratic interest in gold, fearing it being drained from the country's reserves. It was not obvious that the issue warranted his intense attention to it. Before he became president he kept clear in his mind the difference between fiscal and monetary policy by the "M" which began the last name of William McChesney Martin Jr., the longstanding chairman of the Federal Reserve Board, which controlled monetary policy.[33] But Kennedy was eager to learn what he did not know but recognized as essential, taking private lessons from leading economists. One said that he earned the equivalent of a graduate degree in economics during his time as president. He did come to believe that one of the legitimate responsibilities of the federal government was helping create conditions for economic growth and prosperity. Toward that end, he was persuaded by his economic advisors, especially Walter Heller—who had been influenced by John Maynard Keynes, the British economist who argued that proper governmental policy was essential in staving off recessions—that a tax cut would help bring the economy out of its then sluggishness. It would do this, so the argument ran, faster than increased social spending. Kennedy was determined to do what he could to prevent the economy from sliding into recession in 1964, as some economists were predicting, when he would be running for re-election. His was a different policy to either Roosevelt's, with its New Deal emphasis on social spending, or Eisenhower's, with its emphasis on balancing the federal budget. The Cold War was never far from his mind, and he observed that if the economy weakened to the point that the nation tumbled into conditions even remotely resembling those of the Great Depression, it would be just what the Communists hoped would happen.

There was little support at first in Congress for across-the-board tax reduction. Many in both parties, including Wilbur Mills of the Ways and Means Committee, were hesitant because of its potential impact on federal deficits. More populist Democrats, such as Albert Gore Sr. of Tennessee, believed Kennedy's proposal would widen economic inequality.[34] In late 1962, Kennedy tried to rally public opinion with a speech at the Economics Club of New York. The present tax system, he argued, was forged during World War Two to direct all resources toward the military, but it was now obsolete and a drag on the economy. Kennedy expected that lower taxes would boost tax revenues overall and contribute to the nation's economic and military strength. He was willing to hold the line on government spending, except for space and defense, to keep inflation at bay. He also maintained that an expanding economy was essential for the millions of young Americans who would be entering the labor force over the next ten years.[35]

And so in early January 1963, Kennedy proposed a reduction in income tax for both individuals and corporations. His plan would lower corporate tax rates from 52 percent to 47 percent and establish a "more sensible range" of individual rates of 14 percent to 65 percent, down from 20 percent to 91 percent.[36] He also advocated the closing of numerous tax loopholes—a daunting legislative task in any era. Kennedy eventually won support for his plan from such disparate groups as the Chamber of Commerce and the American Federation of Labor and Congress of Industrial Organizations (AFL-CIO). The House passed a version of the bill in September of 1963, with the Senate set to consider it in November. Most of Kennedy's original proposal became law as part of the Revenue Act of 1964. Within two years the economy was growing at more than 6 percent a year, exceeding even Kennedy's expectations; businesses of all sizes enjoyed rising profits, unemployment dropped to 4 percent—which economists consider virtually full employment—and inflation, which some critics of Kennedy's plan feared would rise sharply, remained low, at just over 1 percent.[37] Economists disagreed as to what extent the Kennedy tax cuts contributed to this robust performance, but he had become educated in economics to the benefit of the nation. One further consequence, most likely unintended, was that rising economic growth and confidence made it more politically possible for a president to launch a national campaign against poverty.

Kennedy had two opportunities to fill vacancies in the Supreme Court, headed by Chief Justice Earl Warren. On a whole range of issues, most notably the *Brown* decision of 1954, Warren had moved the court in a more liberal direction, using its power to correct a variety of what he and other like-minded justices considered problems in American life that had constitutional remedies. Two justices who had generally aligned with the conservatives on the court retired in 1962. Kennedy's first appointment was Byron "Whizzer" White, a Rhodes scholar, former All-American in football, and navy veteran whose biography appealed to Kennedy. More immediately, he had a strong reputation as the number two man under Bobby Kennedy in the Department of Justice and was sympathetic to the civil rights movement. He had no judicial experience, however. Once on the court, he proved to be moderate and occasionally conservative. His tenure is best remembered for his dissenting opinion in *Roe v. Wade,* when he found no constitutional grounds for the court's 1973 decision legalizing abortion. Kennedy's other nominee, Secretary of Labor Arthur Goldberg, with whom he had a close working relationship, proved to be more conventionally liberal; he became an important part of the Warren court during his short time on it (he resigned in 1965 to become ambassador to the United Nations), including its banning of the death penalty. In an era when Supreme Court nominations were rarely politicized, both White and Goldberg were confirmed by the Senate on voice votes.

Looking back over his time in office in 1963, John F. Kennedy told an aide that he never imagined that civil rights would become such a defining issue of his presidency.[38] As with other leading politicians in the decades after World War Two, his political ambitions were not initially motivated by a desire to advance the long struggle of African-Americans for racial equality. He had little experience of popular, mass campaigns by groups on the margins of society, clamoring to secure their basic rights. He was probably aware of efforts by Daniel O'Connell in mobilizing Irish Catholics to overturn systemic and historically rooted discrimination, but that was a distant historical memory. Before becoming president he had spent his adult life inside well-established American institutions: Harvard University, the United States Navy, the Democratic Party, and Congress. When his own national ambitions emerged in the middle of the 1950s, concurrently with the budding civil rights movement, Kennedy viewed the latter primarily through the lens of politics. Given that white southerners remained among the most dependable Democratic voting blocs in the country, he struggled to find a middle ground on civil rights. In 1960, this had proven to be a difficult balancing act. During the campaign he asked Harris Wofford, an advisor on the subject, to "tick off the ten things a president ought to do to clean up this goddam civil rights mess."[39] Kennedy, as with nearly all white Americans, was not sure what to make of this unprecedented movement for change, one grounded in the most contentious and tragic question in all of American history. Unlike economic issues, where he favored cool, rational discussion, the civil rights movement *was* marked by grand passions sweeping across the nation. And he knew that the Democratic Party's, and his, newfound commitment to the federal government's role in upholding the constitutional rights of African-Americans had cost him votes in the Deep South in 1960.

In his inaugural address, which was meant to inspire the nation, Kennedy passed up the opportunity to address the matter of civil rights, making only a passing reference to it. He liked to remind the American people and the world that the United States had its own revolutionary tradition, one worthy of respect and emulation, yet he was slow to grasp how essential the civil rights movement and the question of race was to this heritage. African-Americans had, after all, fought in every war in the nation's history, starting with their service in George Washington's Continental Army. The Civil War was largely to do with the question of freedom for all, as Abraham Lincoln came to realize. But even the racial and cultural divisions that gave rise to that conflict were not fully settled a century later.

The Centennial Commission created to oversee commemorations of the Civil War presented it almost as a massive football game between blue and grey; words that might remind Americans of their problems, such as "negro," "slavery," and "emancipation," were deliberately left out of its publicity.[40] At the first official meeting of the commission, in Charleston, South Carolina in early 1961, a black delegate from New Jersey complained that she was unable to rent a hotel room because of her race. In solidarity with her, the delegations of four northern states announced they would boycott the proceedings. President Kennedy, recently inaugurated, tried to find a compromise by suggesting that the commission meet at the Charleston Navy Yard, where he served during World War Two, as federal property was not segregated. The South Carolina delegation took such umbrage at this that, in a resounding echo from 1861, it seceded from the national commission. Two separate meetings were held, one integrated and one segregated.[41] Although no shots were fired on Fort Sumter in Charleston Harbor that spring, it was clear that that the new birth of freedom that Lincoln spoke of at Gettysburg had not yet been fully realized

Whether he meant to or not, Kennedy raised hopes on the civil rights front from start of his presidency. John Lewis, emerging as a leader in the civil rights community through the Student Nonviolent Coordinating Committee, (SNCC) said, "John F. Kennedy's very election ushered in a sense of optimism—of great expectation. There was something about the Kennedy presidency—about the man—that touched black people almost immediately."[42] Kennedy, however, did not respond by summoning a grand civil rights crusade. Civil rights were not at first his paramount domestic issue. He did, however, act affirmatively on behalf of the cause from the beginning. Noting that there were no black faces in the Coast Guard delegation as it marched by him at the inaugural parade, he ordered an inquiry into the matter. It turned out that no African-American had been admitted to the Coast Guard Academy in all its 86 years of existence; the first one entered in 1962. This was the strategy he favored initially; acting as an ally of civil rights on a case-by-case basis and through executive orders. He did not think that the time was right to send Congress comprehensive legislation in this area. Acutely aware of his narrow margin of victory, he kept in mind Jefferson's words: "Great innovations should not be imposed on slender majorities."

Kennedy did score one important procedural victory in his first days in office, however. Speaker of the House Sam Rayburn, an early skeptic of Kennedy who came around to become an enthusiastic supporter over the course of the 1960 campaign, led efforts to expand the membership of the Rules Committee. Many a liberal bill had died an unceremonious death in this committee, which had the power to prevent any legislation from reaching the full House for a vote and was chaired by a conservative Virginia Democrat. By a narrow margin, Rayburn was victorious in late January of 1961, increasing the chances that major civil rights legislation might someday become law.

Throughout his political career, John F. Kennedy often spoke and wrote of courage, finding it in astronauts, athletes, soldiers, and politicians. Courage was also very much on display in Alabama and Mississippi during the spring of 1961. Volunteers from the Congress on Racial Equality (CORE) and SNCC, building on sit-ins at lunch counters, decided to test a recent Supreme Court decision outlawing segregated interstate travel facilities in bus stations. The Interstate Commerce Commission, with jurisdiction in this matter, was slow to enforce the court's decisions. Influenced by the non-violent doctrine of Martin Luther King Jr. and the Southern Christian Leadership Conference (SCLC), they anticipated a violent response from arch-segregationists, which they expected would lead in turn to positive action by the Kennedy administration.

Starting out from Washington, D.C. in two buses, the plan was for the white and black volunteers to sit down in waiting rooms and coffee shops at bus stations that had long been segregated by law and custom. On the first part of their trip there were only minor disturbances, but this changed dramatically when one of the buses reached Anniston, Alabama. There it was attacked and firebombed by a mob, apparently organized by the Ku Klux Klan (KKK)—presently experiencing a revival of sorts with the dawning of the modern civil rights movement. The Freedom Riders, as the volunteers called themselves, were beaten by weapon-wielding Klansmen and others. Twelve of them were injured so badly they were taken to hospitals, where, speaking from their beds, they vowed to persevere until the bus terminals were integrated. Photos of the burning bus were published in newspapers all round the world. Meanwhile, the other bus made its way toward Birmingham, Alabama, where Police Commissioner Bull Connor, who was open in his racism and hatred for black people, promised the local Klan 15 minutes to assault the Freedom Riders before his police officers would intervene.[43] FBI agents, whose director, J. Edgar Hoover, was generally hostile to the civil rights movement, were on the scene but did nothing other than take notes.

As he prepared to leave for his first trip to Europe as president, Kennedy wanted above all for the violence to end. He was concerned that the chaos surrounding the Freedom Rides would damage the nation's—and his—reputation overseas. Ordering civil rights aide Harris Wofford to bring the Freedom Rides to a halt, he barked at him: "Tell them to call it off! Stop them!"[44] Kennedy's appeals for law and order disappointed civil rights leaders. But Attorney General Bobby Kennedy was more proactive, sending aide John Seigenthaler from his office to Alabama. There, while trying to protect Freedom Riders from a mob, Seigenthaler was himself attacked by a club-wielding assailant and left concussed on the street. An infuriated attorney general sent aide Byron White and 500 U.S. marshals to Alabama to both protect the Freedom Riders and preserve law and order, something local and state authorities had clearly failed to do. The marshals, with help from state police and some National Guard units, barely managed to protect a congregation of 1500 black people gathered in a Baptist church to hear Martin Luther King Jr. speak.

Bobby Kennedy kept the pressure on, as the Department of Justice filed an injunction against the KKK to prevent it from interfering with interstate travel. And in late May, in the immediate aftermath of the violence in Alabama, he requested that the Interstate Commerce Commission (ICC) strengthen its enforcement of the Supreme Court decision on desegregating bus terminals. Secretary of State Dean Rusk presented evidence to the ICC that the photos of the burning bus had done harm to the image of the United States around the world.[45] Bus terminals across the South, including those in Alabama and Mississippi, began to take down their "white" and "colored" signs. By the end of 1962, CORE declared the campaign a success. There was a price to be paid for this politically, however, in parts of the South. In Louisiana, a state Kennedy had carried in 1960, the legislature adopted a resolution denouncing the administration for conducting a "Hate the South" campaign, even though Kennedy had not made any bold or unequivocal public statements on behalf of civil rights, nor did he have any plans to submit major legislation to Congress.[46] It was becoming clear, however, that the civil rights movement had an ally in the nation's attorney general, and another advocate, albeit one less committed, in the White House.

The Freedom Riders' experience in Mississippi was more orderly than in Alabama but equally traumatic in its own way. When the Riders reached Jackson, the state capital, under an agreement reached by Robert Kennedy and U.S. Senator James Eastland, an avowed segregationist, they were promptly arrested. Most were sent to the infamous Parchman Farm, a prison in the Delta, where they were badly treated. Even by the standards of other southern states, Mississippi was a world apart in the early 1960s. A largely rural inland state, it had experienced little of the immigration, urbanization, and industrialization that had re-shaped much of the rest of the nation over the preceding century. Its dominant attitude on racial matters was rooted deep in the past, its system of enforced segregation similar to South African apartheid.

Even as the "winds of change" began to blow across the United States, Africa, and Asia, Jim Crow, as white supremacy and racial segregation was known, became ever more entrenched in Mississippi. In 1960, a plurality of its voters had rejected both John F. Kennedy and Richard Nixon in favor of a segregationist candidate. In the years immediately after the *Brown* decision, the number of African-Americans registered to vote dropped nearly in half; every school district in the state remained segregated, and unequally so.[47] Mississippi's defensive culture led one critic in the early 1960s to describe it as a "closed society."[48] Across the state, African-Americans suffered from a pervasive poverty akin to Third World conditions, a lack of even basic education, near-universal denial of the right to vote, low life expectancy, and a deeply ingrained sense that they were inferior to whites.

It was in this environment that James Meredith, the grandson of enslaved Mississippians, an Air Force veteran, and an African-American inspired by Kennedy's election and inaugural address, applied to the University of Mississippi, in Oxford. Known as "'Ole Miss," its registrar refused to consider his application, but the National Association for the Advancement of Colored People (NAACP), which focused on the legal side of the civil rights struggle, took up his case. The Supreme Court eventually rejected Ole Miss's claim that it was not segregated by noting, "the hard fact to get around is that no person known to be a Negro has ever attended the University." It then ordered Meredith admitted to the university for the fall semester of 1962.

This set the stage for one of the most dramatic episodes of the entire Civil Rights era. The Kennedy brothers hoped to avoid a situation like that of Little Rock, Arkansas, in 1957, when President Eisenhower sent in the U.S. Army to ensure the peaceful integration of a high school. They also feared a highly public crisis which would endanger moderate southern Democrats in the upcoming elections. To these ends they decided to work closely with Governor Ross Barnett of Mississippi, in the hope that he would comply with the court order and oversee the peaceful registration of Meredith. This proved to be a serious miscalculation on their part. The son of a Confederate war veteran, Barnett was fully committed to segregation, including in the state's universities. He was a leader of limited capacities, heavily influenced by the white supremacist Citizens' Councils of America which had arisen in the wake of the *Brown* decision. Barnett and his government made their case for keeping James Meredith out of the University of Mississippi on the grounds of states' rights, the tenth amendment to the U.S. Constitution, which reserved all rights not expressly delegated to the federal government, and the doctrine of interposition. The latter, by which states reserved the right to defy federal laws with which they disagreed, had a long tradition in the South, including John C. Calhoun of South Carolina's theory of nullification from the 1830s.

Meredith was first escorted onto the Ole Miss campus on September 20 by a team of U.S. marshals, as a large crowd chanted, "Go home nigger." [49] At the registrar's office, he was met by none other than Governor Barnett, who denied Meredith admission to the university in dramatic fashion. Barnett and Attorney General Kennedy followed this with a surreal conversation, in which the latter asked the governor if Mississippi was "getting out of the union." Barnett had earlier declared: "I won't agree to let that boy get to Ole Miss. I will never agree to that. I would rather spend the rest of my life in a penitentiary than do that." [50] Barnett blocked Meredith's registration a second time, but the Kennedys had the advantage of broad and growing bipartisan support for their position, including that of moderate southerners outside Mississippi. The Kennedys continued to try to work with Barnett behind the scenes, the president saying to him of Meredith, "I didn't put him in the university, but on the other hand, I have to carry out the [court's] orders."[51] The legalistic tone of Kennedy's remarks did not move the recalcitrant Mississippian. Kennedy was able to build a constructive rapport with a wide range of world leaders, but he and the state governor talked past one another, each asserting their responsibilities as they understood them. Kennedy also began to work with the Pentagon in case he did decide to send the army into Oxford, and U.S. Army generals began to pore over maps of Mississippi in preparation of this possibility.

Now the Kennedys began to move with more authority. Backed up by further court orders, they sent a contingent of U.S. marshals and other federal officials to register Meredith once and for all, keeping army troops on standby in neighboring Memphis. The president appealed to Barnett to use state police to help effect Meredith's peaceful registration. The night before Meredith again tried to register, however, Barnett gave a brief but impassioned speech at halftime at an Ole Miss football game, declaring his love for the people of Mississippi and their "heritage and customs." Using his full powers, President Kennedy then federalized the Mississippi National Guard and authorized Secretary of Defense McNamara to enforce all existing federal court orders, including the deployment of "the armed forces of the United States as he may deem necessary."[52]

As U.S. marshals converged on Oxford, so did white southerners, many of them armed with guns and mobilized by the KKK and Citizens' Councils. At 10 p.m. on the night of September 30, Kennedy went on national television to explain the situation in Mississippi. As he spoke, a riot broke out on the Ole Miss campus, Governor Barnett having broken his earlier pledge to use state police to maintain order. Kennedy, as he had throughout this crisis, explained that he was executing a court order and listed the names and states of the southern judges on the federal district court who had made the most recent decision in this matter—in effect, forcing Barnett's hand. He adopted a conciliatory tone, saying, "Neither Mississippi nor any other southern state deserves to be charged with all the accumulated wrongs of the last hundred years of race relations."[53] As he had often done during the 1960 campaign, Kennedy appealed to his audience's military heritage and patriotism, speaking well of Lucius Lamar, a Mississippi politician of the Reconstruction era whom Kennedy had featured in *Profiles in Courage,* for putting "the national good ahead of sectional interest."[54] Speaking directly to Ole Miss students, Kennedy reminded them, "You have a great tradition to uphold, a tradition of honor and courage, won on the field of battle, and on the gridiron as well the university campus."[55] What he did not do in evoking the state's legacy in war and football was make a moral or ethical case for Meredith's admittance to the university.

Kennedy's remarks did not meet the moment. He underestimated the ferocity of the white Mississippians who swarmed about the campus as he spoke, shooting about three dozen U.S. marshals and killing two other people, including Paul Guihard, a French journalist who declared in his last report, with the evidence all around him, that "the Civil War has never ended."[56] The White House ordered 23,000 U.S. troops to Oxford from Memphis. Logistical problems caused them to be delayed, which enraged Kennedy. His subsequent conversation with Secretary of the Army Cyrus Vance, said Bobby Kennedy, was "one of the worst and harshest conversations" he ever heard his brother engage in.[57] The troops did eventually arrive and restore order. James Meredith was finally enrolled at Ole Miss, graduating the next year.

Kennedy's actions in Mississippi were given generally high marks by the public and many civil rights activists (although some younger African-Americans thought Kennedy had failed to connect the Meredith case to the larger struggle for equality), and by African leaders as well. In the aftermath of Oxford, the president himself was chiefly concerned with the army's logistical snafus, keeping this in mind the following month when his generals called for an invasion of Cuba.[58] His brother the attorney general, however, showed he had grasped the implications of what had happened in Mississippi when, a week later, he said emphatically in a speech, "James Meredith brought to a head and lent his name to another chapter in the mightiest internal struggle of our time."[59] White Mississippians, for their part, did not forget what they considered an illegal invasion of their state by the federal government. In 1964, Barry Goldwater carried Mississippi with an astonishing 87 percent of the vote. He was the first Republican presidential candidate to do so since 1872, when Ulysses S. Grant carried the state during Reconstruction.

After Mississippi, Kennedy maintained a certain caution and restraint on civil rights. In November 1962, with the fall elections safely behind him, he signed a long-awaited executive order banning racial discrimination in public housing (more than a few members of Congress from northern states, with their own racial problems, asked Kennedy for the delay). He had promised to do it with "the stroke of a pen" during the 1960 campaign, but once in office he delayed in doing so, prompting civil rights activists to organize a "Pens for Jack" campaign. When pens began to flood into the White House, Kennedy was annoyed and directed the White House mailroom to send them to the office of Harris Wofford, his civil rights advisor. He told Bobby that he could not understand how he made that promise, muttering to himself: 'Who put those words in my mouth?" But he did sign the order, one of many the Kennedy administration pursued, often out of the glare of publicity. Through Secretary of the Interior Stewart Udall, it pressured the Washington Redskins football team to integrate its lineup or lose access to its stadium in the District of Columbia. After some resistance, the longtime Redskins owner, George Marshall, relented and his team began to sign black players.

President Kennedy appointed more than 40 African-Americans to posts in his administration and hoped to make Robert Weaver the first black cabinet secretary of a proposed department of urban affairs. Congress refused to create such a department, however. He also appointed several African-American judges, including Thurgood Marshall—although to gain congressional approval he had to make a trade, appointing a segregationist judge, William Cox, to the federal bench in the South. The White House also hosted several social events for African-Americans, and, after some initial hesitation, Kennedy met with Dr. Martin Luther King Jr. in the Oval Office.

Robert Kennedy's Department of Justice continued to file a wide range of suits on behalf of those whose voting rights were being systematically violated. His brother, in his State of the Union address in January of 1963, reminded the nation briefly that on the centennial of the Emancipation Proclamation, millions of Americans were still denied this fundamental right on the grounds of race and color.[60] The Kennedys quietly encouraged civil rights leaders to focus on voter registration, seeing that as having a sounder constitutional basis than a broad-based public accommodations bill, which might be vigorously opposed on the grounds of property rights and right of association. Certain senators committed to segregation privately acknowledged that it was very hard to deny on constitutional grounds that African-Americans possessed the right to vote. The Kennedy administration came out in support of a proposed amendment to the U.S. Constitution outlawing poll taxes, which had often been used to thwart voting. It became the twenty-fourth amendment to the U.S. Constitution in January 1964.

The next round of momentous events occurred a few months later in Birmingham, Alabama. The powers that be in Birmingham, a city so dedicated to segregation that it willingly gave up its minor league baseball team rather than permit integrated competition, maintained the strictest of social and economic divides between white and black.[61] The racial climate in Alabama was perhaps a shade more humane than that of Mississippi, but the difference was small. When George Wallace was inaugurated governor in January of 1963, he cried: "From the cradle of the confederacy, this very heart of the great Anglo-Saxon Southland, I draw the line in the dust and toss the gauntlet before the feet of tyranny. And I say, Segregation now! Segregation tomorrow! Segregation forever!"[62] This put Wallace and

Birmingham's Bull Connor on a collision course with Martin Luther King Jr. and the civil rights movement. King, in part to force a confrontation that would once and for all draw the Kennedy administration into full support of civil rights, led a march in April of 1963 without a permit and was promptly arrested. While in jail he wrote to his fellow clergy, comparing the plight of African-Americans to the progress being made around the world: "The nations of Asia and Africa are moving with jet-like speed toward gaining political independence, but we still creep at horse and buggy pace toward gaining a cup of coffee at a lunch counter."[63] He rejected the counsel of those who urged restraint, caution, and yet more waiting (although he did not mention President Kennedy by name, he might have), an attitude he found patronizing and inadequate to the moment.

Once released from prison, King commenced another march that included schoolchildren, risking their safety for the good of the cause. As he expected, Bull Connor's police force unleashed a spate of violence on the demonstrators, some of whom, breaking with King's ideal of non-violence, responded in kind by throwing bricks at the police. Photographers captured snarling police dogs lunging at protesters. The pictures, which President Kennedy said "made him sick," were broadcast throughout the nation and the world, providing widespread outrage among both American and international observers. Agents of the Soviet Union made sure African leaders saw them.[64] Now more than ever engaged by civil rights, Kennedy said to leaders of Americans for Democratic Action, a liberal group he had avoided as a young politician: "I think it's terrible, the picture in the paper [of the events in Birmingham] . . . I am not saying anybody ought to be patient."[65] The federal government sent mediators to help calm the situation and Kennedy ordered federal troops to be stationed near Birmingham in case they were needed to quell any further disturbances. Unlike the Freedom Rides and the Mississippi crisis, however, there was no direct involvement by the federal government in Birmingham. The events there (and the worldwide circulation of the images) spurred Kennedy to begin work on comprehensive civil rights legislation, which he had studiously avoided during his first two years in office.

The focus of the nation with regard to racial matters had been on the South, and rightly so. But what Kennedy came to call the "fires of frustration and discord" were beginning to burn in northern cities as well. African-Americans had started moving from the rural South to the urban northern states in significant numbers in 1917, triggering race riots over the next few years. More serious clashes between whites and blacks occurred in Detroit during World War Two. Most African-Americans resided in the older and poorer neighborhoods of cities in the Northeast and Midwest, never having been fully integrated into the wider communities where they lived. Their children were educated in segregated, less well-funded schools, and the employment prospects for many, as jobs moved out of the inner cities after the war, were only marginally better than those of families who remained in the South. Local civil rights leaders bemoaned a pattern of unfair and illegal treatment from the nearly all-white police forces in these cities.

Desperation among African-Americans was so pronounced that some turned to the radical Nation of Islam and its message of racial division. In the spring of 1963, James Baldwin, a leading African-American writer, published *The Fire Next Time,* in which he gave voice to the growing anger felt by black Americans in the north of the country. New leaders such as Malcolm X began to question the efficacy of Martin Luther King's message of non-violence and racial reconciliation. And King himself let it be known that he would not be able to restrain much longer those who were increasingly impatient with the path of peaceful change. Emboldened by developments in the South, African-Americans in the northern states took to the streets as part of what was becoming called "the Negro Revolt of 1963."[66] Significant protests were held in Philadelphia, New York City, New Jersey, Boston, Detroit, and Chicago. None erupted into full-scale violence, but neither did they go unnoticed in the White House. The growing radicalism of these protests stunned even civil rights leaders, as not only King came in for criticism, but James Meredith, the presumptive hero of the siege of Oxford, was booed in Chicago by a black audience when he questioned the tactics of northern civil rights activists.[67]

Back in Dixie, Governor Wallace pledged to stop integration at the University of Alabama, his state being the last in the nation to maintain racial segregation at its institutions of higher learning. After some tense negotiations, conducted mainly by Bobby Kennedy and his team but with some help from the president, Wallace—after a last public display of defiance—reluctantly gave way, and permitted two African-Americans, Vivian Malone and Jimmy Hood, to enroll at the University of Alabama in Tuscaloosa in June of 1963. Compared to the mayhem at Oxford, Mississippi, the previous year, Alabama proved to be a victory for both racial equality and the Constitution.

Kennedy used this more hopeful moment to speak to the nation on civil rights in a way he had not done previously. On June 11, the day after he asked the nation to re-examine some of the basic assumptions of the Cold War in his speech at American University, he went before network television cameras. Not having his speech fully prepared as he went on the air, he improvised toward the end, and the results were a highlight of his presidency. After explaining events in Alabama, Kennedy put the struggle in a global context: "Today we are committed to a worldwide struggle to promote and protect the rights of all who wish to be free. When Americans are sent to Vietnam or West Berlin, we do not ask for whites only."[68] He also said, "We preach freedom around the world, and we mean it . . . but are we to say to the world, and, much more importantly to each other, that this is the land of the free except for the Negroes?"[69] Careful not to cast too much blame on the South, Kennedy said, "This is not a sectional issue. Difficulties over segregation and discrimination exist in every city, in every state of the Union, producing in many cities a rising tide of discontent that threatens the public safety."[70] And finally, Kennedy addressed the heart of the centuries' long struggle of African-Americans for freedom: "We are confronted primarily with a moral issue. It is as old as the Scriptures and is as clear as the American Constitution."[71] He outlined his plans to submit major civil rights legislation to Congress, which included a strong public accommodation section and vigorous federal action to protect the right to vote for African-Americans.

Kennedy's address, which came later than many hoped, nonetheless galvanized civil rights advocates. Jackie Robinson, a Republican whose skepticism toward Kennedy in 1960 was unmatched among African-Americans, announced that he would vote for Kennedy in the next election.[72] In Jackson, Mississippi, Medgar Evers, a veteran of World War Two and leader of the NAACP in that troubled state, was returning home to his family, buoyed up after hearing Kennedy's speech on the radio. As he got out of his car he was shot in the back in his own driveway by a Klansman, Byron De La Beckwith, and died a short time later, a victim of what has been described as "the first political assassination of the 1960s."[73] After two mistrials in the years soon afterward, Beckwith was finally convicted of murder in 1994.

John F. Kennedy's thinking on civil rights changed that season. He met with Medgar Evers' family in the White House two weeks after the murder. He mentioned to Arthur Schlesinger that he had been reading the work of historian C. Vann Woodward, who offered a revisionist view of southern history and Reconstruction, one which led Kennedy to question some of his assumptions on the South and race. "I don't understand the South. I'm coming to believe that Thaddeus Stevens was right."[74] Stevens was a Radical Republican from Pennsylvania who fiercely defended the rights of African-Americans during Reconstruction and Kennedy had painted a highly negative portrayal of him in the pages of *Profiles in Courage*.

Now fully committed to the cause of civil rights, Kennedy enlisted leading members of his government to lobby on behalf of his bill. Testifying in Congress, Secretary of State Rusk reiterated the persistent attempts by the Soviet Union to portray the United States as profoundly racist, and this a natural result of the alienation produced by capitalism. Attorney General Robert Kennedy spoke long and passionately before the Senate Judiciary Committee, pointing out, among other things, the profound absurdity that in some southern communities, dogs, if accompanied by a white person, were welcomed at certain hotels that denied black people accommodation.[75]

President Kennedy himself was hopeful that the civil rights bill of 1963 would be enacted before the coming election year and so not become a central issue in the campaign. He was aware that his approval among southern whites dipped immediately after his June 11 speech, although later it did rebound somewhat. African-Americans, despite the earlier misgivings of civil rights leaders, now saw Kennedy in a different light. One poll in September of 1963 had Kennedy garnering 95 percent support among black voters in a potential race against Senator Barry Goldwater, and enjoying only slightly less overwhelming support in a potential matchup with New York Governor Nelson Rockefeller, himself widely known to be a supporter of civil rights.[76] And while Kennedy understood that Mississippi and Alabama would almost certainly be lost to him in 1964, on his trip to Arkansas in the fall of 1963 he spoke hopefully of "a new South" of growing industry, education and opportunity for all its people.[77]

In part to build support for Kennedy's comprehensive civil rights bill, which would, among other measures, outlaw racial segregation in all places of public accommodation, civil rights activists planned a march on Washington in the summer of 1963. Its official name was the March for Jobs and Freedom, which reflected the economic struggles of black people all over the United States. The White House was originally skeptical of the proposed march, with Kennedy telling civil rights leaders: "We want success in Washington, not just a big show at the Capitol."[78] He and his aides eventually came to see such a march as supportive of the civil rights bill. What Kennedy and his advisors did not want was for it to become unruly. If it did, it would allow moderates of both parties to claim they were being unduly pressured and thus have a convenient reason for opposing Kennedy's legislation. On August 28, 1963, Martin Luther King Jr. stirred a vast and peaceful throng, estimated at 250,000 Americans, mostly but not entirely black, in the shadow of the Lincoln Memorial. A couple of miles away, an admiring president, watching live coverage of the event on television, said of King, "He's damn good."[79] Relieved that the massive event had gone off well, Kennedy invited civil rights leaders to the White House afterwards, greeting King with, "I have a dream."[80] A polite but spirited discussion followed on what strategies to pursue to ensure success of Kennedy's civil rights bill. Later that fall, the House Judiciary Committee approved it. With most of Kennedy's original proposal intact, it was passed by bipartisan majorities in Congress and signed into law the next summer by President Lyndon Johnson as the Civil Rights Act of 1964, one of America's landmark pieces of social legislation.

Civil rights activist and Kennedy administration official Roger Wilkins, looking back on the 1960s, said African-Americans assumed during those years that nearly all whites were to some degree racist and that the best one could hope for was a leader who was open to being educated. That, he said, described John F. Kennedy at his best.[81] He had not made his mark in civil rights early on in his career, as did Hubert Humphrey. Critics of Kennedy before 1960 had legitimate reason to question his commitment to civil rights, given his record in Congress, and his initial hesitation as president was reproached by those who indeed had waited too long. Once he came to see the issues in a new light in May and June of 1963—and with a politician's calculation of how it might impact his own fortunes—Kennedy threw the full weight of his presidency behind this struggle. Some of the problems that concerned African-Americans, such as persistent poverty and residential and educational segregation both north and south, remained far beyond the scope of Kennedy's presidency. On the most important domestic question of his presidency, and the era, John F. Kennedy had acted to help his nation overcome.

CHAPTER 8

"A Long Twilight Struggle"

In October of 1962, British scholar Isaiah Berlin met President John F. Kennedy at a dinner on the evening of the very day that Kennedy was shown photographic evidence of Soviet missiles in Cuba. Berlin found Kennedy to be gracious, charming, and not at all preoccupied, despite the burdens of his office—made incalculably heavier just hours before. This he chalked up to an extraordinary exertion of self-control. Berlin, with a wealth of Old World knowledge and experience, described Kennedy as intense, with exceptional powers of concentration. "I've never known a man," he said, "who listened to every single word that was uttered more attentively."[1] Kennedy was curious about things, he found, but not idly so. He asked direct questions, expecting similar answers in return. Although Kennedy was a man of obvious charisma and charm, Berlin did not see in him a natural ease. In his view, Kennedy "thought of life as a series of hurdles which had to be overcome," not "in the easy, jaunty fashion which obviously Roosevelt must have done."[2] Berlin understood Kennedy to have a strong sense of his own destiny and that, with his "very, very personalized view of history," he was particularly interested in how great men dealt with the major issues of their times.[3] Kennedy impressed him as a natural leader, who saw himself as marching "at the head of a small, dedicated band of men, with shining eyes."[4] The reserved British philosopher and historian, although not starstruck by Kennedy, found all this fascinating but also potentially dangerous.

Kennedy had been at the center of various political enterprises since 1946; everything that was done around him was intended to advance his career. His needs and interests came first, and this almost inevitably created a certain self-centeredness.[5] He did not socialize with the people he worked with; his determination to keep separate these parts of his life extended even to his brother Bobby, who, to his disappointment, was never invited to the private living quarters of the White House. Even so, reporters and others noted a devotion to Kennedy among his staff that was unique, bordering on love. Many an exposé has been written about Kennedy, but none by a member of his personal staff or his administration. And more than one individual who knew him praised his ability to raise people's spirits, a noble trait for prince or pauper.[6]

Kennedy's character had various dimensions to it. His journalist friend, Benjamin Bradlee, understood him as having a two-sided nature: one part tough and pragmatic Irish-American politician, the other more intellectual, refined, and cultivated.[7] Knowing the importance of establishing and maintaining good relations with reporters, editors, and publishers, he could have a thin skin when it came to criticism. He canceled the White House subscription to one major newspaper when its coverage displeased him. And Tom Wicker, then a young reporter for the *New York Times*, recalled keeping Kennedy waiting as Air Force One prepared to take off. He sheepishly made his way through the presidential cabin. "I'd like to report that we exchanged jovial remarks. But he only glared, as if he wanted no further interruption."[8] What impressed him most about Kennedy, however, was his quality of leadership. "My strongest impression of him has nothing to do with sex or health—it's of a man able to draw about him in Washington a large group of talented people and remain always not just their titular 'boss' but, more important, their leader by natural force. Among the political figures I have known, few have had that naturally dominant quality to the extent that Kennedy did."[9]

What kind of man was John F. Kennedy, as he served as his nation's thirty-fifth president? In his mid-forties, Kennedy was about six foot one in height, with a full head of brownish-red hair. Although his general health improved through a variety of medicines and treatments—some administered daily—Bobby Kennedy said later that his brother was in pain nearly every day of his life. And the strain of the job took its toll as it does with all presidents; by his third year in office he had begun to noticeably age and intimates observed that his habit of fidgeting with his hands had become more pronounced. Even so, Kennedy once told a friend that he never had an unhappy day in his life, medical problems notwithstanding. Even with the burdens of high office, he never lost a genuine light-heartedness. One friend said, "Jack's attitude made you feel like you were at a fair or something."[10] Despite the strains and pressures, Kennedy enjoyed being president. After an underwhelming legislative career in the House and Senate, he was happy in his work, famously telling one news conference that the ancient Greek's definition of happiness was "using one's full powers along lines of excellence," and he now had the opportunity for that.

Kennedy faced some of the same crises that any other middle-aged person does. His father's stroke at the end of 1961 was a devastating event for the Kennedys. Along with other members of his family, he flew to Florida to be with his father, who had showed signs of an impending event but refused medical treatment until he fell ill. He was left partially paralyzed and all but unable to speak. His oldest surviving son said after the stroke that he missed talking to his father, even if he did not often take his advice. One of the last times they saw each other, at the family compound on Cape Cod, Kennedy remarked to an aide how his father had "made all this possible, and now look at him." For a family that prided itself on presenting an image of strength and vigor, Joe's extended paralysis (he died in 1969) must have been especially difficult to accept.

Kennedy's relationship with his wife Jackie was changed by his becoming president. A more normal routine was possible, with Kennedy working from home and not having to travel as often. Given the demands of his office, Jackie tried to make their living quarters a haven from his responsibilities. The Kennedys often had small dinner parties during the week, with Jackie steering the conversation away from politics and matters of state as much as possible. Late to parenthood, Kennedy clearly enjoyed being a father and loved spending time with his children, rolling around on the floor with them as they did their exercises, following fitness expert Jack LaLanne on the television.[11] When Jackie was away (frequently enough for comedians to say in jest, "Goodnight Mrs. Kennedy, wherever you are"), the president instructed his press team to let news photographers have access to the children, something their mother generally discouraged. There were widely published photos in magazines such as *Time, Life,* and *Look,* which featured the Kennedys at the White House and on vacation in Massachusetts and Florida, frolicking on beaches, playing touch football, and riding horses. All of this was designed to present the image of a healthy, high-spirited, close-knit, and active American family.

But outside of the happy pictures, the Kennedy marriage continued to have its serious problems. Jack told a friend before he was inaugurated that he "hoped to keep the White House white," but, however much he might have meant that, he continued with his long-established pattern of sexual affairs. The presidency not only enhanced Kennedy's appeal to women, it provided him with a protected bubble of security and privacy. One of Kennedy's more serious relationships was with Mary Pinchot Meyer, sister-in-law of his friend Benjamin Bradlee, editor of the *Washington Post.* She was three years younger than Kennedy and they had known each other since 1938. If this had been his only extramarital affair, his behavior might be easier to comprehend. Kennedy's sexual encounters included Jackie Kennedy's personal assistants, movie stars, and actresses, women he scarcely knew (such as a 19-year-old White House intern) and others he apparently did not know at all, prostitutes brought to him by aides or friends. Secret service agents committed to protecting the president were aghast when ordered to let unfamiliar women without formal security clearance pass through them to Kennedy. Showing extremely poor judgment, Kennedy became involved with a young woman named Judith Campbell, who was also sexually linked with leaders of organized crime. FBI director, J. Edgar Hoover, who had known for years about Kennedy's sexual escapades and very much disapproved of them, suggested strongly he cease contact with Exner, which he eventually did. As disturbing, or even worse, was his affair with Ellen Rometsch, who had lived in East Germany before defecting and may have had ties with the East German secret police. Again on the advice of Hoover and the FBI, Rometsch was sent back to West Germany. Such recklessness exposed him to the possibility of blackmail from both internal and external enemies of the United States.

What explains this puzzlingly wild behavior? Kennedy was unable, or unwilling, to change his ways. If he had not had a political career, he might well have remained a bachelor; that lifestyle seemed to suit him best. Some who knew him found he had a certain adolescent immaturity when it came to matters of women and sex. His father, for whom he had enormous admiration and respect, set a bad example in this area that he chose to follow, whether consciously or subconsciously. In a later day, Kennedy might be understood as addicted to sex; he once more or less said that himself to Macmillan the British Prime Minister.[12] Some of the many medications he took may have added to his already prodigious sexual drive.

His determination to squeeze all he could out of every day and every hour was in many ways admirable, courageous, and profoundly human. At the same time, it led Kennedy into areas that were dangerous and, according to most ethical systems, immoral. For him, the great evils were boredom, routine, and convention. His restlessness was obvious to those who knew him best. The nation he led, however, held up as an ideal the monogamous marriage at the center of the traditional nuclear family. For public and political reasons, the Kennedys maintained their own version of this image. John F. Kennedy was able, to an extraordinary degree, to compartmentalize his life, keeping friends, family, political allies, and staff in separate chambers. It may also be that he believed something essential was lacking in his marriage, allowing him to rationalize his adultery. Being with a variety of women could have bolstered Kennedy's confidence, or he might have justified his actions to himself as a necessary release from the crushing burdens of office.

John F. Kennedy also did not want to live his life under any constraints, rules, or limitations imposed from outside. How he reconciled this attitude with Catholicism, or whether he even attempted to do so, is unclear. Ted

Sorensen, who spent countless hours with him over the course of a decade, said of Kennedy's sexual behavior: "[He] knew it was wrong . . . he had a conscience, and there must have been times when his conscience tortured him."[13] What he said about these matters to the priests in the confessional—and he regularly partook of this sacrament, as did nearly all Catholics at the time—is also unknown and presumably will be forever. Jackie Kennedy said nothing publicly about that painful aspect of her marriage when interviewed by Arthur Schlesinger in 1964 about life with her husband, although she is understood to have been more critical in private. Given how disciplined he was and how committed he was to his political career, Kennedy's "girling," as he referred to it, is all the more puzzling.

Kennedy was fortunate that the media personnel of the day, overwhelmingly male and mostly working for the major newspapers and magazines, never questioned Kennedy at his press conferences about the persistent rumors and speculations concerning his sexual life. A number of them were engaged in similar affairs themselves; in addition, a politician's private life was generally considered off limits. The Kennedys had long cultivated influential journalists, editors, and publishers, and Kennedy himself was on good terms with nearly all of them. On overseas trips, many reporters broke with protocol and called the president "Jack." A few fringe publications had tried for years to make Kennedy's philandering a public issue, but those efforts went largely unnoticed. If he had lived to complete a second term, he might not have been so fortunate, as the relationship between the media and established authority became more confrontational in the later 1960s. One friend speculated that, had his affairs been exposed by powerful and respected sources, Kennedy might have resigned the presidency, in the British tradition of politics he so admired. Whether this was a Shakespearean flaw in an otherwise great man, as Kennedy admirers maintain, or part of a larger pattern of deception, selfishness, and dereliction of duty, as his most severe critics charge, is a question not easily answered. What is clear, though, is that with this behavior he failed to meet his responsibilities, not only to his wife and children, but to the nation and the Western alliance he led.

Despite their troubles, the Kennedys may have grown closer together in the final months of their marriage. Not since Grover Cleveland in the late nineteenth century had a child been born to a president, and there was much anticipation within the Kennedy family and in the national media about a newborn baby in the White House when Jackie's pregnancy was announced in the spring of 1963. In August, however, Patrick Bouvier Kennedy was born prematurely, before his lungs had fully developed. His father flew immediately up from Washington to Otis Air Force base on Cape Cod, praying the rosary on the plane. In later decades, Patrick's chance of survival would have been much greater. Despite intensive and experimental efforts to save his life, the little boy lived only two days, his father holding his hand as he died at a Boston hospital. Understandably distraught at the loss of his son, Kennedy was inconsolable at the private funeral mass said by Cardinal Cushing. His aides made sure to keep any prying cameras at bay. Later that fall, Kennedy slipped away from a Harvard football game to visit Patrick's grave at the family cemetery in Brookline, making sure that no reporters followed him.[14] The Kennedy marriage was apparently never easy, but the shared grief over their son's Patrick's death, the kind of tragedy which can irreparably harm a marriage, in their case seemed to afford them at least the chance of a new beginning. Some of their friends noticed a new closeness between them; other observers saw their relationship as still troubled.

After physically recovering from the ordeal, Jackie Kennedy agreed to go with her husband on a political swing into two important southern states, Florida and Texas, in November of 1963. The trip was in preparation for the 1964 election, about which Kennedy had good reason to feel confident. His standing in the last Gallup Poll taken during his presidency was just a shade under 60 percent, having rebounded somewhat after a loss of support following his civil rights speech in June. He looked especially strong in potential matchups against Republican Senator Barry Goldwater of Arizona, the emerging spokesman for a more ideological conservatism. He and Kennedy were on friendly terms, and even discussed the possibility of flying around the nation together on Air Force One, stopping for debates, in a jet-age version of the Lincoln-Douglas encounters. And Kennedy's 1960 opponent, Richard Nixon, had lost a gubernatorial race in California in 1962, trailed far behind Kennedy in polls done of a potential rematch, and seemingly faced the end of his political career. At the height of his confidence and power in the late fall of 1963, the third year of his presidency, Kennedy had become something of a master politician. At both home and abroad, things were generally moving in a direction that he liked and had helped to steer. At his last official press conference, he exuberantly predicted that Congress would eventually enact his legislative program, including crucial bills on civil rights and taxes.[15]

Yet, even at this moment American politics was beginning to change in ways that would have enormous consequences for the nation over the next several decades. In 1962, the Students for a Democratic Society (SDS), originally based at the University of Michigan, where Kennedy had first suggested the idea of a Peace Corps, issued a manifesto that became known as the Port Huron Statement. Inspired by the civil rights movement, frustrated with the seeming stalemate of the Cold War, angered at the increasing gap between rich and poor and the growing technocratic character of a political culture grown stale and unimaginative, they called for a more vibrant, participatory democracy. The incumbent president did not come in for criticism or praise, although some of the manifesto's authors were vaguely inspired by him. Kennedy himself shared certain of their sentiments, musing to advisors about the upcoming campaign, "we've got so mechanical an operation here in Washington [that ordinary people find it increasingly difficult to identify with their government]."[16] The SDS became an important part of the New Left that led the protests against the Vietnam War in the later 1960s.

On the political right, Young Americans for Freedom (YAF) organized in 1960, and issued its own critique of the current situation, the Sharon Statement. It was written at the Connecticut home of conservative William F. Buckley Jr. The YAF was also chafing at politics defined by the moderate, non-ideological major parties, and called for outright victory in the Cold War and federal government responsibilities limited largely to national defense. Within a decade, the energies that emerged in the early 1960s produced national candidates more ideologically driven than either Kennedy or Nixon had been in their contest for the White House. Both Barry Goldwater in 1964 and Democrat George McGovern in 1972 suffered crushing defeats at the polls, but each helped to transform their parties, one becoming more stridently conservative, the other more self-consciously leftist.

Most of this was still over the horizon when the Kennedys went to Texas in late November 1963, the week before Thanksgiving. Kennedy was looking forward to 1964, and as with his previous campaigns, was determined to get an early start. Always looking to harness new technologies to his political advantage, Kennedy was intrigued by the idea of presenting some of the 1964 Democratic convention in color, which was just beginning to replace the traditional black and white pictures most Americans saw on their television sets.[17] And Texas loomed as an important state in 1964, as it had three years earlier when Kennedy won it narrowly. He was also expecting to raise money for his campaign with a series of events there. Vice President Johnson, who accompanied Kennedy in Texas, was caught up in a growing political feud in the state between the Democratic Party's dominant conservative wing, led by his protégé, Governor John Connally, and a more populist faction associated with Senator Ralph Yarborough. With the battle over the civil rights bill approaching, it would not be in Kennedy's interest in 1964 to have the Democratic Party divided in the most populous southern state. Kennedy had real concerns about Johnson's suitability as a potential president, but he certainly planned to run for re-election with him in 1964. After nearly three years together as president and vice president, however, the two were still, in political terms, rivals as much as partners.

On Friday morning, November 22, 1963, the Kennedys woke up in the Hotel Texas in Fort Worth. President Kennedy spoke at two events before boarding Air Force Two (Air Force One was flying his cabinet to Japan for meetings) for the short flight to Dallas. The first of these was in a parking lot near the hotel, before a crowd that was in high spirits despite the early hour and light rain. Kennedy touched on three major issues of his presidency, tailoring his remarks to his Texan audience. Praising Fort Worth for its role in the nation's defense, he noted that the next generation of fighter planes was being developed in the city, highlighted Texas's role in space exploration, and emphasized that the United States would soon launch a booster rocket, "putting us ahead of the Soviet Union [in this area] for the first time." He concluded by stressing that the United States was now outstripping the Soviet Union in economic growth. Kennedy wanted Texans to know that his administration remained committed to building the nation's strength.

There had been some trepidation within the Kennedy administration about his visiting Dallas. A month earlier there, U.N. Ambassador Adlai Stevenson had been heckled, hit on the head with a sign, and spat on by a right-wing crowd, some of whom handed out handbills with President Kennedy's picture and the words, "Wanted For Treason."[18] But Kennedy had a history of success in Texas, including his address to the Houston ministers in 1960 and his 1962 speech at Rice University on the space program. Avoiding potentially dangerous situations was not in his nature, although he remarked fatalistically, "we are heading into nut country today," and mused that anyone with a high-powered rival might easily shoot him from a high building.

Kennedy was greeted by at least one Confederate flag at the Dallas airport; there was also an advertisement in the city's paper that day condemning him again for alleged treason. With good reason, the Secret Service and other agencies responsible for Kennedy's safety in Dallas were most concerned with potential threats coming from right-wing extremists.[19]

As his motorcade rolled into Dallas that day, Kennedy was enveloped by large, boisterous, cheering crowds—in a city where he was not thought to be particularly popular—and protected by associates who were committed to him beyond the call of duty. One observer of Kennedy's staff during the Cuban Missile Crisis believed they would, if necessary, "take a bullet" for him. Members of the Secret Service assigned to protect Kennedy had also grown quite devoted to him. Their agency was much smaller than it later became, and procedures for protecting the president were strengthened in later years. Some of the agents on duty in Dallas never got over what happened that day.

Kennedy had ordered the presidential limousine's bubble top removed after the weather had cleared, to give the crowds lining the streets a better look at him and Jackie. As the car made its way through a section of Dallas where the crowds were less dense and when the motorcade only five minutes from its destination, Nellie Connally, wife of the governor, took the opportunity to say to Kennedy "Well, Mr. President, you can't say that Texas doesn't love you." A moment later, a man named Lee Harvey Oswald intervened in history, firing a shot at Kennedy from his sniper's nest in a warehouse. That first volley missed its target, but a second hit Kennedy in the neck, his arms jerking up involuntarily in response. Kennedy may well have realized what was happening to him in those final moments. There was a third and final shot, to the head. The president was rushed to the nearest hospital and news of the shooting immediately flashed across the country. Kennedy was pronounced dead within the hour.

Every death, even when expected, comes with a jolt. Kennedy, however, was the most widely known person on the planet—charismatic, exuding youth and vitality, and with extraordinary power at his disposal. He had become such a familiar and powerful figure that millions were flabbergasted to learn that he had died so suddenly and violently. The headline in the *Boston Globe* the next day spoke for millions when it proclaimed starkly: "Shock . . . Disbelief . . . Grief." Kennedy's death came so out of the blue that it seemed unfathomable, becoming an existential moment for countless individuals who never forgot where they were and what they were doing when they first heard the news. Protected from the horrors of World War Two by two oceans, many Americans in 1963 assumed that war, chaos, coups, and the murder of national leaders only happened in distant, less fortunate, and unstable lands. Although John F. Kennedy was the fourth president of the United States to be the victim of an assassination (a word that had fallen out of common usage), only Abraham Lincoln's death had remained in the national memory, and that was nearly a century earlier.

Within moments of the shooting, CBS interrupted *As the World Turns*, a daytime drama, to report the first fragmentary news from Dallas. Anchorman Walter Cronkite's voice was heard, but there was no picture, because in 1963 it took a while for television cameras to warm up. Once they were operational, his and the other networks stayed on the air nearly round the clock for the next four days, enhancing the importance and credibility of television news. Many of the images on television and in newspapers and magazines in the days and weeks following the event entered the nation's collective historical memory. Among them were those of Jackie Kennedy standing by Lyndon Johnson as he was sworn in as president on the same plane that had taken them to Texas, her skirt stained with her husband's blood; John F. Kennedy Jr. saluting his father's casket as it made its way to Arlington National Cemetery, pulled by horses, one horse left riderless, its stirrups reversed, in honor of the fallen leader. Leaders of many nations flew to Washington, marching in Kennedy's funeral procession to St. Matthew's Cathedral. At the end of the funeral Mass, which was not televised, Cardinal Cushing, longtime friend of the Kennedys and an emotional man, broke from the traditional Latin liturgy and cried out in a spontaneous prayer, "May God, dear Jack, lead you into Paradise."[20] Other unforgettable scenes included people waiting quietly in long lines to pay their respect to Kennedy as his body lay in state at the U.S. Capitol. Jackie Kennedy, who modeled her husband's funeral on that of Lincoln's, orchestrated much of this somber pageantry.

Within the Kennedy family, Rose turned to her Catholic faith for solace but wondered why her son had died just then, "when he had everything to live for."[21] On Cape Cod, Ted and Eunice Kennedy broke the news as gently as they could to their invalid father, telling him "Jack is in heaven, Daddy." The elder Kennedy understood and wept silently. When Eunice Kennedy Shriver learned that her brother had been wounded, one of her hopeful initial thoughts was that after all he had been through, he would survive this as well.[22] Bobby Kennedy was devastated, seemingly beyond consolation; his recovery from the trauma of Dallas was a long time coming. Jacqueline Kennedy bore up admirably during the funeral and burial of her husband, but she too grieved deeply. For those who worked closest with Kennedy and viewed him as their hero, his death marked the end of what they considered the great adventure of their lives. Ted Sorensen, who had been with Kennedy for a decade, later recalled: "His death hit me much harder than had the death of my own father."[23] Some of Kennedy's aides stayed on with President Johnson, at his request; their hearts no longer in their work, they quietly left the White House at a later date. Countless others who had never met the man felt similarly. Civil rights activist John Lewis said, "We were robbed of something."[24]

Alongside the scenes of restrained and somber dignity that weekend was a gruesome and disturbing one. On live television that Sunday, a mentally unstable bystander gunned down Lee Harvey Oswald as he was being transferred between jails. Oswald, 24-years old, had lived an unusual and largely unsuccessful life. Although troubled and alienated, he did not lack a certain intelligence and curiosity. He came to speak Russian fluently, for example. A native of New Orleans, he lived briefly in New York City, where he first encountered radical politics, and then served in the Marine Corps, becoming sufficiently skilled at shooting a rifle to qualify as a marksman. Disillusioned with American society, he denounced the whole country and gravitated toward Marxism-Leninism—so much so that he moved to the Soviet Union in 1959. This strange decision put him in a very small subset of young American men of the time. He ended up working in a factory in Minsk, which was not exactly the heroic socialist life he envisioned for himself in his adopted homeland. Oswald eventually came to view the Soviet Union as more a bureaucratic state than a communist utopia, and furthermore, one that failed to recognize his potential greatness. He returned to the United States in 1962 with Marina, his young Russian wife, and their baby girl. Taking a violent turn, in April of 1963 Oswald fired a shot into the

Dallas home of retired General Edwin Walker, a controversial right-wing general whom Oswald considered a "fascist" and whom President Kennedy had earlier relieved of his command for unprofessional conduct. Oswald, his anger spilling out at home, began to physically assault Marina.

Still holding out hope for Castro's revolution, Oswald became associated with the Fair Play For Cuba Committee, apparently hoping to defect to Cuba. One can easily imagine that plan ultimately not working out for him either, but nonetheless he stood on street corners in New Orleans passing out leaflets demanding that the United States change its policy toward Castro's government. A loner and a habitual liar, Oswald was at a loose end and moved to Dallas, where he filled book orders in a warehouse, work he considered far beneath his abilities. Despite the realities of his life, he continued to think of himself as a man of destiny, worthy of an important place in history. Most Americans were no doubt relieved that Cuba had grown quiet after the Bay of Pigs and the missile crisis. For Lee Harvey Oswald, however, it remained a fixation. In early September of 1963, Fidel Castro said: "United States leaders should be mindful that if they are aiding terrorist plans to eliminate Cuban leaders, they themselves will not be safe."[25] These comments were published in the New Orleans papers, where Oswald was living at the time, and may have spurred him to take action. At night in his Dallas rooming house he listened to Radio Havana's English language broadcasts, in which the state-run service vehemently condemned the United States in general and President Kennedy in particular for alleged crimes against Cuba.[26] After a speech in Florida by the president, a headline in the *Dallas Times Herald* of November 19, 1963, declared, "Kennedy Virtually Invites Cuban Coup."[27] For Oswald, this was just the latest in a long string of provocations by the Kennedy government. A few days later, he decided to act both in defense of Fidel Castro, whom he greatly admired, and to close the excruciating gap between his dreams of greatness and the squalor of his daily existence. John F. Kennedy had been caught up in the private torment of someone unknown to him and the antagonisms arising from the Cold War that still bubbled in some fevered imaginations.

In Oswald's motives, as best as they can be determined, lies one of the paradoxes of Kennedy's assassination. Just seconds after the last shot found its mark, Jackie Kennedy screamed, "*They've* killed my husband" (emphasis added). That Kennedy was murdered in Dallas—the most right-wing city of a largely conservative state, in a region where his popularity had ebbed over the previous year—took on great significance for some. In the years ahead, conspiracy theories regarding what has rightly been called the crime of the century abounded, most assuming the existence of a sinister cabal that viewed Kennedy as too soft on communism and too liberal on the domestic front. Since Oswald could not be brought to trial, President Johnson appointed a blue ribbon commission headed by Chief Justice Earl Warren to investigate Kennedy's death. Its members included Richard Russell of Georgia, Gerald Ford of Michigan, and John Sherman Cooper of Kentucky. Kennedy and Ford had been on friendly terms since serving together in the House in the late 1940s and Cooper was among Kennedy's closest friends while in the Senate. Charges that such men and others on the commission, including the chief justice, became knowing accomplices in a conspiracy to murder the president of the United States requires a high standard of proof, one that has never been approached. The Warren Commission, as it became known, did not follow every lead into the darker corners of the Kennedy presidency, nor did it investigate every conspiracy theory. It is also true that not every government agency cooperated fully with the commission (the CIA did not, for instance). But its essential findings—that Oswald, acting alone, fired three shots at Kennedy—have never been seriously challenged, despite a raft of books (and one movie that achieved great success at the box office) making wild claims of conspiracy. A special congressional committee in the late 1970s, its members not nearly as well regarded as those who sat on the Warren Commission, affirmed that Oswald had killed Kennedy, but speculated that he may well have been part of a conspiracy, though not one they could identify. The claim that Oswald acted as part of a conspiracy has never been proven. Kennedy once told a friend that he accepted the idea of death. The nation he led has had a difficult time coming to terms with his.

One of the ironies of Kennedy's death is that he was killed by a left-wing radical in a city with a reputation for right wing-extremism. Had Kennedy been shot in Dallas by a sniper akin to the Klansman who gunned down Medgar Evers, his death could have been folded into the struggle for civil rights, for example. But history often does not follow such neat paths. Communists and socialists had long been on the forefront of calling for racial equality in the United States; presumably Lee Harvey Oswald approved of John F. Kennedy's 1963 position on civil rights. Dallas police asked Oswald if he had any animosity toward Catholics; the accused assassin, who denied all charges of wrongdoing, said that he did not.[28] Scattered anecdotal evidence suggests that those who applauded Kennedy's death included die-hard segregationists, a few anti-Catholic bigots, and fanatical anti-communists who thought Kennedy had sold out to Moscow. They were a small minority that November weekend and afterward, however. Despite having made substantial progress in improving the U.S. relationship with the Soviet Union, John F. Kennedy could not ultimately escape the Cold War.

News of Kennedy's death reverberated around the world. In Moscow, a stunned Nikita Khrushchev, whose government quietly assured Washington that it was not involved in the assassination, went to the U.S. embassy and signed the condolence book. Having learned he could work with

Kennedy over the previous year, he appeared genuinely saddened at his death.[29] The reaction of the world's other leading communist power, however, was quite different. The *Daily Worker,* the official organ of the government in China, whose relations with the United States remained at low ebb in the early 1960s, printed a cartoon of a figure lying in a pool of blood, dollar signs on his tie, with the caption, "Kennedy Bites the Dust."[30] On the far right of international politics, a leading official of the apartheid government of South Africa denounced Kennedy as "an unremitting enemy of South Africa and an opponent of her race policies."[31]

These were rare notes of hostility, however. Coming just a few months after his triumphant visit to Ireland, Kennedy's death was taken particularly hard in that nation, where people made their way to church to pray in stunned silence. In Denmark, a country Kennedy had never visited, thousands held a candlelight vigil outside the U.S. embassy in Copenhagen.[32] Outside Europe, reactions were no less strong. In Africa, Tom Mboya, a rising young politician, noted how powerfully Kennedy's death had affected his fellow Kenyans: "It was the first time that the death of a foreigner, and a foreign head of state, had registered so sharply. . . . I saw very clearly that President Kennedy's personality had penetrated deep in the villages. . . . [He] gave the world that much more hope."[33] Ordinary people, at least vaguely aware of his support for civil rights in the United States and appreciative of his interest in Africa, were deeply upset, many of them seeking out pictures of Kennedy to place in their homes. And for leaders such as Julius Nyerere of Tanzania and Sekou Toure of Guinea, Kennedy was a rarity, a Western leader who took their concerns seriously and tried to understand Africa. In the Middle East, there was grief in both Israel and its neighboring Arab states; both Golda Meir and Gamal Nasser were touched by Kennedy's death. And Lleras Camargo, former president of Colombia, said, "For Latin America, Kennedy's passing is a blackening, a tunnel, a gust of cloud and smoke."[34] Kennedy had been especially well known and popular on much of the continent, where many had reason to value the Peace Corps and the Alliance for Progress. As in Africa and elsewhere, Kennedy's picture went up in the most humble of homes.

It was in the United States, of course, that John F. Kennedy's death was felt most acutely and where he is most remembered. His gravesite at Arlington has drawn a steady stream of visitors over the decades, as has a museum in Dallas concerned with his assassination. A major airport, a university, countless streets, Irish-American fraternal organizations, schools both public and Catholic, and a major cultural center in Washington all bear his name. The presidential library and museum dedicated to him which opened in Boston in 1979 have been an important part of maintaining Kennedy's memory and encouraging scholarly interest in his career, with the emphasis, not surprisingly, on the positive. Nearby is the John F. Kennedy School of Government at Harvard University, his alma mater. Books about Kennedy—his presidency, his life and death, his family—have been fixtures on best-seller lists for decades. In a way that is unusual for a political figure, Kennedy has evolved into something of a popular culture favorite, his name and image featured alongside those of Elvis Presley and Marilyn Monroe in magazines and television, on the walls of restaurants, and in many other places.

Toward the end of his life, Henry Cabot Lodge Jr. graciously said of his old rival that Kennedy was "a man for all seasons."[35] He may have been overly generous in his remarks. Kennedy was above all a politician. In closing his 1965 biography of his late boss and friend, Ted Sorensen declared: "all of us are better for having lived in the days of Kennedy," an echo of his White House colleague Arthur Schlesinger's historical work on the Ages of Jackson and Roosevelt.[36] But we have not come to think of the 1960s as the Age of Kennedy, however, as swift and dramatic changes in American society later in the decade dimed memories of his presidency from the early 1960s. Yet Kennedy himself has endured in the American imagination. Part of the reason for this is his family's continued prominence in politics and elsewhere. Robert Kennedy was elected to the U.S. Senate in 1964 from New York, joining his brother Ted in that body. In 1968, he ran an insurgent campaign for the Democratic nomination for president, challenging his old rival, Lyndon Johnson, now in the White House.

Driven by his evolving views on fundamental issues such as war and poverty and out of political necessity, Bobby Kennedy assembled a coalition of outsiders: African-Americans, Hispanics, American Indians, and part of the booming number of young people; he also drew older ethnic working-class whites, as well as intellectuals, to his banner. Running against the war in Vietnam, where President Johnson had greatly enlarged John Kennedy's commitment, Bobby wore his hair longer than he and his brother had a few years earlier, flashed the peace sign, and campaigned in poor neighborhoods and rural areas that few national politicians had ever seen. His death by an assassin at the age of 42 in June of 1968, while celebrating a major victory in the Democratic primaries and following the murder of Martin Luther King Jr. by a sniper two months earlier, brought the hope and promise of the decade to a tragic end for many Americans. Kennedy's funeral train from New York City to his resting place at Arlington, down the hill from his brother, was saluted along the railroad tracks by white and black Americans of modest circumstances, many holding handmade signs. The more professionally choreographed political theater of later decades has rarely yielded images so powerful and authentic.

At Boston's Faneuil Hall in late 1979, the youngest and lone surviving Kennedy brother, Ted—whose ambitions for national office were presumed to have ended a decade earlier when a young woman died in a car accident for which he was responsible—announced his plans to seek the Democratic presidential nomination. Like his brother in 1968, he challenged an incumbent president of his own party, in this case Jimmy Carter. Kennedy deemed him too conservative and an ineffectual leader. Although Kennedy survived the campaign, galvanized much of the liberal wing of his party, and won several major primaries, he failed to topple Carter. His stirring speech at the Democratic Convention in 1980 signaled for many the end of an era in American presidential politics. Ted Kennedy remained a stalwart in the Senate until his death in 2009, carving out a legacy of legislative achievement for which his older brothers had neither the time nor the temperament.

Another reason that John F. Kennedy has been remembered so vividly is that his death for many marked a breaking point between a simpler and more stable postwar era and the chaotic and turbulent times of the later 1960s and early 1970s. The bitter debate over the U.S. role in the Vietnam War, barely begun during Kennedy's presidency, shattered the Cold War consensus and deeply divided the Democratic Party. The explosion of poor and predominantly black neighborhoods in the urban north in 1967 and 1968 had some beginnings in the summer of 1963. But the riots of the late 1960s were far more extensive, the worst such disturbances since the Civil War. Their repercussions stalled the historic progress on the vexing matter of racial equality that John F. Kennedy had come around to calling for in the final year of his presidency. This upheaval complicated matters for American liberalism, as many traditionally Democratic, white, working-class voters, seeing the party as prioritizing civil rights and ignoring their concerns, migrated to the Republican Party in the 1970s and 1980s. Kennedy was spared the twin agonies of Vietnam at its worst and the "fires of frustration and discord burning in every city" of his 1963 civil rights speech. In 1975, however, his birthplace in Brookline, Massachusetts, made a National Historic Site in 1967, was firebombed. The assailants were angry at Ted Kennedy for his support of court-ordered busing, which required public schools in Boston to be racially mixed, provoking strong opposition from working-class whites, many of Irish Catholic heritage who had admired and supported the Kennedys for decades.

Much of American culture was transformed in the years after John F. Kennedy's death. Changing attitudes toward the family, sex, the role of women, religion, food, clothes, and authority in American life—all underwent what has been accurately described as a cultural revolution. These new values were reflected in music, movies, literature, and clothes, and most noticeably expressed by the young. We now know that many of these changes were already underway by the early 1960s. The Beats, for example, a loose collection of writers and poets, saw American society and culture as profoundly corrupt and in need of radical change.[37] Popular music, which was at the heart of the rebellious youth culture of the late 1960s and early 1970s, was on the cusp of a great transformation. Bob Dylan, an enigmatic folk singer, and rock and roll bands from England, including the Beatles and the Rolling Stones, had already begun to make their mark by the end of 1963. To what extent, if any, John F. Kennedy was aware of this is unclear.[38] Although young for a world leader (his grandmother was alive at the time of his death and people born the year of his birth, 1917, were still living in 2013), he was nonetheless well into middle age in 1963. While one can easily imagine Kennedy appreciating the new attitudes toward sex, other changes in American society might have puzzled him as much as they did his contemporaries.

One of the most important results of the upheavals that followed Kennedy's death was the marked decline in people's trust in government and other established institutions after Vietnam and the Watergate scandal of the 1970s. There was also surprise and some disappointment felt at the revelations, beginning to emerge in the 1970s and continuing into the twenty-first century, concerning Kennedy's personal life. They may have contributed in their way to the greater cynicism about politicians and government. The carefully crafted images of the Kennedys in the White House as the prototypical American family have been shown to be less idyllic than they appeared at the time. Even so, John F. Kennedy has remained popular in the public mind, invariably near the top of public opinions polls that ask respondents to rate U.S. presidents—a measure of debatable validity but one indication of his ongoing appeal.

Since 1963, his memory has had special meaning for African-Americans, Catholics, liberals, and Democrats, among others. Leading members of Kennedy's own political party have gone to great lengths to identify with him. In 1984, one of the first-tier candidates for the Democratic presidential nomination, Gary Hart, named his son after Kennedy and even went so far as to adopt some of Kennedy's gestures in public. In 1988, the Democrats chose another nominee from Massachusetts, Michael Dukakis, who also selected a Texan, Lloyd Bentsen, as his running mate. In an echo of 1960, Dukakis claimed that the "Boston-Austin Axis" was back; it wasn't, but that did not dissuade a successful Democratic presidential candidate, Bill Clinton, four years later, from openly identifying with Kennedy as well. The young Arkansas governor made much in his campaign commercials of a video recording of his brief meeting with Kennedy on the White House lawn when a teenager. The Democratic convention of 2000, held in Los Angeles, featured Caroline Kennedy as a main speaker. Delegates and the national viewing audience were reminded frequently that it was in that same city 40 years earlier that John F. Kennedy had claimed the party's presidential nomination.

The nomination of Joseph Lieberman for vice president, the first Jewish American so selected, also evoked Kennedy's breaking of another religious barrier in 1960. Then in 2004, the Democrats nominated John F. Kerry, a senator from Massachusetts, an Ivy League-educated Catholic, and a naval war veteran. The similarities between the two practically spoke for themselves, but that did not stop Kerry from invoking Kennedy's legacy whenever he could. Later in the twenty-first century, Barack Obama's candidacy was given a boost in 2008 when Caroline and Ted Kennedy endorsed him over former first lady Hillary Clinton. Both compared Obama's youthful idealism to that of President Kennedy, as the late president continued to be a star in the Democratic sky nearly 50 years after his death.

Leading Republicans have looked to Kennedy as well, sometimes to the consternation of their Democratic counterparts. Jack Kemp and Dan Quayle in 1988 and Newt Gingrich and Paul Ryan in 2012 all invoked Kennedy's memory, citing his youth, his idealism, his tax cuts, the Peace Corps, and the space program in support of their own political ambitions. It was Ronald Reagan, however, a conservative Republican who was quite critical of John F. Kennedy in 1960, labeling his domestic program as Marxist, who as president in 1985 captured something of Kennedy's character at a private fundraiser for the Kennedy presidential library. His predecessor, he said, was "a man of the most interesting contradictions, very American contradictions. . . . He was self-deprecating yet proud, ironic yet easily moved, highly literary yet utterly at home with the common speech of the ordinary man." Reagan, who survived a serious attempt on his own life while president, said in contemplating Kennedy's humanity: "One sensed that he loved mankind as it was, in spite of itself, and that he had little patience with those who would perfect what was really not meant to be perfect." And he recognized Kennedy's inspirational role in encouraging his fellow citizens to enter into public service, hailing him as "a patriot who summoned patriotism from the heart of a sated country."[39]

On a sadder note, memories of Kennedy family tragedies became front and center once more in the summer of 1999, when John F. Kennedy Jr., not yet 40 years old, was killed in a crash of his private jet, along with his wife and sister-in-law. He had been the subject of speculation about a possible political career, but at the time of his death it remained just that. His mother Jacqueline had died quietly five years earlier. Caroline Kennedy made an abortive run at the U.S. Senate seat from New York in 2008 that did not contribute to the family's political legacy. The children of Bobby and Ted Kennedy have had their own successes in politics, and in 2012, Joseph P. Kennedy III, grandson of Bobby Kennedy and great-grandson of Joe and Rose, was elected to the U.S. House of Representatives from Massachusetts. Members of the Kennedy family have fared much better politically than those who worked for John F. Kennedy; three of his aides, including Ted Sorensen, lost electoral bids in the years following Dallas.

John Kennedy's liberalism was shaped by the Cold War. It was in mind when he spoke often of national greatness, challenging Americans to do better across a wide range of endeavors, and spoke of responsibilities and sacrifices as much as or more than he did of rights. The more individualist liberalism of later decades emphasized personal liberation. But after Vietnam and the riots of the late 1960s, which exposed the nation to its deeply rooted and ongoing inequities of race and class, some intellectuals began to conceive of the United States not as a land of promise and freedom but rather an intolerant place deeply marked by the evils of racism and greed. From Christopher Columbus—now cast as a harbinger of plunder and slavery—onward, the history of the nation was recast. A new generation of historians and other scholars of the New Left, influenced by Marxism, brought to light compelling evidence of how the United States over the centuries had fallen short of its stated ideals of equality and freedom for all Americans. The United States was now seen as primarily to blame for the most recent decade of the Cold War, with Vietnam portrayed as the ultimate American crime. But others on the American left came to understand that viewing the United States as a nation beyond all hope and redemption was damaging to the cause of creating a better nation and world. Such a standpoint could cripple progress toward pragmatic reforms, realized through political means, even if they fell short of a sweeping, radical change.[40] It was there, in what Arthur Schlesinger Jr. described as the "vital center," between the extremes of right and left, that much of Kennedy's politics could ultimately be found.

John F. Kennedy had little reason to question the fundamental assumptions about government and economics on which the United States was based. When he fully committed himself to the cause of civil rights, for example, he saw the history of Reconstruction not as a matter of overweening federal tyranny but a noble effort to create opportunity for freed slaves. Neither satisfied nor smug about where the country stood in the early 1960s, Kennedy had little patience with those who were complacent. As he gained his footing as the nation's leader, he increasingly called on his fellow Americans to face the realities of its problems and help craft solutions to solve them. The federal government, in his reckoning, had a central role in such efforts. Kennedy hewed to certain Cold War orthodoxies until the end, as his remarks in Fort Worth, Texas on the last day of his life attest. Not everyone in future generations was as convinced of the certainties he espoused, especially at the start of his presidency. Yet he managed to avoid letting those beliefs overwhelm reason and make a devastating conflict more likely. Indeed, at the crucial moment of his presidency, he helped steer the world away from a war beyond imagining.

Kennedy's mistakes, hesitancies, and personal failings give his detractors credence when they argue that he falls far short of greatness. His admirers, who constitute the larger group, think otherwise, and the debate will go on. There are many ways to think about John F. Kennedy. One is that he boldly stepped forward at a defining hour in the history of the Cold War, reminding his fellow citizens that their nation's revolutionary spirit was not yet spent. In rightly encouraging them to see that they had more to offer each other, and the world, than the mere sum of their wealth and the might of their arms, he became an unforgettable character in the American story.

PART **II**

DOCUMENTS

JOHN F. KENNEDY, CONCLUSION OF *WHY ENGLAND SLEPT*, 1940

In 1940, John F. Kennedy published a revised version of his senior thesis at Harvard. In its final pages, he summarized what he considered the lessons from Britain's agonizing and ultimately unsuccessful efforts to stave off war with Nazi Germany. As a young man in his early twenties, Kennedy pondered the broader problem of democracies in relation to dictatorships on matters of war and peace. He wrestled with these questions for the rest of his life, which shaped his thinking on the Cold War when he became president 20 years after the publication of his first book.

Much of the cause of England's failure may be attributed to the leaders. The great advantage a democracy is presumed to have over a dictatorship is that ability and not brute force is the qualification for leadership. Therefore, if a democracy cannot produce able leaders, its chance for survival is slight. I say, therefore, that many of the very factors intrinsic in democracy resulted in England's falling further and further behind. For democracy and capitalism are institutions which are geared for a world at peace. It is our problem to find a method of protecting them in a world at war. What does this signify for our country? We must be prepared to recognize democracy's weaknesses and capitalism's weaknesses in competition with a totalitarian form of government. We must realize that one is a system geared for peace, the other for war. We must recognize that while one may have greater endurance, it is not immune to swift destruction by the other. It means that in preparing for war today, which takes such a long time and is so expensive, a democracy may be struck such a knockout blow by a totalitarian form of government, which has prepared for war over a long period, that she will not be able to bring in the latent advantages that she possesses.

It is only in the long war that the advantages of a greater spirit and determination among the people will be effective. And we must realize that a democracy finds it difficult to keep up this sustained effort over a long period of time, for the interests of the individual are not directly concerned with armaments. He must make a great personal sacrifice to build them up, and it is hard to maintain this sacrifice year in and year out. Especially is it complicated by the fact that a democracy's free press gives the speeches of the totalitarian leaders, who state their case in such a "reasonable" manner that it is hard always to see them as a menace. Taking all these factors into consideration, to prepare for modern warfare, where all the energies of a country must be subordinated to this task, a totalitarian state does have a great advantage. A democracy will, indeed, be two years behind a dictatorship. Coupled with these internal disadvantages, are the more obvious advantages that a dictator has in foreign policy. He can bring the might of a unified nation into any issue, whether he is strongly supported by his followers or not.

[. . .]

The representatives of a democracy cannot run contrary to the basic wishes of the people in any game of bluff. When the decision must be whether it will be peace or war, the fundamental instinct of man against war binds the hands of democratic leaders. In a dictatorship, on the other hand, people are often powerless to impress their wishes on the dictator until it is too late. The democracies know this; they know that the weight of public opinion in the dictatorship, which would ordinarily be inclined on the side of peace, will not be of decisive importance; they can't count on it to slow up the dictator. On the other hand, the dictator is able to know exactly how much the democracy is bluffing, because of the free press, radio, and so forth, and so can plan his moves accordingly. These great advantages of a dictatorship must be recognized if we are ever to hope for a survival of our system.

[. . .]

We must always keep our armaments equal to our commitments. Munich should teach us that; we must realize that any bluff will be called. We cannot tell anyone to keep out of our hemisphere unless our armaments and the people behind these armaments are prepared to back up the command, even to the ultimate point of going to war. There must be no doubt in anyone's mind, the decision must be automatic: if we debate, if we hesitate, if we question, it will be too late. And if the decision goes to the British, we must be prepared to take our part in setting up a world order that will prevent the rise of a militaristic dictatorship. We withdrew from Europe in 1920 and refused to do anything to preserve the democracy we had helped to save. We thought that it made no difference to us what happened in Europe. We are beginning to realize that it does.

[. . .]

Now that the world is ablaze, America has awakened to the problems facing it. But in the past, we have repeatedly refused to appropriate money for defense. We can't escape the fact that democracy in America, like democracy in England, has been asleep at the switch. If we had not been surrounded by oceans three and five thousand miles wide, we ourselves might be caving in at some Munich of the Western World. To say that democracy has been awakened by the events of the last few weeks is not enough. Any person will awaken when the house is burning down. What we need is an armed guard that will wake up when the fire first starts or, better yet, one that will not permit a fire to start at all. We should profit by the lesson of England and make our democracy work. We must make it work right now. Any system of government will work when everything is going well. It's the system that functions in the pinches that survives.

SOURCE

John F. Kennedy, *Why England Slept* (n.p: Wilifred Funk, 1940; reprint Greenwood Press, 1981), 225–231. Reprinted with permission of Greenwood Press.

JOHN F. KENNEDY, OPENING STATEMENT OF FIRST DEBATE WITH VICE PRESIDENT RICHARD NIXON, CHICAGO, ILLINOIS, SEPTEMBER 26, 1960

In the first televised presidential debate in U.S. history, Senator John F. Kennedy and Vice President Richard M. Nixon met in a Chicago television studio in late September. Kennedy was still lesser known than his Republican opponent, who had a reputation as a formidable debater. Although the subject of the debate was domestic policy, Kennedy from the outset seized the initiative, making the claim for the urgency of solving problems at home with an eye toward prevailing in the Cold War.

Appearing relaxed and well rested, Kennedy made a strong impression on the nation-wide television audience. Nixon, despite his experience and a solid command of the issues, looked wan and haggard, as he had recently been hospitalized with a knee problem. For much of the debate, he found himself reacting to Kennedy's proposals for national improvement. One result of the first debate was to elevate Kennedy's stature to the equal of his previously better-known opponent.

———

MR. SMITH, MR. NIXON:

In the election of 1860, Abraham Lincoln said the question was whether this nation could exist half slave or half free. In the election of 1960, and with the world around us, the question is whether the world will exist half slave or half free, whether it will move in the direction of freedom, in the direction of the road that we are taking, or whether it will move in the direction of slavery. I think it will depend in great measure upon what we do here in the

United States, on the kind of society that we build, on the kind of strength that we maintain. We discuss tonight domestic issues, but I would not want there to be . . . any implication to be given that this does not involve directly our struggle with Mr. Khrushchev for survival.

Mr. Khrushchev is in New York, and he maintains the Communist offensive throughout the world because of the productive power of the Soviet Union, itself. [. . .] The kind of country we have here, the kind of society we have, the kind of strength we build in the United States will be the defense of freedom. If we do well here, if we meet our obligations, if we are moving ahead, then I think freedom will be secure around the world. If we fail, then freedom fails.

Therefore, I think the question before the American people is: Are we doing as much as we can do? Are we as strong as we should be? Are we as strong as we must be if we are going to maintain our independence, and if we're going to maintain and hold out the hand of friendship to those who look to us for assistance, to those who look to us for survival? I should make it very clear that I do not think we're doing enough, that I am not satisfied as an American with the progress that we are making. This is a great country, but I think it could be a greater country; and this is a powerful country but I think it could be a more powerful country.

I'm not satisfied to have 50 percent of our steel-mill capacity unused. I'm not satisfied when the United States had last year the lowest rate of economic growth of any major industrialized society in the world. Because economic growth means strength and vitality. It means we're able to sustain our defenses; it means we're able to meet our commitments abroad.

I'm not satisfied, when we have over $9 billion dollars worth of food, some of it rotting even though there is a hungry world and even though 4 million Americans wait every month for a food package from the Government, which averages 5 cents a day per individual. I saw cases in West Virginia, here in the United States, where children took home part of their school lunch in order to feed their families because I don't think we're meeting our obligations toward these Americans.

I'm not satisfied when the Soviet Union is turning out twice as many scientists and engineers as we are. I'm not satisfied when many of our teachers are inadequately paid, or when our children go to school part-time shifts. I think we should have an educational system second to none. I'm not satisfied when I see men like Jimmy Hoffa, in charge of the largest union in the United States, still free. I'm not satisfied when we are failing to develop the natural resources of the United States to the fullest. Here in the United States, which developed the Tennessee Valley and which built the Grand Coulee and the other dams in the Northwest United States, at the present rate of hydropower production—and that is the hallmark of an industrialized society—the Soviet Union by 1975 will be producing more power than we are. These are all the things I think in this country that can make our society strong, or can mean that it stands still.

I'm not satisfied until every American enjoys his full constitutional rights. If a Negro baby is born, and this is true also of Puerto Ricans and Mexicans in some of our cities, he has about one-half as much chance to get through high school as a white baby. He has one-third as much chance to get through college as a white student. He has about a third as much chance to be a professional man, and about half as much chance to own a house. He has about four times as much chance that he'll be out of work in his life as the white baby. I think we can do better. I don't want the talents of any American to go to waste. I know that there are those who want to turn everything over to the Government. I don't at all. I want the individuals to meet their responsibilities and I want the States to meet their responsibilities. But I think there is also a national responsibility. The argument has been used against every piece of social legislation in the last 25 years. The people of the United States individually could not have developed the Tennessee Valley; collectively they could have. A cotton farmer in Georgia, or a peanut farmer or a dairy farmer in Wisconsin and Minnesota, he cannot protect himself against the forces of supply and demand in the marketplace, but working together in effective governmental programs he can do so.

Seventeen million Americans, who live over 65 on an average social security check of about $78 a month, they're not able to sustain themselves individually, but they can sustain themselves through the social security system. I don't believe in big government, but I believe in effective governmental action, and I think that's the only way that the United States is going to maintain its freedom; it's the only way that we're going to move ahead. I think we can do a better job. I think we're going to have to do a better job if we are going to meet the responsibilities which time and events have placed upon us.

We cannot turn the job over to anyone else. If the United States fails, then the whole cause of freedom fails, and I think it depends in great measure on what we do here in this country. [. . .] I want people in Latin America and Africa and Asia to start to look to America to see how we're doing things, to wonder what the President of the United States is doing, and not to look at Khrushchev, or look at the Chinese Communists. That is the obligation upon our generation. The question now is: Can freedom be maintained under the most severe attack it has ever known? I think it can be. And I think in the final analysis it depends upon what we do here. I think it's time America started moving again.

Source

John F. Kennedy Presidential Library and Museum Website

INAUGURAL ADDRESS, WASHINGTON, D.C., JANUARY 20, 1961

Upon his swearing in as the nation's thirty-fifth president, John F. Kennedy immediately set the tone for his presidency. Despite a snowstorm the previous day and freezing temperatures, he spoke without a topcoat or hat, delivering one of the more memorable inaugural addresses of the twentieth century. Focusing almost entirely on international affairs and the Cold War, Kennedy reaffirmed his commitment to the defense of the Western alliance and the role of the United States in leading it. He made it a special point to acknowledge the concerns and aspirations of the emerging nations of the Third World, and also held out the possibility of greater cooperation between the United States and its communist rivals in the Cold War. The ringing phrases of this ambitious speech have been considered an important part of the Kennedy legacy ever since.

We observe today not a victory of party but a celebration of freedom—symbolizing an end as well as a beginning, signifying renewal as well as change. For I have sworn before you and Almighty God the same solemn oath our forbears prescribed nearly a century and three-quarters ago.

The world is very different now. For man holds in his mortal hands the power to abolish all forms of human poverty and all forms of human life. And yet the same revolutionary beliefs for which our forebears fought are still at issue around the globe—the belief that the rights of man come not from the generosity of the state but from the hand of God.

We dare not forget today that we are the heirs of that first revolution. Let the word go forth from this time and place, to friend and foe alike, that the torch has been passed to a new generation of Americans—born in this century, tempered by war, disciplined by a hard and bitter peace, proud of our ancient heritage, and unwilling to witness or permit the slow undoing of those human rights to which this nation has always been committed, and to which we are committed today at home and around the world. Let every nation know, whether it wishes us well or ill, that we shall pay any price, bear any burden, meet any hardship, support any friend, oppose any foe to assure the survival and the success of liberty.

This much we pledge—and more.

To those old allies whose cultural and spiritual origins we share, we pledge the loyalty of faithful friends. United there is little we cannot do in a host of cooperative ventures. Divided there is little we can do—for we dare not meet a powerful challenge at odds and split asunder.

To those new states whom we welcome to the ranks of the free, we pledge our word that one form of colonial control shall not have passed away merely to be replaced by a far more iron tyranny. We shall not always expect to find them supporting our view. But we shall always hope to find them strongly supporting their own freedom—and to remember that, in the past, those who foolishly sought power by riding the back of the tiger ended up inside.

To those people in the huts and villages of half the globe struggling to break the bonds of mass misery, we pledge our best efforts to help them help themselves, for whatever period is required—not because the communists may be doing it, not because we seek their votes, but because it is right. If a free society cannot help the many who are poor, it cannot save the few who are rich.

To our sister republics south of our border, we offer a special pledge: to convert our good words into good deeds in a new alliance for progress, to assist free men and free governments in casting off the chains of poverty. But this peaceful revolution of hope cannot become the prey of hostile powers. Let all our neighbors know that we shall join with them to oppose aggression or subversion anywhere in the Americas. And let every other power know that this Hemisphere intends to remain the master of its own house.

To that world assembly of sovereign states, the United Nations, our last best hope in an age where the instruments of war have far outpaced the instruments of peace, we renew our pledge of support—to prevent it from becoming merely a forum for invective, to strengthen its shield of the new and the weak, and to enlarge the area in which its writ may run.

Finally, to those nations who would make themselves our adversary, we offer not a pledge but a request: that both sides begin anew the quest for peace, before the dark powers of destruction unleashed by science engulf all humanity in planned or accidental self-destruction.

We dare not tempt them with weakness. For only when our arms are sufficient beyond doubt can we be certain beyond doubt that they will never be employed. But neither can two great and powerful groups of nations take comfort from our present course—both sides overburdened by the cost of modern weapons, both rightly alarmed by the steady spread of the deadly atom, yet both racing to alter that uncertain balance of terror that stays the hand of mankind's final war.

So let us begin anew—remembering on both sides that civility is not a sign of weakness, and sincerity is always subject to proof. Let us never negotiate out of fear. But let us never fear to negotiate. Let both sides explore what problems unite us instead of belaboring those problems which divide us. Let both sides, for the first time, formulate serious and precise proposals for the inspection and control of arms—and bring the absolute power to destroy other nations under the absolute control of all nations. Let both sides seek to invoke the wonders of science instead of its terrors. Together let us explore the stars, conquer the deserts, eradicate disease, tap the ocean depths and encourage the arts and commerce.

Let both sides unite to heed in all corners of the earth the command of Isaiah—to "undo the heavy burdens . . . (and) let the oppressed go free." And if a beachhead of cooperation may push back the jungle of suspicion, let both sides join in creating a new endeavor, not a new balance of power, but a new world of law, where the strong are just and the weak secure and the peace preserved. All this will not be finished in the first one hundred days. Nor will it be finished in the first one thousand days, nor in the life of this Administration, nor even perhaps in our lifetime on this planet. But let us begin. In your hands, my fellow citizens, more than mine, will rest the final success or failure of our course. Since this country was founded, each generation of Americans has been summoned to give testimony to its national loyalty. The graves of young Americans who answered the call to service surround the globe.

Now the trumpet summons us again, not as a call to bear arms—though arms we need—not as a call to battle—though embattled we are—but a call to bear the burden of a long twilight struggle, year in and year out, "rejoicing in hope, patient in tribulation"—a struggle against the common enemies of man: tyranny, poverty, disease and war itself.

Can we forge against these enemies a grand and global alliance, North and South, East and West, that can assure a more fruitful life for all mankind? Will you join in that historic effort?

In the long history of the world, only a few generations have been granted the role of defending freedom in its hour of maximum danger. I do not shrink from this responsibility—I welcome it. I do not believe that any of us would exchange places with any other people or any other generation. The energy, the faith, the devotion which we bring to this endeavor will light our country and all who serve it—and the glow from that fire can truly light the world.

And so, my fellow Americans: ask not what your country can do for you—ask what you can do for your country. My fellow citizens of the world: ask not what America will do for you, but what together we can do for the freedom of man.

Finally, whether you are citizens of America or citizens of the world, ask of us here the same high standards of strength and sacrifice which we ask of you. With a good conscience our only sure reward, with history the final judge of our deeds, let us go forth to lead the land we love, asking His blessing and His help, but knowing that here on earth God's work must truly be our own.

Source

John F. Kennedy Presidential Library and Museum Website

MESSAGE TO CHAIRMAN KHRUSHCHEV CONCERNING THE EVENTS IN CUBA, APRIL 18, 1961

As the failed U.S.-backed invasion of Cuba was unfolding, President Kennedy took the opportunity at an extraordinarily tense moment at the start of his presidency to address Soviet leader Nikita Khrushchev via a direct communication. Kennedy outlined his nation's reason for opposing the Castro government, claiming that the United States was on the side of the Cuban people against what he characterized as the dictatorship of Cuban leader Fidel Castro. Although Kennedy stated that the United States was not planning a direct invasion of Cuba, he warned Khrushchev not to use the present crisis on that island to move against Western interests elsewhere in the world, nor to interfere with the internal matters of the Western Hemisphere. The two dramatically different understandings of the Cuban revolution led the following year to the most dangerous moments of the Cold War, when the Soviet Union put nuclear missiles in Cuba.

––––––––––

MR. CHAIRMAN:

You are under a serious misapprehension in regard to events in Cuba. For months there has been evident and growing resistance to the Castro dictatorship. More than 100,000 refugees have recently fled from Cuba into neighboring countries. Their urgent hope is naturally to assist their fellow Cubans in their struggle for freedom. Many of these refugees fought along side Dr. Castro against the Batista dictatorship; among them are prominent leaders of his own original movement and government.

These are unmistakable signs that Cubans find intolerable the denial of democratic liberties and the subversion of the 26th of July Movement by an alien-dominated regime. It cannot be surprising that, as resistance within Cuba grows, refugees have been using whatever means are available to return and support their countrymen in the continuing struggle for freedom. Where people are denied the right of choice, recourse to such struggle is the only means of achieving their liberties.

I have previously stated, and I repeat now, that the United States intends no military intervention in Cuba. In the event of any military intervention by outside force we will immediately honor our obligations under the inter-American system to protect this hemisphere against external aggression. While refraining from military intervention in Cuba, the people of the United States do not conceal their admiration for Cuban patriots who wish to see a democratic system in an independent Cuba. The United States government can take no action to stifle the spirit of liberty.

I have taken careful note of your statement that the events in Cuba might affect peace in all parts of the world. I trust that this does not mean that the Soviet government, using the situation in Cuba as a pretext, is planning to inflame other areas of the world. I would like to think that your government has too great a sense of responsibility to embark upon any enterprise so dangerous to general peace.

I agree with you as to the desirability of steps to improve the international atmosphere. I continue to hope that you will cooperate in opportunities now available to this end. A prompt cease-fire and peaceful settlement of the dangerous situation in Laos, cooperation with the United Nations in the Congo and a speedy conclusion of an acceptable treaty for the banning of nuclear tests would be constructive steps in this direction. The regime in Cuba could make a similar contribution by permitting the Cuban people freely to determine their own future by democratic processes and freely to cooperate with their Latin American neighbors.

I believe, Mr. Chairman, that you should recognize that free peoples in all parts of the world do not accept the claim of historical inevitability for the Communist revolution. What your government believes is its own business; what it does in the world is the world's business. The great revolution in the history of man, past, present and future, is the revolution of those determined to be free.

JOHN F. KENNEDY

SOURCE

The American Presidency Project, University of California at Santa Barbara

RADIO AND TELEVISION REPORT TO THE AMERICAN PEOPLE ON THE SOVIET MILITARY BUILDUP IN CUBA, OCTOBER 22, 1962

After asking for time from the leading broadcast networks on a matter of the "highest national urgency," a drawn but resolute John F. Kennedy revealed the discovery of offensive Soviet nuclear weapons on Cuba. In what was among the most sobering and chilling addresses ever given by a U.S. president, Kennedy accused the Soviet Union of lying about its intentions in the Caribbean and installing missiles with the capacity to strike the mainland of the United States. Determined to above all secure the removal of the missiles, Kennedy announced a policy of quarantine—in effect a blockade, which under international law was considered an act of war—and cast the showdown as one between an aggressive Soviet Union and the nations of the Western Hemisphere. Bringing enormous diplomatic, political, and military pressure to bear, Kennedy warned in the starkest of terms that any missile launched from Cuba against the United States would result in a massive nuclear attack upon the Soviet Union. Kennedy's speech brought the crisis in Cuba to its highest level of tension as the world was left to contemplate the prospect of a nuclear war.

———

Good evening my fellow citizens.

This Government, as promised, has maintained the closest surveillance of the Soviet Military buildup on the island of Cuba. Within the past week, unmistakable evidence has established the fact that a series of offensive missile sites is now in preparation on that imprisoned island. The purpose of these bases can be none other than to provide a nuclear strike capability against the Western Hemisphere.

[...]

The characteristics of these new missile sites indicate two distinct types of installations. Several of them include medium range ballistic missiles capable of carrying a nuclear warhead for a distance of more than 1,000 nautical miles. Each of these missiles, in short, is capable of striking Washington, D.C., the Panama Canal, Cape Canaveral, Mexico City, or any other city in the southeastern part of the United States, in Central America, or in the Caribbean area.

Additional sites not yet completed appear to be designed for intermediate range ballistic missiles capable of traveling more than twice as far—and thus capable of striking most of the major cities in the Western Hemisphere, ranging as far north as Hudson Bay, Canada, and as far south as Lima, Peru. In addition, jet bombers, capable of carrying nuclear weapons, are now being uncrated and assembled in Cuba, while the necessary air bases are being prepared.

This urgent transformation of Cuba into an important strategic base—by the presence of these large, long range, and clearly offensive weapons of sudden mass destruction—constitutes an explicit threat to the peace and security of all the Americas, in flagrant and deliberate defiance of the Rio Pact of 1947, the traditions of this Nation and hemisphere, the joint resolution of the 87th Congress, the Charter of the United Nations, and my own public warnings to the Soviets on September 4 and 13. This action also contradicts the repeated assurances of Soviet spokesmen, both publicly and privately delivered, that the arms buildup in Cuba would retain its original defensive character, and that the Soviet Union had no need or desire to station strategic missiles on the territory of any other nation.

The size of this undertaking makes clear that it has been planned for some months. Yet only last month, after I had made clear the distinction between any introduction of ground-to-ground missiles and the existence of defensive antiaircraft missiles, the Soviet Government publicly stated on September 11, and I quote, "the armaments and military equipment sent to Cuba are designed exclusively for defensive purposes," that, and I quote the Soviet Government, "there is no need for the Soviet Government to shift its weapons for a retaliatory blow to any other country, for instance Cuba," and that, and I quote their government, "The Soviet Union has so powerful rockets to carry these nuclear warheads that there is no need to search for sites for them beyond the boundaries of the Soviet Union." That statement was false.

Only last Thursday, as evidence of this rapid offensive buildup was already in my hand, Soviet Foreign Minister Gromyko told me in my office that he was instructed to make it clear once again, as he said his government had already done, that Soviet assistance to Cuba, and I quote, "pursued solely the purpose of contributing to the defense capabilities of Cuba," that, and I quote him, "training by Soviet specialists of Cuban nationals in handling defensive armaments was by no means offensive, and if it were otherwise," Mr. Gromyko went on, "the Soviet Government would never become involved in rendering such assistance." That statement also was false.

Neither the United States of America nor the world community of nations can tolerate deliberate deception and offensive threats on the part of any nation, large or small. We no longer live in a world where only the actual firing of weapons represents a sufficient challenge to a nation's security to constitute maximum peril. Nuclear weapons are so destructive and ballistic missiles are so swift, that any substantially increased possibility of their use or any sudden change in their deployment may well be regarded as a definite threat to peace.

For many years both the Soviet Union and the United States, recognizing this fact, have deployed strategic nuclear weapons with great care, never upsetting the precarious status quo which insured that these weapons would not be used in the absence of some vital challenge. Our own strategic missiles have never been transferred to the territory of any other nation under a cloak of secrecy and deception; and our history—unlike that of the Soviets since the end of World War II—demonstrates that we have no desire to dominate or conquer any other nation or impose our system upon its people. Nevertheless, American citizens have become adjusted to living daily on the bull's-eye of Soviet missiles located inside the U.S.S.R. or in submarines.

In that sense, missiles in Cuba add to an already clear and present danger—although it should be noted the nations of Latin America have never previously been subjected to a potential nuclear threat. But this secret, swift, and extraordinary buildup of Communist missiles—in an area well known to have a special and historical relationship to the United States and the nations of the Western Hemisphere, in violation of Soviet assurances, and in defiance of American and hemispheric policy—this sudden, clandestine decision to station strategic weapons for the first time outside of Soviet soil is a deliberately provocative and unjustified change in the status quo which cannot be accepted by this country, if our courage and our commitments are ever to be trusted again by either friend or foe.

The 1930s taught us a clear lesson: aggressive conduct, if allowed to go unchecked and unchallenged ultimately leads to war. This nation is opposed to war. We are also true to our word. Our unswerving objective, therefore, must be to prevent the use of these missiles against this or any other country, and to secure their withdrawal or elimination from the Western Hemisphere. Our policy has been one of patience and restraint, as befits a peaceful and powerful nation, which leads a worldwide alliance. We have been determined not to be diverted from our central concerns by mere irritants and fanatics. But now further action is required—and it is underway, and these actions may only be the beginning. We will not prematurely or unnecessarily risk the costs of worldwide nuclear war in which even the fruits of victory would be ashes in our mouth—but neither will we shrink from that risk at any time it must be faced.

Acting, therefore, in the defense of our own security and of the entire Western Hemisphere, and under the authority entrusted to me by the Constitution as endorsed by the resolution of the Congress, I have directed that the following initial steps be taken immediately:

First: To halt this offensive buildup, a strict quarantine on all offensive military equipment under shipment to Cuba is being initiated. All ships of any kind bound for Cuba from whatever nation or port will, if found to contain cargoes of offensive weapons, be turned back. This quarantine will be extended, if needed, to other types of cargo and carriers. We are not at this time, however, denying the necessities of life as the Soviets attempted to do in their Berlin blockade of 1948.

Second: I have directed the continued and increased close surveillance of Cuba and its military buildup. The foreign ministers of the OAS, in their communiqué of October 6, rejected secrecy in such matters in this hemisphere. Should these offensive military preparations continue, thus increasing the threat to the hemisphere, further action will be justified. I have directed the Armed Forces to prepare for any eventualities; and I trust that in the interest of both the Cuban people and the Soviet technicians at the sites, the hazards to all concerned in continuing this threat will be recognized.

Third: It shall be the policy of this Nation to regard any nuclear missile launched from Cuba against any nation in the Western Hemisphere as an attack by the Soviet Union on the United States, requiring a full retaliatory response upon the Soviet Union.

Fourth: As a necessary military precaution, I have reinforced our base at Guantanamo, evacuated today the dependents of our personnel there, and ordered additional military units to be on a standby alert basis.

Fifth: We are calling tonight for an immediate meeting of the Organ of Consultation under the Organization of American States, to consider this threat to hemispheric security and to invoke articles 6 and 8 of the Rio Treaty in support of all necessary action. The United Nations Charter allows for regional security arrangements—and the nations of this hemisphere decided long ago against the military presence of outside powers. Our other allies around the world have also been alerted.

Sixth: Under the Charter of the United Nations, we are asking tonight that an emergency meeting of the Security Council be convoked without delay to take action against this latest Soviet threat to world peace. Our resolution will call for the prompt dismantling and withdrawal of all offensive weapons in Cuba, under the supervision of U.N. observers, before the quarantine can be lifted.

Seventh and finally: I call upon Chairman Khrushchev to halt and eliminate this clandestine, reckless and provocative threat to world peace and to stable relations between our two nations. I call upon him further to abandon this course of world domination, and to join in an historic effort to end the perilous arms race and to transform the history of man. He has an opportunity now to move the world back from the abyss of destruction—by returning to his government's own words that it had no need to station missiles outside its own territory and withdrawing these weapons from Cuba, by refraining from any action which will widen or deepen the present crisis, and then by participating in a search for peaceful and permanent solutions.

[. . .]

We are prepared to discuss new proposals for the removal of tensions on both sides—including the possibility of a genuinely independent Cuba, free to determine its own destiny. We have no wish to war with the Soviet Union—for we are a peaceful people who desire to live in peace with all other peoples.

But it is difficult to settle or even discuss these problems in an atmosphere of intimidation. That is why this latest Soviet threat—or any other threat which is made either independently or in response to our actions this week—must and will be met with determination. Any hostile move anywhere in the world against the safety and freedom of peoples to whom we are committed—including in particular the brave people of West Berlin—will be met by whatever action is needed.

[. . .]

My fellow citizens, let no one doubt that this is a difficult and dangerous effort on which we have set out. No one can see precisely what course it will take or what costs or casualties will be incurred. Many months of sacrifice and self-discipline lie ahead—months in which our patience and our will be tested—months in which many threats and denunciations will keep us aware of our dangers. But the greatest danger of all would be to do nothing.

The path we have chosen for the present is full of hazards, as all paths are—but it is the one most consistent with our character and courage as a nation and our commitments around the world. The cost of freedom is always high—and Americans have always paid it. And one path we shall never choose, and that is the path of surrender or submission.

Our goal is not the victory of might, but the vindication of right—not peace at the expense of freedom, but both peace and freedom, here in this hemisphere, and, we hope, around the world. God willing, that goal will be achieved.

Source

John F. Kennedy Presidential Library and Museum Website

COMMENCEMENT ADDRESS AT AMERICAN UNIVERSITY, WASHINGTON, D.C., JUNE 10, 1963

Less than a year after the peaceful resolution of the Cuban Missile Crisis, President Kennedy spoke about making the world situation less dangerous. Asking the nation to re-examine its attitude toward the Soviet Union and toward the Cold War itself, he proposed that a new era of peace was possible, one based on the mutual recognition that no side wanted war, especially a nuclear one. Known as the "peace speech" within the Kennedy administration, his remarks helped move forward progress on a test ban treaty, one that the Soviet Union, the United Kingdom, and the United States agreed to in August of 1963.

———————

I speak of peace, therefore, as the necessary rational end of rational men. I realize that the pursuit of peace is not as dramatic as the pursuit of war— and frequently the words of the pursuer fall on deaf ears. But we have no more urgent task. Some say that it is useless to speak of world peace or world law or world disarmament—and that it will be useless until the leaders of the Soviet Union adopt a more enlightened attitude. I hope they do. I believe we can help them do it. But I also believe that we must reexamine our own attitude—as individuals and as a nation—for our attitude is as essential as theirs. And every graduate of this school, every thoughtful citizen who despairs of war and wishes to bring peace, should begin by looking inward—by examining his own attitude toward the possibilities of peace, toward the Soviet Union, toward the course of the cold war and toward freedom and peace here at home.

First: Let us examine our attitude toward peace itself. Too many of us think it is impossible. Too many think it unreal. But that is a dangerous, defeatist belief. It leads to the conclusion that war is inevitable, that mankind is doomed, that we are gripped by forces we cannot control.

We need not accept that view. Our problems are manmade—therefore, they can be solved by man. And man can be as big as he wants. No problem of human destiny is beyond human beings. Man's reason and spirit have often solved the seemingly unsolvable—and we believe they can do it again. I am not referring to the absolute, infinite concept of peace and good will of which some fantasies and fanatics dream. I do not deny the value of hopes and dreams, but we merely invite discouragement and incredulity by making that our only and immediate goal.

[. . .]

And history teaches us that enmities between nations, as between individuals, do not last forever. However fixed our likes and dislikes may seem, the tide of time and events will often bring surprising changes in the relations between nations and neighbors.

So let us persevere. Peace need not be impracticable, and war need not be inevitable. By defining our goal more clearly, by making it seem more manageable and less remote, we can help all peoples to see it, to draw hope from it, and to move irresistibly toward it.

Second: Let us reexamine our attitude toward the Soviet Union. It is discouraging to think that their leaders may actually believe what their propagandists write. It is discouraging to read a recent authoritative Soviet text on Military Strategy and find, on page after page, wholly baseless and incredible claims—such as the allegation that "American imperialist circles are preparing to unleash different types of wars . . . that there is a very real threat of a preventive war being unleashed by American imperialists against the Soviet Union . . . (and that) the political aims of the American imperialists are to enslave economically and politically the European and other capitalist countries . . . (and) to achieve world domination . . . by means of aggressive wars."

[. . .] It is sad to read these Soviet statements—to realize the extent of the gulf between us. But it is also a warning—a warning to the American people not to fall into the same trap as the Soviets, not to see only a distorted and desperate view of the other side, not to see conflict as inevitable, accommodation as impossible, and communication as nothing more than an exchange of threats.

No government or social system is so evil that its people must be considered as lacking in virtue. As Americans, we find communism profoundly repugnant as a negation of personal freedom and dignity. But we can still hail the Russian people for their many achievements—in science and space, in economic and industrial growth, in culture and in acts of courage.

Among the many traits the peoples of our two countries have in common, none is stronger than our mutual abhorrence of war. Almost unique among the major world powers, we have never been at war with each other. And no nation in the history of battle ever suffered more than the Soviet Union suffered in the course of the Second World War. At least 20 million lost their lives. Countless millions of homes and farms were burned or sacked. A third of the nation's territory, including nearly two-thirds of its industrial base, was turned into a wasteland—a loss equivalent to the devastation of this country east of Chicago.

Today, should total war ever break out again—no matter how—our two countries would become the primary targets. It is an ironic but accurate fact that the two strongest powers are the two in the most danger of devastation. All we have built, all we have worked for, would be destroyed in the first 24 hours. And even in the Cold War, which brings burdens and dangers to so many nations, including this nation's closest allies—our two countries bear the heaviest burdens. For we are both devoting massive sums of money to weapons that could be better devoted to combating ignorance, poverty, and disease. We are both caught up in a vicious and dangerous cycle in which suspicion on one side breeds suspicion on the other, and new weapons beget counter-weapons.

In short, both the United States and its allies, and the Soviet Union and its allies, have a mutually deep interest in a just and genuine peace and in halting the arms race. Agreements to this end are in the interests of the Soviet Union as well as ours—and even the most hostile nations can be relied upon to accept and keep those treaty obligations, and only those treaty obligations, which are in their own interest. So, let us not be blind to our differences—but let us also direct attention to our common interests and to the means by which those differences can be resolved. And if we cannot end now our differences, at least we can help make the world safe for diversity. For, in the final analysis, our most basic common link is that we all inhabit this small planet. We all breathe the same air. We all cherish our children's future. And we are all mortal.

Third: Let us reexamine our attitude toward the Cold War, remembering that we are not engaged in a debate, seeking to pile up debating points. We are not here distributing blame or pointing the finger of judgment. We must deal with the world as it is, and not as it might have been had the history of the last 18 years been different. We must, therefore, persevere in the search for peace in the hope that constructive changes within the Communist bloc might bring within reach solutions which now seem beyond us. We must conduct our affairs in such a way that it becomes in the Communists' interest to agree on a genuine peace. Above all, while defending our own vital interests, nuclear powers must avert those confrontations which bring an adversary to a choice of either a humiliating retreat or a nuclear war. To adopt that kind of course in the nuclear age would be evidence only of the bankruptcy of our policy—or of a collective death-wish for the world.

[. . .]

For we can seek a relaxation of tension without relaxing our guard. And, for our part, we do not need to use threats to prove that we are resolute. We do not need to jam foreign broadcasts out of fear our faith will be eroded. We are unwilling to impose our system on any unwilling people—but we are willing and able to engage in peaceful competition with any people on earth.

Meanwhile, we seek to strengthen the United Nations, to help solve its financial problems, to make it a more effective instrument for peace, to develop it into a genuine world security system—a system capable of resolving disputes on the basis of law, of insuring the security of the large and the small, and of creating conditions under which arms can finally be abolished.

[. . .]

Speaking of other nations, I wish to make one point clear. We are bound to many nations by alliances. Those alliances exist because our concern and theirs substantially overlap. Our commitment to defend Western Europe and West Berlin, for example, stands undiminished because of the identity of our vital interests. The United States will make no deal with the Soviet Union at the expense of other nations and other peoples, not merely because they are our partners, but also because their interests and ours converge.

Our interests converge, however, not only in defending the frontiers of freedom, but in pursuing the paths of peace. It is our hope—and the purpose of allied policies—to convince the Soviet Union that she, too, should let each nation choose its own future, so long as that choice does not interfere with the choices of others. The Communist drive to impose their political and economic system on others is the primary cause of world tension today. For there can be no doubt that, if all nations could refrain from interfering in the self-determination of others, the peace would be much more assured.

This will require a new effort to achieve world law—a new context for world discussions. It will require increased understanding between the Soviets and ourselves. And increased understanding will require increased contact and communication. One step in this direction is the proposed arrangement for a direct line between Moscow and Washington, to avoid on each side the dangerous delays, misunderstandings, and misreadings of the other's actions which might occur at a time of crisis. We have also been talking in Geneva about other first-step measures of arms control designed to limit the intensity of the arms race and to reduce the risks of accidental war. Our primary long-range interest in Geneva, however, is general and complete disarmament—designed to take place by stages, permitting parallel political developments to build the new institutions of peace which would take the place of arms. The pursuit of disarmament has been an effort of this government since the 1920s. It has been urgently sought by the past three administrations. And however dim the prospects may be today, we intend to continue this effort [. . .].

The one major area of these negotiations where the end is in sight, yet where a fresh start is badly needed, is in a treaty to outlaw nuclear tests. The conclusion of such a treaty, so near and yet so far, would check the spiraling arms race in one of its most dangerous areas. It would place the nuclear powers in a position to deal more effectively with one of the greatest hazards which man faces in 1963, the further spread of nuclear arms. It would increase our security—it would decrease the prospects of war. Surely this goal is sufficiently important to require our steady pursuit, yielding neither to the temptation to give up the whole effort nor the temptation to give up our insistence on vital and responsible safeguards. I am taking this opportunity, therefore, to announce two important decisions in this regard.

First: Chairman Khrushchev, Prime Minister Macmillan, and I have agreed that high-level discussions will shortly begin in Moscow looking toward early agreement on a comprehensive test ban treaty. Our hopes must be tempered with the caution of history—but with our hopes go the hopes of all mankind.

Second: To make clear our good faith and solemn convictions on the matter, I now declare that the United States does not propose to conduct nuclear tests in the atmosphere so long as other states do not do so. We will not be the first to resume. Such a declaration is no substitute for a formal binding treaty, but I hope it will help us achieve one. Nor would such a treaty be a substitute for disarmament, but I hope it will help us achieve it.

Finally, my fellow Americans, let us examine our attitude toward peace and freedom here at home. The quality and spirit of our own society must justify and support our efforts abroad. We must show it in the dedication of our own lives—as many of you who are graduating today will have a unique opportunity to do, by serving without pay in the Peace Corps abroad or in the proposed National Service Corps here at home. But wherever we are, we must all, in our daily lives, live up to the age-old faith that peace and freedom walk together. In too many of our cities today, the peace is not secure because the freedom is incomplete.

[. . .]

The United States, as the world knows, will never start a war. We do not want a war. We do not now expect a war. This generation of Americans has already had enough—more than enough—of war and hate and oppression. We shall be prepared if others wish it. We shall be alert to try to stop it. But we shall also do our part to build a world of peace where the weak are safe and the strong are just. We are not helpless before that task or hopeless of its success. Confident and unafraid, we labor on—not toward a strategy of annihilation but toward a strategy of peace.

SOURCE

John F. Kennedy Presidential Library and Museum Website

REPORT TO THE AMERICAN PEOPLE ON CIVIL RIGHTS, JUNE 11, 1963

Angered by the brutal treatment by authorities in Birmingham, Alabama, the previous month toward civil rights demonstrators, which included the arrest of Martin Luther King Jr., Kennedy took decisive action on civil rights after two and a half years of a cautious and piecemeal approach to the problem. Focused not only on the moral aspect of civil rights, Kennedy was also concerned with how racial discrimination made the United States look in the eyes of the world during the Cold War. Calling for Congress to enact comprehensive civil rights legislation, Kennedy became the first U.S. president to put the full weight of the office behind sweeping and thoroughgoing reform on this difficult question in American life.

––––––––––

Good evening my fellow citizens.

[. . .]

I hope that every American, regardless of where he lives, will stop and examine his conscience. . . . This Nation was founded by men of many nations and backgrounds. It was founded on the principle that all men are created equal, and that the rights of every man are diminished when the rights of one man are threatened.

Today we are committed to a worldwide struggle to promote and protect the rights of all who wish to be free. And when Americans are sent to Vietnam or West Berlin, we do not ask for whites only. It ought to be possible, therefore, for American students of any color to attend any public institution they select without having to be backed up by troops. It ought to be possible for American consumers of any color to receive equal service in places of public accommodation, such as hotels and restaurants and theaters and retail stores, without interference or fear of reprisal. It ought to be possible, in short, for every American to enjoy the privileges of being American without regard to his race or his color. In short, every American ought to have the right to be treated as he would wish to be treated, as one would wish his children to be treated. But this is not the case. The Negro baby born in America today, regardless of the section of the Nation in which he is born, has about one-half as much chance of completing a high school as a white baby born in the same place on the same day, one-third as much chance of completing college, one-third as much chance of becoming a professional man, twice as much chance of becoming unemployed, about one-seventh as much chance of earning $10,000 a year, a life expectancy which is seven years shorter, and the prospects of earning only half as much.

This is not a sectional issue. Difficulties over segregation and discrimination exist in every city, in every State of the Union, producing in many cities a rising tide of discontent that threatens the public safety. Nor is this a partisan issue. In a time of domestic crisis men of good will and generosity should be able to unite regardless of party or politics. This is not even a legal or legislative issue alone. It is better to settle these matters in the courts than on the streets, and new laws are needed at every level, but law alone cannot make men see right.

We are confronted primarily with a moral issue. It is as old as the Scriptures and is as clear as the American Constitution. The heart of the question is whether all Americans are to be afforded equal rights and equal opportunities, whether we are going to treat our fellow Americans as we want to be treated. If an American, because his skin is dark, cannot eat lunch in a restaurant open to the public, if he cannot send his children to the best public school available, if he cannot vote for the public officials who will represent him, if, in short, he cannot enjoy the full and free life which all of us want, then who among us would be content to have the color of his skin changed and stand in his place? Who among us would then be content with the counsels of patience and delay?

One hundred years of delay have passed since President Lincoln freed the slaves, yet their heirs, their grandsons, are not fully free. They are not yet freed from the bonds of injustice. They are not yet freed from social and economic oppression. And this Nation, for all its hopes and all its boasts, will not be fully free until all its citizens are free. We preach freedom around the world, and we mean it, and we cherish our freedom here at home, but are we to say to the world, and much more importantly, to each other that this is the land of the free except for the Negroes; that we have no second-class citizens except Negroes; that we have no class or caste system, no ghettoes, no master race except with respect to Negroes? Now the time has come for this Nation to fulfill its promise. The events in Birmingham and elsewhere have so increased the cries for equality that no city or State or legislative body can prudently choose to ignore them.

The fires of frustration and discord are burning in every city, North and South, where legal remedies are not at hand. Redress is sought in the streets, in demonstrations, parades, and protests which create tensions and threaten violence and threaten lives. We face, therefore, a moral crisis as a country and as a people. It cannot be met by repressive police action. It cannot be left to increased demonstrations in the streets. It cannot be quieted by token moves or talk. It is time to act in the Congress, in your State and local legislative body and, above all, in all of our daily lives.

It is not enough to pin the blame on others, to say this is a problem of one section of the country or another, or deplore the fact that we face. A great change is at hand, and our task, our obligation, is to make that revolution, that change, peaceful and constructive for all. Those who do nothing are inviting shame as well as violence. Those who act boldly are recognizing right as well as reality.

Next week I shall ask the Congress of the United States to act, to make a commitment it has not fully made in this century to the proposition that race has no place in American life or law. The Federal judiciary has upheld that proposition in the conduct of its affairs, including the employment of Federal personnel, the use of Federal facilities, and the sale of federally financed housing. But there are other necessary measures which only the Congress can provide, and they must be provided at this session. The old code of equity law under which we live commands for every wrong a remedy, but in too many communities, in too many parts of the country, wrongs are inflicted on Negro citizens and there are no remedies at law. Unless the Congress acts, their only remedy is in the street.

I am, therefore, asking the Congress to enact legislation giving all Americans the right to be served in facilities which are open to the public—hotels, restaurants, theaters, retail stores, and similar establishments. This seems to me to be an elementary right. Its denial is an arbitrary indignity that no American in 1963 should have to endure, but many do.

[. . .]

I am also asking the Congress to authorize the Federal Government to participate more fully in lawsuits designed to end segregation in public education. We have succeeded in persuading many districts to desegregate voluntarily. Dozens have admitted Negroes without violence. Today a Negro is attending a State-supported institution in every one of our 50 States, but the pace is very slow. Too many Negro children entering segregated grade schools at the time of the Supreme Court's decision nine years ago will enter segregated high schools this fall, having suffered a loss which can never be restored. The lack of an adequate education denies the Negro a chance to get a decent job.

The orderly implementation of the Supreme Court decision, therefore, cannot be left solely to those who may not have the economic resources to carry the legal action or who may be subject to harassment. Other features will also be requested, including greater protection for the right to vote. But legislation, I repeat, cannot solve this problem alone. It must be solved in the homes of every American in every community across our country. In this respect I want to pay tribute to those citizens North and South who have been working in their communities to make life better for all. They are acting not out of a sense of legal duty but out of a sense of human decency [. . .].

My fellow Americans, this is a problem which faces us all—in every city of the North as well as the South. Today there are Negroes unemployed, two or three times as many compared to whites, inadequate in education, moving into the large cities, unable to find work, young people particularly out of work without hope, denied equal rights, denied the opportunity to eat at a restaurant or lunch counter or go to a movie theater, denied the right to a decent education, denied almost today the right to attend a State university even though qualified. It seems to me that these are matters which concern us all, not merely Presidents or Congressmen or Governors, but every citizen of the United States.

This is one country. It has become one country because all of us and all the people who came here had an equal chance to develop their talents. We cannot say to 10 percent of the population that you can't have that right; that your children cannot have the chance to develop whatever talents they have; that the only way that they are going to get their rights is to go into the streets and demonstrate. I think we owe them and we owe ourselves a better country than that. Therefore, I am asking for your help in making it easier for us to move ahead and to provide the kind of equality of treatment which we would want ourselves; to give a chance for every child to be educated to the limit of his talents.

[. . .]

We have a right to expect that the Negro community will be responsible, will uphold the law, but they have a right to expect that the law will be fair, that the Constitution will be color blind, as Justice Harlan said at the turn of the century. This is what we are talking about and this is a matter which concerns this country and what it stands for, and in meeting it I ask the support of all our citizens.

Thank you very much.

Source

John F. Kennedy Presidential Library and Museum Website

TELEVISION INTERVIEW WITH WALTER CRONKITE OF CBS NEWS, HYANNIS PORT, MA, SEPTEMBER 2, 1963

President Kennedy sat down with CBS anchorman Walter Cronkite at his home on Cape Cod, Massachusetts, to discuss a range of issues. Toward the end of the interview, Cronkite asked Kennedy about U.S. involvement in Vietnam. Kennedy asserted that ultimately the fate of South Vietnam rested with the people and government of that nation, and that the U.S. role would remain one of assisting them in their efforts. He also signaled that the United States was running out of patience with the Diem government over its relations with the people of South Vietnam and its conduct of the war; indeed, the United States was at that moment working with members of the South Vietnamese military in what two months later became a coup against the Diem regime. Kennedy also maintained that the United States would not be withdrawing from Vietnam. His comments on this occasion reflected his ambivalent views on Vietnam, as he never reached a definite conclusion about the direction of U.S. policy toward that nation.

MR. CRONKITE: Mr. President, the only hot war we've got running at the moment is of course the one in Vietnam, and we have our difficulties there, quite obviously.

THE PRESIDENT: I don't think that unless a greater effort is made by the government to win popular support that the war can be won out there. In the final analysis, it is their war. They are the ones who have to win it or lose it. We can help them, we can give them equipment, we can send our men out there as advisers, but they have to win it, the people of Vietnam, against the Communists.

We are prepared to continue to assist them, but I don't think that the war can be won unless the people support the effort and, in my opinion, in the last two months, the government has gotten out of touch with the people.

The repressions against the Buddhists, we felt, were very unwise. Now all we can do is to make it very clear that we don't think this is the way to win. It is my hope that this will become increasingly obvious to the government, that they will take steps to try to bring back popular support for this very essential struggle.

MR. CRONKITE: Do you think this government still has time to regain the support of the people?

THE PRESIDENT: I do. With changes in policy and perhaps with personnel I think it can. If it doesn't make those changes, I would think that the chances of winning it would not be very good.

MR. CRONKITE: Hasn't every indication from Saigon been that President Diem has no intention of changing his pattern?

THE PRESIDENT: If he does not change it, of course, that is his decision. He has been there ten years and, as I say, he has carried this burden when he has been counted out on a number of occasions.

Our best judgment is that he can't be successful on this basis. We hope that he comes to see that, but in the final analysis it is the people and the government itself who have to win or lose this struggle. All we can do is help, and we are making it very clear, but I don't agree with those who say we should withdraw. That would be a great mistake. I know people don't like Americans to be engaged in this kind of an effort. Forty-seven Americans have been killed in combat with the enemy, but this is a very important struggle even though it is far away.

We took all this—made this effort to defend Europe. Now Europe is quite secure. We also have to participate—we may not like it—in the defense of Asia.

MR. CRONKITE: Mr. President, have you made an assessment as to what President de Gaulle was up to in his statement on Vietnam last week?

THE PRESIDENT: No. I guess it was an expression of his general view, but he doesn't have any forces there or any program of economic assistance, so that while these expressions are welcome, the burden is carried, as it usually is, by the United States and the people there. But I think anything General de Gaulle says should be listened to, and we listened.

What, of course, makes Americans somewhat impatient is that after carrying this load for 18 years, we are glad to get counsel, but we would like a little more assistance, real assistance. But we are going to meet our responsibility anyway.

It doesn't do us any good to say, "Well, why don't we all just go home and leave the world to those who are our enemies."

General de Gaulle is not our enemy. He is our friend and candid friend—and, there, sometimes difficulty [sic]—but he is not the object of our hostility.

MR. CRONKITE: Mr. President, the sending of Henry Cabot Lodge, who after all has been a political enemy of yours over the years at one point or another in your career, and his—sending him out to Saigon might raise some speculation that perhaps you are trying to keep this from being a political issue in 1964.

THE PRESIDENT: No. Ambassador Lodge wanted to go out to Saigon. If he were as careful as some politicians are, of course, he would not have wanted to go there. He would have maybe liked to have some safe job. But he is energetic and he has strong feelings about the United States and, surprisingly as it seems, he put this ahead of his political career. Sometimes politicians do those things, Walter.

MR. CRONKITE: Thank you very much, Mr. President.

THE PRESIDENT: And we are fortunate to have him.

MR. CRONKITE: Thank you, sir.

Source

The American Presidency Project, University of California at Santa Barbara

THOMAS G. PATERSON, "BEARING THE BURDEN: A CRITICAL LOOK AT JFK'S FOREIGN POLICY," 1978

Writing in a period of national disillusionment following the U.S. defeat in the Vietnam War and the Watergate crisis, Professor Thomas Paterson offered an early revisionist critique of Kennedy's foreign policy from a New Left perspective. Taking Kennedy to task for prosecuting the Cold War in a more vigorous and ultimately more dangerous way than did his predecessors, Paterson found Kennedy too often reckless, acting out of personal motives, and deeply mired in Cold War ways of thinking.

————————

The once elevated and exaggerated reputation of John F. Kennedy as the triumphant diplomatist has collided in recent years not only with the skepticism of journalists, political scientists, and historians but also with the facts, the realities themselves. Rich historical documents and oral histories housed at the John F. Kennedy Library as well as revelations in the *Pentagon Papers* and congressional hearings on CIA activities have joined the eulogistic memoirs of Kennedy advisers to recommend a critical retrospective view of the years of Camelot. [. . .] We must also grapple with the question of rhetoric. JFK said so many grand things so elegantly. One can easily get caught up in the eloquent phrasing and noble appeals to human uplift and overlook contradictions between word and deed or the coercive components of American foreign policy. Kennedy also said so many hackneyed things so superficially, both publicly and privately. He often spoke of the "Communist offensive" or the "free world" as monoliths, ignoring complexities. Kennedy defenders like Schlesinger ask us to dismiss such statements as mere political rhetoric or as State Department "boilerplate." That simple advice won't do, for Kennedy seemed to say what he meant.

Ambiguity also dogs us. Kennedy's foreign policy was a mixture of sincere idealism and traditional anti-Communist fervor. The President sent Peace Corps volunteers into hungry and appreciative villages in Latin America to grow food. But he also sent the Green Berets to destroy village life in Southeast Asia. We're left, then, with part hawk and part dove, an administration which had serious doubts about the clichés of the Cold War but never shed them.

[. . .]

What made Kennedy's foreign policy tick? *First,* the historical imperatives of experience and ideology which linked Kennedy's generation to a past of compelling lessons. *Second,* the conspicuous style, personality, and mood of the president and his advisers, who were determined to win the Cold War by bold action. And *third,* counter-revolutionary thought, best summarized by the phrases "nation-building" and "modernization," demanding a high degree of activism in the Third World." The difference between the Kennedy and Eisenhower administrations," Special Assistant Walt W. Rostow has written, "is not one of 180 degrees. The difference was a shift from defensive reaction to initiative. . . ."

The first explanation, the power of historical conditioning, derives from the truism that we are creatures of our pasts, that long-held assumptions, traditional behavior, and habits tug at us in the present. John F. Kennedy and his advisers were captives of an influential past. They constituted the political generation of the 1940s. Many of them came to political maturity during World War II and the early years of the Cold War. Kennedy himself served with honor during the Second World War on PT 109 and was elected to Congress in 1946, just a few months before the enunciation of the Truman or containment doctrine, the most commanding American principle of the Cold War. Kennedy and his advisers were members of what we might call the "containment generation," which enjoyed what they considered the triumphs of aid to Greece and Turkey, the Marshall Plan, the Berlin Blockade crisis, NATO.

[. . .]

Kennedy's "containment generation" imbibed several lessons from the postwar years of the Soviet-American confrontation: that toughness against communism works; that a nation must negotiate from strength; that precautions must be taken to avoid compromises or sell-outs in negotiations; that communism was monolithic; that communism was a cancer feeding on poverty and economic dislocation; that it had to be contained through counter-force on a global scale; that revolutions and civil wars were usually Communist-inspired; and that a powerful United States almost alone had the duty to protect a threatened world. Many of these lessons were exaggerated, ill-defined, superficial, or downright mistaken, yet a generation of Americans committed them to memory in the 1940s. That generation, once in positions of governmental authority in the 1960s, would constantly look back to that earlier decade for inspiration and guidelines.

John F. Kennedy wrote a senior thesis at Harvard and published it in 1940 as *Why England Slept*. Its theme was direct: the English revealed weakness before the Nazi threat and should have employed force. For Kennedy's generation, the Munich agreement became the Munich "syndrome" or lesson, a vivid example of the costs of softness. In his televised address to the nation on October 22, 1962, in the terrible throes of the Cuban Missile Crisis, Kennedy tapped that historical legacy for a rationale: "The 1930s taught us a clear lesson: aggressive conduct, if allowed to go unchecked and unchallenged, ultimately leads to war." The Kennedy team, then, came to office with considerable historical baggage. They felt, too, that the Eisenhower Administration, complacent and indifferent in the 1950s, had let American power and prestige slip and had thereby permitted the lessons of the 1930's and 1940s to slump from underwork and passivity. They craved triumphs like those over Nazism and Stalinism. They charged, with remarkable exaggeration, that Eisenhower was unwilling to enter the new battleground of the Cold War, the Third World—that he was consigning it to communism without a fight. "I think it's time America started moving again," proclaimed John F. Kennedy.

In his campaign speeches, Kennedy, who said he didn't mind being called Truman with a Harvard accent, hammered away on the issue of Cuba and the Cold War. He urged pressure on Castro and aid to Cuban rebels to overthrow him. "I wasn't the vice president who presided over the communization of Cuba," he declared. "I'm not impressed with those who say they stood up to Khrushchev when Castro has defied them 90 miles away." In Alexandria, Virginia, in August, he announced that "I think there is a danger that history will make a judgment that these were the days when the tide began to run out for the United States. These were the times when the communist tide began to pour in." A month later he embellished his rhetoric: "The enemy is lean and hungry and the United States is the only sentinel at the gate." Or in Salt Lake City: "The enemy is the Communist system itself—implacable, unceasing in its drive for world domination. For this is not a struggle for the supremacy of arms alone—it is also a struggle for supremacy between two conflicting ideologies: Freedom under God versus ruthless, godless tyranny." John Foster Dulles could not have said it better.

[...]

Handsome, articulate, witty, ingratiating, dynamic, energetic, competitive, athletic, cultured, bright, self-confident, cool, analytical, mathematical, zealous—these were the traits universally ascribed to the young president. People often listened not to what he said, but how he said it, and he usually said it with verve and conviction. He simply overwhelmed. Dean Rusk remembered him as an "incandescent man. He was on fire, and he set people around him on fire." For Schlesinger, JFK had "enormous confidence in his own luck," and "everyone around him thought he had the Midas touch and could not lose." Style and personality are important to how diplomacy is conducted; how we behave obviously affects how others read us and respond to us, and our personal characteristics and needs generate measurable behavior. Many of his friends have commented that John F. Kennedy was driven by a desire for power, because power ensured winning. Furthermore, he personalized issues, converting them into tests of will. Politics became a matter of crises and races. His father, Joe Kennedy, demanded excellence. As James Barber has pointed out in his book, *The Presidential Character,* old Joe "pressed his children hard to compete, never to be satisfied with anything but first place. The point was not just to try; the point was to win." John developed a "fighting spirit," a thirst for victory, a self-image as the vigorous man. Aroused in the campaign of 1960 by the stings of anti-Catholic bias, by misplaced right-wing charges that he was "soft on communism," and by his narrow victory over Nixon, Kennedy seemed eager to prove his toughness once in office.

Kennedy took up challenges with zest. Soon Americans watched for box scores on the missile race, the arms race, and the space race. There was also the race for influence in the Third World, Even the noblest of his programs, the Peace Corps, was part of the game. When JFK learned in 1961 that both Ghana and Guinea had requested Peace Corps volunteers, he told Rusk: "If we can successfully crack Ghana and Guinea, Mali may even turn to the West. If so, these would be the first Communist-oriented countries to turn from Moscow to us."

The Kennedy people considered themselves "can-do" types, who with rationality and careful calculation could revive an ailing nation and world. Theodore H. White has tagged them "the Action Intellectuals." They believed that they could *manage* affairs. "Management" became one of the catchwords of the time. For example, the new program for the military, called "flexible response," was devised to account for all military contingencies, from nuclear to conventional to guerilla warfare.

[. . .]

That toughness was evident in Kennedy's alarmist Inaugural Address. Its swollen Cold War language was matched only by the pompous phrasing that "the torch has been passed to a new generation." He paid homage to historical memories when he noted that that generation had been "tempered by war" and "disciplined by a hard and bitter peace. . . ." Then came those moving, but in hindsight rather frightening words: "Let every nation know that we shall pay any price, bear any burden, meet any hardship, support any friend, oppose any foe to assure the survival and the success of liberty." No halfway measures here. Kennedy and his assistants thought they could lick anything. They were impatient. As Schlesinger recalled, the Kennedy Administration "put a premium on quick, tough, laconic, decided people. . . ."

The Cuban Missile Crisis provided an opportunity for the exercise of management skills and toughness. What is most telling about Kennedy's response to the reckless Soviet installation of missiles in Cuba is that he essentially suspended diplomacy and chose a television address, rather than a direct approach to Moscow, to inform Khrushchev that his flagrant action would not be tolerated. Kennedy chose public rather than private diplomacy and thereby significantly increased the chances of war. Why? Ever since the Bay of Pigs muddle, the Kennedy team had nurtured a sense of revenge. The president himself was stunned by the failure and in a speech on April 20, 1961, he spelled out the lessons he had drawn: "Let the record show that our restraint is not inexhaustible," he declared. He pledged that the United States would take up the "relentless struggle" with communism in "every corner of the globe." It was clear, he went on, that the "complacent, the self-indulgent, the soft societies are about to be swept away with the debris of history. Only the strong . . . can possibly survive." Finally, with his customary appeals for the supreme sacrifice, Kennedy announced that "I am determined upon our system's survival and success, *regardless* of the cost and *regardless* of the peril!"

[. . .]

The point is that when the missiles were discovered in Cuba in October, 1962, Kennedy was poised for boldness, for another test of will. It was an eyeball-to-eyeball confrontation, and remember, said Dean Rusk, the Russians blinked first. [. . .] Kennedy himself put it this way in a letter to Prime Minister Harold MacMillan of Great Britain: "What is essential at this moment of highest test is that Khrushchev should discover that if he is counting on weakness or irresolution, he has miscalculated." Personality and style alone did not determine the American reaction in the Cuban Missile Crisis. There were obvious strategic calculations of national interest. What I am suggesting is that the *way*, the *manner* in which Kennedy responded was molded by the "action intellectuals" style and mood. The president's desire to score a victory, to recapture previous losses, and to flex his muscle accentuated the crisis and obstructed diplomacy. Public statements via television are not calculated to defuse a crisis; Kennedy gave Khrushchev no chance to withdraw his mistake or to save face. Kennedy never probed deeply for

Soviet motivations. He left little room for bargaining but instead issued a public ultimatum and seemed willing to destroy, in Strangelovian fashion, millions in the process.

[. . .]

The result? Russia was humiliated publicly. Having its own pride, recognizing its nuclear inferiority, and being harangued by the Chinese as "capitulationist," Moscow launched a massive arms build-up. "Never will we be caught like this again," concluded the Soviet deputy foreign minister. The American lessons for the Cuban Missile Crisis, according to political scientist James Nathan, illustrate my point: "force and toughness became enshrined as instruments of policy." Indeed, "the policy of toughness became dogma to such an extent that non-military solutions to political problems were excluded. The 1962 "victory" in Cuba may have emboldened the Kennedy administration to take firmer action in Vietnam.

[. . .]

The nation-building concept also over-estimated the power of the United States to shape other nations. It assumed that soldiers from Vermont, Iowa, Connecticut, and North Carolina could manage "natives" abroad, much as they had done in the Philippines at the turn of the century or in Latin America through part of the 20th century. But unable to force reform on others, they often ended up violating our principles by supporting the elite or the military or by trying to topple regimes, such as that of Diem in Vietnam. Strategic hamlets, part of counter-insurgency in Vietnam, proved to be disruptive of village life. Villages bitterly resented resettlement. It made the Viet Cong appear to be Robin Hoods. The tasks were too great for the United States. We learned that even our massive air power, our B-52s, could not knock Vietnamese from their environment.

[. . .]

The Kennedy Administration, propelled by Cold War history, by its own bumptious "can-do" style, and by its grandiose theories for world revival, bequeathed a dubious legacy in foreign policy. Would JFK have changed had he lived? Unlikely. He would have had to fire the hard-line advisers who persistently clung to their theories. The Cold War was too ingrained in Kennedy's experience to permit too much adjustment. Moreover, it is likely that he would not have shed his penchant for personalization or bold action. And, like all people who must make decisions they need to justify, he would probably have persisted in defending his mistakes with the distortions necessary.

There is no question that he temporarily quieted the crisis in Laos and followed a cautious policy in the Congo, that some of his policies had a touch of humanity, and that just before his death Kennedy had doubts about Vietnam and about the rigidities of his Cold War stance. His June 1963 address at American University is often cited as the example of his change of heart, for therein he expressed an uneasiness with high weapons expenditures, called for a reexamination of American Cold War attitudes, suggested that conflict with the Soviet Union was not inevitable, and appealed for disarmament. It was a high-minded speech and seemingly reflected a willingness to negotiate—one product of which was the test ban treaty. Still, "one speech is not enough," George F. Kennan has remarked. This speech was not *typical* of Kennedy or his advisers, many of whom stayed on to work with President Lyndon B. Johnson.

[. . .]

The Kennedy Administration continued a tired, antiquated policy of non-recognition toward the People's Republic of China. As Kennedy simply remarked on the Sino-Soviet split: "A dispute over how to bury the West is no grounds for Western rejoicing."

[. . .]

Kennedy did not act like a Cold Warrior because he was pressured by recalcitrant right-wingers, a Cold War Congress, or an out-of-control bureaucracy. And, although the Russians were belligerent and uncooperative, they had been so for much of the postwar period. What changed in 1961 was not Soviet diplomacy but the inauguration of a new administration in Washington. Kennedy believed in Cold War dogmas and gave them a new vigor. He was thus not only a maker of history but a victim of it.

SOURCE

Virginia Quarterly Review, Spring 1978. Reprinted by permission.

WILLIAM F. BUCKLEY, "WORSHIPPING JFK: 40 YEARS LATER," 2003

William F. Buckley (1925–2008) was a leading conservative public intellectual of the second half of the twentieth century. His background was similar in many ways to that of John F. Kennedy: both were raised in wealthy Catholic families in the Northeast, both had Irish ancestry, both were educated in Ivy League colleges, and each was the son of a successful and flamboyant father. Buckley, however, emerged as a sharp critic of liberalism in the pages of his opinion journal, *The National Review*. Buckley argued that liberals pushed relentlessly for the expansion of the state at the expense of individual liberty and that they were at the same time weak prosecutors of the Cold War. In this retrospective on Kennedy 40 years after his death, Buckley sees Kennedy's ongoing appeal as based on superficial characteristics and the shock of his assassination. On matters of substance, Buckley argued, the Kennedy legacy was thin.

———

I was asked by a television network to comment on the career of President Kennedy.

[. . .]

But the question I was asked didn't have to do with who killed JFK, but with what was his legacy. It was, said I, entirely personal. Nothing that Mr. Kennedy did in the way of public policy was either singular or enduring in effect. In foreign policy, he lost out on Berlin [. . .]. He did not consummate his war against Castro at any level. At the military level, he failed in the Bay of Pigs. At the dirty-dog level, he failed in four or five attempts to assassinate

Castro; failed with toxic cigars, impregnated wetsuits, and poison pills. At the diplomatic level, we focus more appropriately on the arrival of Soviet nuclear missiles in Cuba than on their withdrawal. It is acknowledged by everyone that we very nearly had a nuclear exchange in October, 1962, and historical adjudications correctly deal rather with the fact of the missiles being deployed there, than of the fact that they were finally shooed away.

It is pointed out, even by the school of political thought least anxious to associate itself with low taxes, that JFK called for tax reduction—which he did, though it was left to Lyndon Johnson to consummate the proposal. Civil Rights is adduced, and it is true that Mr. Kennedy came eloquently to the cause—after hearing Martin Luther King give his great speech, and weighing the implications of it. He arrived finally (sooner than I did) to the cause of equality under the law, but was a recruit to it, spurred by others. It was only in the summer of his last year that he turned to the subject of a Civil Rights Bill.

In Vietnam, he engaged the Communist aggressors intending two things, the first, to abide by George Kennan's long-standing doctrine of Containment, the second, to challenge the evaluation of him by Khrushchev as a "pygmy." That was the character reading by Khrushchev, who proceeded, after their personal encounter in Vienna, to build the Berlin Wall, and to send missiles to Cuba. Maybe, if Kennedy had lived, he'd have reversed the course he took in Vietnam, adopted by his successor, Lyndon Johnson, who continued to press the doctrine of containment. But it is asking too much, at eulogy time, to compliment a dead man on the grounds that you feel certain he'd have proceeded, if he had lived, to undo what he did when alive. I can think of any number of reforms I would myself undertake, after I am dead.

What I said to the interviewer was that the legacy of John F. Kennedy is his sheer ... beauty. I have visited yurts in Mongolia, adobe huts in Mexico, and rural redoubts in Turkey and seen framed pictures of John F. Kennedy. He was all-American, splendid to look at, his expression of confident joy in life and work transfiguring. Add to this that he was slaughtered, almost always a mythogenic act, and what we came to know about the awful physical afflictions he suffered, making his appearances as a whole, vigorous man, the equivalent of seeing FDR rise from his wheelchair and play touch football.

That is why JFK is worshipped, which word exactly describes the attitude we have toward him.

SOURCE

National Review Online, November 21, 2003. © 2003 by National Review, Inc. Reprinted by permission.

NOTES

John F. Kennedy Presidential Library and Museum has been abbreviated to JFKPLM in the Notes.

INTRODUCTION

1. Peter Beinart, *The Good Fight: Why Liberals—and Only Liberals—Can Win the War on Terror and Make America Great Again* (New York: Harper Perennial, 2008), 23.
2. Ted Widmer (ed.), *Listening In: The Secret White House Recordings of John F. Kennedy* (New York: Hyperion, 2012), 39.

CHAPTER 1

1. Quoted in Thomas Maier, *The Kennedys: America's Emerald Kings* (New York: Basic Books, 2003), 55.
2. Edmund Burke to Sir Hercules Langrishe, 1792, in Peter Stanlis (ed.) *Edmund Burke: Selected Writings and Speeches* (New York: Anchor Books, 1963), 265.
3. Kerry Miller, quoted in Maier, *The Kennedys*, 37.
4. Maier, *The Kennedys*, 37.
5. Kerby Miller and Paul Wagner, *Out of Ireland: The Story of Irish Emigration to America* (Washington, D.C.: Elliot and Clark Publishing, 1994), 114.
6. Maier, *The Kennedys*, 36.
7. June 8, 1961, *The Reporter*.
8. Thomas Bartlett, *Ireland: A History* (Cambridge, U.K.: Cambridge University Press, 2010), 293.
9. Maier, *The Kennedys*, 54.
10. Rose Fitzgerald Kennedy, *Times To Remember* (Garden City, N.Y.: Doubleday & Company, 1974), 52.
11. Doris Kearns Goodwin, *The Fitzgeralds and the Kennedys: An American Saga* (New York: Simon and Schuster, 1987), 235.
12. Robert Dallek, *An Unfinished Life: John F. Kennedy, 1917–1963* (Boston: Little, Brown and Company, 2003), 21.
13. Dallek, *An Unfinished Life*, 29.
14. Maier, *The Kennedys*, 80.
15. Maier, *The Kennedys*, 80.
16. Dallek, *An Unfinished Life*, 31.
17. Maier, *The Kennedys*, 76.
18. Maier, *The Kennedys*, 88.
19. David Nasaw, *The Patriarch: The Remarkable Life and Turbulent Times of Joseph P. Kennedy* (New York: The Penguin Press, 2012), 241.

20. Nasaw, *The Patriarch*, 90–91.
21. Nasaw, *The Patriarch*, 63.
22. Nasaw, *The Patriarch*, 63.
23. Kay Halle, Oral History Interview, John F. Kennedy Library.
24. Rose Kennedy, *Times to Remember*, 111.
25. Rose Kennedy, *Times to Remember*, 94.
26. Dallek, *An Unfinished Life*, 70.
27. David Burner, *John F. Kennedy and a New Generation* (The Library of American Biography series, New York: Pearson Longman, 2009), 33.
28. Kearns Goodwin, *The Fitzgeralds and the Kennedys*, 464.
29. Nigel Hamilton, *JFK: Reckless Youth* (New York: Random House, 1992), 107.
30. Herbert Parmet, *Jack: The Struggles of John F. Kennedy* (New York: Dial Press, 1982), 36.
31. David Pitts, *Jack and Lem: John F. Kennedy and Lem Billings – The Untold Story of an Extraordinary Friendship* (New York: Da Capo Press, 2007), 17.
32. Kearns Goodwin, *The Fitzgeralds and the Kennedys*, 436.
33. Dallek, *An Unfinished Life*, 21.
34. Dallek, *An Unfinished Life*, 43.
35. Dallek, *An Unfinished Life*, 45.
36. C. J. Friedrich to Clifford Shipton, August 3, 1964, JFKPLM, Personal Papers, Series 3.1, Box 2, Folder "Miscellaneous Materials, 1946–1964".
37. Dallek, *An Unfinished Life*, 45.
38. Dallek, *An Unfinished Life*, 31.
39. *Fortune Magazine*, fortune.com, January 1963.
40. Maier, *The Kennedys*, 118.
41. Joseph P. Kennedy to John F. Kennedy, August 2, 1940 in Amanda Smith (ed.), *Hostage to Fortune: The Letters of Joseph P. Kennedy* (New York: Viking Press, 2001), 453.
42. John F. Kennedy, *While England Slept*, Wilfred Funk, 1940 (Westport, CT: Greenwood Press, repr. 1981), xvi.
43. Kennedy, *While England Slept*, 229.
44. Harvard Crimson, June 9, 1940, JFKPLM, Personal Papers, Series 3.1, Harvard Records, Folder "Activities, 1939–1940."
45. Kennedy, *While England Slept*, 225.
46. James MacGregor Burns, *John Kennedy: A Political Profile* (New York: Avon Book Division, 1960), 53.
47. Burns, *John Kennedy*, 56.
48. David Burner and Thomas R. West, *The Torch is Passed: The Kennedy Brothers and American Liberalism* (New York: Athenium, 1984), 30.
49. Nasaw, *The Patriarch*, 485–486.

CHAPTER 2

1. Robert Dallek, *An Unfinished Life: John F. Kennedy, 1917–1963* (Boston: Little, Brown and Company, 2003), 67.
2. David Nasaw, *The Patriarch: The Remarkable Life and Turbulent Times of Joseph P. Kennedy* (New York: The Penguin Press, 2012) 514–515.
3. Theodore C. Sorensen, *Kennedy* (New York: Harper & Row Publishers, 1965), 32.
4. Peter Collier and David Horowitz, *The Kennedys: An American Drama* (New York: Encounter Books, 1984), 94.
5. Rose Fitzgerald Kennedy, *Times to Remember* (Garden City, N.Y.: Doubleday and Company, 1974), 286.
6. Dallek, *An Unfinished Life*, 181.
7. Nasaw, *The Patriarch*, 540–542.

8. Inga Arvad to John F. Kennedy, January 26, 1942, Correspondence 1933–1950, Arvad, Inga. JFKPLM.
9. Edward J. Renehan Jr., *The Kennedys at War, 1937–1945* (New York: Doubleday, 2002), 224.
10. Dallek, *An Unfinished Life,* 91.
11. Nigel Hamilton, *JFK: Reckless Youth* (New York: Random House, 1992), 505.
12. Hamilton, *JFK,* 543.
13. Hamilton, *JFK,* 544.
14. Robert J. Donovan, *PT 109: John F. Kennedy in World War II* (New York: McGraw-Hill Book Company, 1961), 35; Dallek, *An Unfinished Life,* 94.
15. Joan and Clay Blair Jr., *The Search for JFK* (New York: Berkley Publishing Corporation, 1974), 240.
16. Dallek, *An Unfinished Life,* 96.
17. Donovan, *PT 109,* 216.
18. Nasaw, *The Patriarch,* 702.
19. David Nasaw, *The Patriarch: The Remarkable Life and Turbulent Times of Joseph P. Kennedy* (New York: The Penguin Press, 2012), 576.
20. Doris Kearns Goodwin, *The Fitzgeralds and the Kennedys: An American Saga* (New York: Simon and Schuster, 1987), 693.
21. *New York Herald-American,* May 9, 1945, Personal Secretary's Files, Folder "Articles by John F. Kennedy in the Hearst Newspaper Files, 1945," JFKPLM.
22. Deidre Henderson (ed.), *Prelude to Leadership: The European Diary of John F. Kennedy, Summer 1945* (Washington, D.C.: Regnery Publishing, 1995), 7.
23. Dallek, *An Unfinished Life,* 117–118.
24. Dallek, *An Unfinished Life,* 120.
25. Blair, *The Search for JFK,* 392.
26. Mark Dalton Oral History Interview #1, JFKPLM.
27. James MacGregor Burns, *John Kennedy: A Political Profile* (New York: Avon Book Division, 1960), 75.
28. Mark Dalton Interview #1, JFKPLM.
29. Dallek, *An Unfinished Life,* 119; Mark Dalton interview #1, JFKPLM.
30. Kenneth P. O'Donnell and David F. Powers, with Joe McCarthy, *"Johnny, We Hardly Knew Ye": Memories of John Fitzgerald Kennedy* (Boston: Little, Brown and Company, 1970), 53.
31. Burns, *John Kennedy,* 76.
32 Dallek, *An Unfinished Life,* 127.
33. Nick Bryant, *The Bystander: John F. Kennedy and the Struggle for Black Equality* (New York: Basic Books, 2006), 15.
34. Bryant, *The Bystander,* 29.
35. Personal Papers, Box 1, Series 1, JFKPLM.
36. Frederick Logevall, *Embers of War: The Fall of an Empire and the Making of America's Vietnam* (New York: Random House, 2012), xii.
37. Logevall, *Embers of War,* xiv.
38. Richard N. Goodwin, *Remembering America: A View from the Sixties* (Boston: Little, Brown and Company, 1988), 745–746.
39. Kay Halle, Oral History Interview, JFKPLM.
40. Thomas J. Whalen, *Kennedy versus Lodge: The 1952 Massachusetts Senate Race* (Boston: Northeastern University Press, 2000), 31.
41. Quoted in Chris Matthews, *Kennedy & Nixon: The Rivalry That Shaped Postwar America* (New York: Simon and Schuster, 1996), 100.
42. FK Personal Papers, Box 1, Series 1, JFKPLM.
43. O'Donnell and Powers, *"Johnny, We Hardly Knew Ye,"* 78.
44. Michael O'Brien, *John F. Kennedy: A Biography* (New York: Thomas Dunne Books, 2005), 254.
45. Chris Matthews, *Jack Kennedy: Elusive Hero* (New York: Simon and Schuster, 2011), 135.

46. Bryant, *The Bystander*, 37–38.
47. Nasaw, *The Patriarch*, 665.
48. Whalen, *Kennedy Versus Lodge*, 149–150.
49. Rose Fitzgerald Kennedy, *Times to Remember*, 327.
50. O'Donnell and Powers, *"Johnny We Hardly Knew Ye,"* 92.
51. Whalen, *Kennedy Versus Lodge*, 158.
52. Whalen, *Kennedy Versus Lodge*, 183–184.
53. Bryant, *The Bystander*, 42.

CHAPTER 3

1. Harry McPherson, quoted in Michael Barone, *Our Country: The Shaping of America From Roosevelt to Reagan* (New York: The Free Press, 1990), 309.
2. Ted Sorensen, *Counselor: A Life at the Edge of History* (New York: Harper Collins Publishers, 2008), 97.
3. Quoted in Robert Dallek, *John F. Kennedy: An Unfinished Life* (Boston: Little, Brown and Company, 2003), 151.
4. Quoted in Peter Collier and David Horowitz, *The Kennedys: An American Drama* (New York: Encounter Books, 2002), 164.
5. Quoted in Michael O'Brien, *John F. Kennedy: A Biography* (New York: Thomas Dunne Books, 2005), 265.
6. Quoted in Robert Dallek, *John F. Kennedy: An Unfinished Life*, 194.
7. Dallek, *An Unfinished Life*, 212.
8. James MacGregor Burns, *John Kennedy: A Political Profile* (New York: Avon Book Division, 1960), 135.
9. Quoted in Thomas Maier, *The Kennedys: America's Emerald Kings* (New York: Basic Books, 2003), 272.
10. Kenneth P. O'Donnell and David F. Powers, with Joe McCarthy, *"Johnny, We Hardly Knew Ye": Memories of John Fitzgerald Kennedy* (Boston: Little, Brown and Company, 1970), 99.
11. Caroline Kennedy and Michael Beschloss (eds.), *Jacqueline Kennedy, Historic Conversations on Life with John F. Kennedy* (New York: Hyperion, 2011), 74.
12. Quoted in Dallek, *An Unfinished Life*, 183.
13. John F. Kennedy, *Profiles in Courage* (New York: Harper & Row, 1956), 17.
14. Sorensen, *Counselor*, 151.
15. Kennedy, *Profiles in Courage*, 181.
16. Nicholas Lemann, *Redemption: The Last Battle of the Civil War* (New York: Farrar, Straus and Giroux, 2007), 207; Nick Bryant, *The Bystander: John F. Kennedy and the Struggle for Black Equality* (New York: Basic Books, 2006), 49.
17. O'Donnell and Powers, *"Johnny, We Hardly Knew Ye,"* 105.
18. Kennedy and Beschloss (eds.) *Jacqueline Kennedy, Historic Conversations*, 9–10.
19. Burns, *John Kennedy*, 173; O'Donnell and Powers, *"Johnny, We Hardly Knew Ye,"* 116.
20. O'Donnell and Powers, *"Johnny, We Hardly Knew Ye,"* 104.
21. John F. Kennedy, Chicago, Illinois, August 16, 1956, JFKPLM Website.
22. *New York Times*, August 14, 1956, A-13.
23. Bryant, *The Bystander*, 60.
24. Bryant, *The Bystander*, 55–56.
25. Arthur Krock, *Memoirs: Sixty Years on the Firing Line* (New York: Funk & Wagnalls, 1968), 359.
26. O'Donnell and Powers, *"Johnny, We Hardly Knew Ye,"* 128.
27. O'Donnell and Powers, *"Johnny, We Hardly Knew Ye,"* 126.
28. Bryant, *The Bystander*, 66.
29. Robert A. Caro, *The Years of Lyndon Johnson, vol. 3, Master of the Senate* (New York: Alfred A. Knopf, 2002), 986.
30. Bryant, *The Bystander*, 68.

31. Maier, *America's Emerald Kings,* 287.
32. Maier, *America's Emerald Kings,* 284.
33. Burns, *John Kennedy,* 208.

CHAPTER 4

1. Statement of Senator John F. Kennedy Announcing His Candidacy for the Presidency of the United States, January 2, 1960. JFKPLM Website.
2. Statement of Senator John F. Kennedy, January 2, 1960.
3. Statement of John F. Kennedy, January 2, 1960.
4. Statement of John F. Kennedy, January 2, 1960.
5. Ted Sorensen, *Counselor: A Life at the Edge of History* (New York: Harper Collins Publishers, 2008), 169.
6. Lawrence O'Brien, *No Final Victories: A Life in Politics from John F. Kennedy to Watergate* (Garden City, N.Y.: Doubleday and Company, 1974), 61.
7. Sorensen, *Counselor,* 176.
8. Of one such Irish-American boss, Dan O'Connell of Albany, New York, Joseph Kennedy later said he was the only one who had not asked him for money in return for supporting his son. William Kennedy, *O Albany!* (New York: Penguin Books, 1983), 275.
9. Robert Dallek, *An Unfinished Life: John F. Kennedy, 1917–1963* (Boston: Little, Brown and Company, 2003), 232.
10. Anthony Burke Smith, *The Look of Catholics: Portrayals in Popular Culture from the Great Depression to the Cold War* (Lawrence, K.S.: University Press of Kansas, 2010), 87.
11. Alexis De Tocqueville, *Democracy in America,* I (New York: Alfred A. Knopf, 1966), 301.
12. Michael Beschloss and Caroline Kennedy (eds.), *Jacqueline Kennedy: Historic Conversations on Life with John F. Kennedy* (New York: Hyperion, 2011), 67–68.
13. Kenneth P. O'Donnell and David Powers with Joe McCarthy, *"Johnny We Hardly Knew Ye": Memories of John Fitzgerald Kennedy* (Boston: Little, Brown and Company, 1970), 157.
14. See the film *Primary* (1961) by Robert Drew, for Kennedy at a Wisconsin campaign rally.
15. W.J. Rorabaugh, *The Real Making of the President: Kennedy, Nixon and the 1960 Campaign* (Lawrence, K.S.: University Press of Kansas, 2009), 51. Whether the worker did so on his own or under orders was unclear.
16. Theodore H. White, *The Making of the President 1960* (New York: Atheneum Publishers, 1961), 96.
17. O'Donnell and Powers, *"Johnny We Hardly Knew Ye,"* 162.
18. Scott Stossel, *Sarge: The Life and Times of Sargent Shriver* (Washington, D.C.: Smithsonian Books, 2004), 117–118.
19. Robert Caro, *The Years of Lyndon Johnson: The Passage of Power* (New York: Alfred A. Knopf, 2012), 84.
20. Beschloss and Kennedy, *Jacqueline Kennedy: Historic Conversations,* 30.
21. Caro, *The Passage of Power,* 61–62.
22. Caro, *The Passage of Power,* 104.
23. Rorabaugh, *The Real Making of the President,* 73.
24. Theodore H. White, *The Making of the President 1960* (New York: Atheneum Publishers, 1961), 159–160.
25. Acceptance Speech at Democratic National Convention, Los Angeles California, July 15, 1960, JFKPLM Website.
26. John F. Kennedy, Acceptance Speech at Democratic National Convention, July 15, 1960.
27. John F. Kennedy, Acceptance Speech at Democratic National Convention, July 15, 1960.
28. White, *The Making of the President,* 1960, 256.
29. Remarks of Senator John F. Kennedy at State Capitol, Albany, New York, September 29, 1960, JFKPLM Website.

30. O'Donnell and Powers, *"Johnny We Hardly Knew Ye,"* 206.
31. James A. Michener, *Report of the County Chairman* (New York: Bantam Books, 1961), 71–72.
32. Address of Senator John F. Kennedy to the Greater Houston Ministerial Association, September 12, 1960, JFKPLM Website.
33. Address of Senator John F. Kennedy to the Greater Houston Ministerial Association, September 12, 1960.
34. Jason K. Duncan, *Citizens or Papists? The Politics of Anti-Catholicism in New York, 1685–1821* (New York: Fordham University Press, 2005), 123–124.
35. Rorabaugh, *The Real Making of the President,* 146.
36. Thomas Maier, *The Kennedys: America's Emerald Kings* (New York: Basic Books, 2003), 350.
37. Rorabaugh, *The Real Making of the President,* 148.
38. "Opening Statement, First Kennedy-Nixon Debate," in Maureen Harrison and Steven Gilbert (eds.) *John F. Kennedy, Word for Word* (La Jolla, C.A.: Excellent Books, 1993), 11.
39. Dallek, *An Unfinished Life,* 286.
40. Rorabaugh, *The Real Making of the President,* 155.
41. Richard Nixon, *Six Crises* (New York: Doubleday, 1962), 340.
42. Nick Bryant, *The Bystander: John F. Kennedy and the Struggle for Black Equality* (New York: Basic Books, 2006), 151.
43. Rorabaugh, *The Real Making of the President,* 124–125.
44. Caro, *The Passage of Power,* 146.
45. Rorabaugh, *The Real Making of the President,* 131–132.
46. Rorabaugh, *The Real Making of the President,* 134.
47. Stossel, *Sarge,* 169–170.
48. Stossel, *Sarge,* 170.
49. Chris Matthews, *Jack Kennedy: Elusive Hero* (New York: Simon and Schuster, 2011), 285.
50. Dallek, *An Unfinished Life,* 288–290.
51. Rorabaugh, *The Real Making of the President,* 173.
52. White, *The Making of the President 1960,* 310.
53. O'Donnell and Powers, *Johnny We Hardly Knew Ye,"* 220.
54. David Nasaw, *The Patriarch: The Remarkable Life and Turbulent Times of Joseph P. Kennedy* (The Penguin Press: New York, 2012), 723–724.
55. Quoted in Rorabaugh, *The Real Making of the President,* 181.
56. Rorabaugh, *The Real Making of the President,* 182
57. Bryant, *The Bystander,* 186.
58. White, *The Making of the President,* 353.

CHAPTER 5

1. Caroline Kennedy and Michael Beschloss (eds.), *Jacqueline Kennedy, Historic Conversations on Life with John F. Kennedy* (New York: Hyperion, 2011), 152–153.
2. Doris Kearns Goodwin describes this moment in *The Kennedys* (PBS, 2011).
3. Rose Fitzgerald Kennedy, *Times to Remember* (Garden City, N.Y.: Doubleday & Company, Inc., 1974), 384.
4. Kenneth P. O'Donnell and David F. Powers with Joe McCarthy, *"Johnny We Hardly Knew Ye": Memories of John Fitzgerald Kennedy* (Boston: Little, Brown and Company, 1970), 237.
5. Arthur M. Schlesinger, *A Thousand Days: John F. Kennedy in the White House* (Boston: Houghton Mifflin Company, 1965), 287.
6. John F. Kennedy, *The Strategy of Peace* (New York: Harper & Row, 1960), 132.
7. Robert Dallek, *An Unfinished Life: John F. Kennedy, 1917–1963* (Boston: Little, Brown and Company, 2003), 358.

8. Harlan Cleveland, quoted in Gerald S. and Deborah H. Strober (eds.), *Let Us Begin Anew: An Oral History of the Kennedy Presidency* (New York: Harper Perennial, 1993), 336.
9. O'Donnell and Powers, "*Johnny We Hardly Knew Ye*," 272.
10. The phrase is generally attributed to Theodore Draper.
11. Richard N. Goodwin, *Remembering America: A Voice from the Sixties* (Boston: Little, Brown and Company, 1988), 182; Schlesinger, *A Thousand Days,* 286.
12. Quoted in W.J. Rorabaugh, *Kennedy and the Promise of the Sixties* (Cambridge, U.K.: Cambridge University Press, 2002), 30.
13. Kennedy and Beschloss, *Historic Conversations,* 185.
14. William Taubman, *Khrushchev: The Man and His Era* (New York: W.W. Norton & Company, 2003), 487.
15. Taubman, *Khrushchev,* 493.
16. Dallek, *An Unfinished Life,* 398–399.
17. Alexsandr Fursenko and Timothy Nattali, *Khrushchev's Cold War: The Inside Story of an American Adversary* (New York: W.W. Norton & Company), 211.
18. George C. Herring, *From Colony to Superpower, U.S. Foreign Relations Since 1776* (New York: Oxford University Press, 2008), 709.
19. Herring, *From Colony to Superpower,* 710.
20. Taubman, *Khrushchev,* 54.
21. Taubman, *Khrushchev,* 533.
22. Taubman, *Khrushchev,* 553.
23. O'Donnell and Powers, "*Johnny, We Hardly Knew Ye,*" 307.
24. Dallek, *An Unfinished Life,* 557–558.
25. Remarks of President Kennedy, October 22, 1962, JFKPLM Website; Sorensen, *Counselor,* 298.
26. Dallek, *An Unfinished Life,* 558–559.
27. Remarks of President Kennedy, October 22, 1962, JFKPLM Website.
28. Remarks of President Kennedy, October 22, 1962, JFKPLM Website.
29. Dallek, *An Unfinished Life,* 554–555.
30. O'Donnell and Powers, "*Johnny We Hardly Knew Ye,*" 316–317.
31. Kennedy and Beschloss, *Historic Conversations,* 185.
32. Robert Kennedy, *Thirteen Days: A Memoir of the Cuban Missiles Crisis* (New York: W.W. Norton & Company, 1969), 69–70.
33. Rorabaugh, *Kennedy and the Promise of the Sixties,* 49.
34. Interactive Exhibit on Cuban Missile Crisis, JFKPLM Website.
35. David Burner, *John F. Kennedy and a New Generation,* 3rd ed. (New York: Pearson Longman, 2009), 102–103.
36. Michael Dobbs, *One Minute to Midnight: Kennedy, Khrushchev and Castro on the Brink of Nuclear War* (New York: Alfred A. Knopf, 2008), 88–90.
37. Taubman, *Khrushchev,* 569.
38. Sorensen, *Counselor,* 305.
39. Taubman, *Khrushchev,* 575.
40. Nikita Khrushchev, *Khrushchev Remembers: The Last Testament* (Boston: Little, Brown and Company, 1974), 512.
41. Taubman, *Khrushchev,* p. 583.
42. Kennedy-Eisenhower Conversation, JFKPLM Library.
43. O'Donnell and Powers, "*Johnny We Hardly Knew Ye,*" 343.
44. John Kenneth Galbraith, quoted in Gerald S. and Deborah H. Strober (eds.) *Let Us Begin Anew,* 261–262.
45. John F. Kennedy, Speech at American University, June 10, 1963, JFKPLM Website.
46. Speech at American University, June 10, 1963.

47. Speech at American University, June 10, 1963.
48. Speech at American University, June 10, 1963.
49. Taubman, *Khrushchev*, 602.
50. Theodore C. Sorensen, *Kennedy* (New York: Harper & Row, 1965), 733.
51. C. Calvin Mackenzie and Robert Weisbrot, *The Liberal Hour: Washington and the Politics of Change in the 1960s* (New York: The Penguin Press, 2008), 278.
52. O'Donnell and Powers with McCarthy, "*Johnny We Hardly Knew Ye*," 361.
53. Mackenzie and Weisbrot, *The Liberal Hour*, 279. Thanks also to the historian Charles Brown of Grand Rapids, Michigan, for bringing this to my attention.
54. *New York Times*, September 25, 1963.

CHAPTER 6

1. James N. Giglio, *The Presidency of John F. Kennedy* (Lawrence, K.A.: University Press of Kansas, 1991), 116.
2. John F. Kennedy, March 1, 1961, JFKPLM Website.
3. Robert Dallek: *An Unfinished Life, John F. Kennedy, 1917–163* (Boston: Little, Brown and Company, 2003), 339.
4. Scott Stossel, *Sarge: The Life and Times of Sargent Shriver* (Washington, D.C.: Smithsonian Books, 2004), 270.
5. Stossel, *Sarge*, 296.
6. Richard N. Goodwin, *Remembering America: A Voice from the Sixties* (Boston, 1988), 147.
7. George Herring, *From Colony to Superpower: U.S. Foreign Relations Since 1776* (New York: Oxford University Press, 2008), 716.
8. John F. Kennedy, March 13, 1961, on JFKPLM Website.
9. Quoted in Steve Rabe, "Controlling Revolutions: Latin America, the Alliance for Progress, and Cold War Anti-Communism," in Thomas G. Paterson (ed.), *Kennedy's Quest for Victory* (New York: Oxford University Press, 1989), 110.
10. Rabe, "Controlling Revolutions," 108, 112.
11. Goodwin, *Remembering America*, 151.
12. Caroline Kennedy and Michael Beschloss (eds.), *Jacqueline Kennedy, Historic Conversations on Life with John F. Kennedy* (New York: Hyperion, 2011), 197–198.
13. Kennedy and Beschloss, *Historic Conversations*, 185
14. Goodwin, *Remembering America*, 160.
15. Goodwin, *Remembering America*, 160.
16. Dallek, *An Unfinished Life*, 468.
17. Bruce Miroff, "The Alliance for Progress," in Clarice Swisher (ed.), *John F. Kennedy* (San Diego, C.A.: Greenhaven Press, 2000), 136.
18. Theodore C. Sorensen, *Kennedy* (New York: Harper & Row, 1965), 535.
19. Sorensen, *Kennedy*, 537.
20. Philip E. Muehlenbeck, *Betting on the Africans: John F. Kennedy's Courting of African Nationalist Leaders* (New York: Oxford University Press, 2012), 45.
21. Thomas J. Noer, "New Frontiers and Old Priorities in Africa, " in Thomas G. Paterson (ed.), *Kennedy's Quest for Victory: American Foreign Policy, 1961–1963* (New York: Oxford University Press, 1989), 257.
22. Muehlenbeck, *Betting on the Africans*, xiii.
23. Arthur M. Schlesinger Jr., *A Thousand Days: John F. Kennedy in the White House* (Boston: Houghton Mifflin Company, 1965), 575–576.
24. Thomas J. Noer, "New Frontiers and Old Priorities in Africa," in Thomas G. Paterson (ed.), *Kennedy's Quest for Victory: American Foreign Policy, 1961–1963* (New York: Oxford University Press, 1989), 263.
25. Schlesinger, *A Thousand Days*, 562–563.

26. Muehlenbeck, *Betting on the Africans,* 110.
27. Schlesinger, *A Thousand Days,* 582.
28. Muehlenbeck, *Betting on the Africans,* 178.
29. Muehlenbeck, *Betting on the Africans,* 182.
30. Muehlenbeck, *Betting on the Africans,* 180, 184.
31. Muehlenbeck, *Betting on the Africans,* 183.
32. Muehlenbeck, *Betting on the Africans,* 191–192.
33. Muehlenbeck, *Betting on the Africans,* 235.
34. Ryan Tubridy, *JFK in Ireland: Four Days That Changed a President* (London: Harper Collins, 2010), 182.
35. David Maranniss, *Barack Obama: The Story* (New York: Simon and Schuster, 2012), 185–186.
36. John F. Kennedy, May 25, 1961, JFKPLM Website.
37. John F. Kennedy, May 25, 1961, JFKPLM Website.
38. Quoted in Dallek, *An Unfinished Life,* 393.
39. "Meeting with James Webb, Jerome Weisner, and Robert Seamans, November 21, 1962," in Ted Widmer (ed.), *Listening In: The Secret House Recordings of John F. Kennedy* (New York: Hyperion, 2012), 220.
40. Meeting with James Webb, *Listening In,* 224.
41. John F. Kennedy, September 12, 1962, Rice University, Houston, Texas, JFKPLM Website.
42. Quoted in Gerald S. and Deborah H. Strober (eds.), *"Let Us Begin Anew," An Oral History of the Kennedy Presidency* (New York: Harper Perennial, 1993), 224.
43. Douglas Little, "From Even Handed to Empty Handed," in Paterson (ed.), *Kennedy's Quest for Victory,* 158.
44. Giglio, *The Presidency of John F. Kennedy,* 230–231.
45. John S. Badeau, *Oral History,* JFKPLM, 10–11; Schlesinger, *A Thousand Days,* 566.
46. Herring, *From Colony to Superpower,* 714.
47. Giglio, *The Presidency of John F. Kennedy,* 232.
48. Little, "From Even Handed to Empty Handed," in Paterson (ed.), *Kennedy's Quest for Victory,* 177.
49. James Fetzer, "Clinging to Containment," in Paterson (ed.), *Kennedy's Quest for Victory,* 185.
50. Schlesinger, *A Thousand Days,* 903–904.
51. W. J. Rorabaugh, *Kennedy and the Promise of the Sixties* (Cambridge, U.K.: Cambridge University Press, 2002), 33.
52. Quoted in Harold Chase and Allen H. Lerman (eds.), *Kennedy and the Press: The News Conferences,* introduction by Pierre Salinger (New York: Thomas Y. Crowell, 1965), 53.
53. Lawrence Freedman, *Kennedy's Wars: Berlin, Cuba, Laos and Vietnam* (New York: Oxford University Press, 2000), 295.
54. Freedman, *Kennedy's Wars,* 299–300.
55. John F. Kennedy, *The Strategy of Peace,* Allen Nevins (ed.) (New York: Harper & Row, 1960), 57.
56. John F. Kennedy, June 1, 1956, JFKPLM Website.
57. John F. Kennedy, June 1, 1956, JFKPLM Website.
58. John F. Kennedy, June 1, 1956, JFKPLM Website.
59. Mackenzie and Weinbrot, *The Liberal Hour,* 294–295.
60. Quoted in Alan Brinkley, *John F. Kennedy,* (New York, 2012), 140.
61. Benjamin C. Bradlee, *Conversations With Kennedy* (New York: Time Books, 1975), 58.
62. Kenneth P. O'Donnell and David F. Powers with Joe McCarthy, *"Johnny We Hardly Knew Ye": Memories of John Fitzgerald Kennedy* (Boston: Little, Brown and Company, 1970), 15.
63. O'Donnell and Powers, *"Johnny We Hardly Knew Ye,"* 15.
64. "Meeting Vietnam Advisors, September 10, 1963, Widmer (ed.), *Listening In,* 243.
65. "John F. Kennedy Criticizes the South Vietnamese Government, 1963" in Robert J. McMahon (ed.), *Major Problems in the History of the Vietnam War* (Lexington, M.A.: D.C. Heath, 1990), 187.
66. "Interview with Walter Cronkite, Inaugurating a CBS TV News Program, September 2, 1963, JFKPLM Website.

67. "Interview with Walter Cronkite, September 2, 1963, JFKPLM Website.
68. "Transcript of NBC Transcript broadcast with Chet Huntley, September 9, 1963, JFKPLM Website.
69. Quoted in Richard Reeves, *President Kennedy: Profile of Power* (New York: Simon and Schuster, 1993), 649.
70. Giglio, *The Presidency of John F. Kennedy,* 253.
71. John F. Kennedy, "Private Dictation, November 4, 1963," in Widmer (ed.), *Listening In,* 245.
72. John F. Kennedy, "Private Dictation, November 4, 1963," in Widmer (ed.), *Listening In,* 246.
73. David Burner, *John F. Kennedy and a New Generation,* 3rd edition (New York: Pearson Longman, 2009), 127,128.
74. O'Donnell and Powers with McCarthy, *"Johnny We Hardly Knew Ye,"* 16.

Chapter 7

1. Arthur M. Schlesinger Jr., *A Thousand Days: John F. Kennedy in the White House* (Boston: Houghton Mifflin Company, 1965), 1007.
2. Lawrence O'Brien, *No Final Victories: A Life in Politics From John F. Kennedy to Watergate* (Garden City, N.Y. Doubleday & Company, Inc., 1974), 126.
3. Schlesinger, Jr., *A Thousand Days,* 1007.
4. Press Conference, July 17, 1963, in Harold W. Chase and Allen H. Lerman (eds.), *Kennedy and the Press* (New York: Thomas Y. Crowell, 1965), 463.
5. Caroline Kennedy and Michael Beschloss (eds.), *Jacqueline Kennedy, Historic Conversations on Life with John F. Kennedy* (New York: Hyperion, 2011), 343–344.
6. Schlesinger, Jr. *A Thousand Days,* 1012.
7. Remarks Before the Protestant Council, November 8, 1963, John F. Kennedy Presidential Library and Museum Website.
8. Press Conference, March 23, 1961, in *Kennedy and the Press,* 55.
9. Irving Bernstein, *Promises Kept: John F. Kennedy's New Frontier* (New York: Hyperion, 1991), 198.
10. Schlesinger Jr., *A Thousand Days,* 1006.
11. Gerald S. and Deborah H. Strober (eds.) *"Let Us Begin Anew:" An Oral History of the Kennedy Presidency,* (New York: Harper Pernnial, 1993), 419.
12. O'Brien, *No Final Victories,* 126–128.
13. Quoted in Allan Nevins (ed.), *The Burden and the Glory* (New York: Harper & Row, 1964), 261–262.
14. Bernstein, *Promises Kept,* 245.
15. Robert Dallek, *John F. Kennedy: An Unfinished Life,* (Boston: Little, Brown and Company, 2003), 327.
16. Special Message to the Congress on Health and Hospital Care, February 9, 1961. Available online at: www.presidency.ucsb.edu/ws/?pid=8222.
17. Quoted in James N. Giglio, *The Presidency of John F. Kennedy* (Lawrence, K.A.: University Press of Kansas, 1991), 102.
18. Giglio, *The Presidency of John F. Kennedy,* 102
19. Bernstein, *Promises Kept,* 253.
20. Bernstein, *Promises Kept,* 256.
21. Ted Widmer (ed.) *Listening In: The Secret White House Recordings of John F. Kennedy* (New York: Hyperion, 2012), 29.
22. Press Conference, November 8, 1961, *Kennedy and the Press,* 130.
23. Giglio, *The Presidency of John F. Kennedy,* 140.
24. Bernstein, *Promises Kept,* 204.
25. Giglio, *The Presidency of John F. Kennedy,* 143.

26. Scott Stossel, *Sarge: The Life and Times of Sargent Shriver* (Washington, D.C.: Smithsonian Books, 2004), 135–136, 261.
27. Quoted in Dallek, *An Unfinished Life,* 484.
28. Press Conference, April 11, 1962, *Kennedy and the Press,* 223.
29. Quoted in Schlesinger Jr., *A Thousand Days,* 635.
30. Dallek, *An Unfinished Life,* 488.
31. John F. Kennedy, Commencement Speech, Yale University, June 11, 1962, John F. Kennedy Presidential Library and Museum Website.
32. John F. Kennedy, Commencement Speech, Yale University, June 11, 1962.
33. Theodore C. Sorensen, *Kennedy* (New York: Harper & Row, 1965), 394.
34. Dallek, *An Unfinished Life,* 584.
35. Giglio, *The Presidency of John F. Kennedy,* 139.
36. State of the Union Address, January 14, 1963, in *The Burden and the Glory,* 23.
37. Giglio, *The Presidency of John F. Kennedy,* 139.
38. Kennedy to Lou Harris, *The Kennedys,* PBS, 1989.
39. Quoted in Nick Bryant, *The Bystander: John F. Kennedy and the Struggle for Racial Equality* (New York: Basic Books, 2006), 155.
40. Maurice Isserman and Michael Kazin, *America Divided: The Civil War of the 1960s* (New York: Oxford University Press, 2000), 1.
41. Isserman and Kazin, *America Divided,* 2.
42. Quoted in *"Let Us Begin Anew,"* 273.
43. Bernstein, *Promises Kept,* 64.
44. Harris Wofford, *Of Kennedys and Kings: Making Sense of the Sixties* (Pittsburgh: University of Pittsburgh Press, 1980), 153.
45. Carl Brauer, *John F. Kennedy and the Second Reconstruction* (New York, 1977), 108.
46. Brauer, *John F. Kennedy and the Second Reconstruction,* 111.
47. Bryant, *The Bystander,* 331.
48. James W. Silver, *Mississippi: The Closed Society* (New York: Harcourt, Brace and World, 1963).
49. Bryant, *The Bystander,* 334.
50. Quoted in Dallek, *An Unfinished Life,* 515.
51. John F. Kennedy and Ross Barnett, September 22, 1962, in Widmer (ed.), *Listening In,* 101.
52. Bernstein, *Promises Kept,* 82.
53. John F. Kennedy, September 30, 1962, in *The Burden and the Glory,* 169.
54. *The Burden and the Glory,* 169.
55. *The Burden and the Glory,* 170.
56. Quoted in Bryant, *The Bystander,* 349.
57. Quoted in Dallek, *An Unfinished Life,* 517.
58. Bryant, *The Bystander,* 357.
59. Quoted in Bryant, *The Bystander,* 353.
60. State of the Union Address, January 14, 1963, in *The Burden and the Glory,* 26.
61. Bernstein, *Promises Kept,* 86.
62. Bernstein, *Promises Kept,* 86–87.
63. "Letter From Birmingham City Jail," in Michael Johnson (ed.), *Reading the American Past: Selected Historical Documents,* 4th edition (Boston: Bedford Books, 2009), 260.
64. Brauer, *John F. Kennedy and the Second Reconstruction,* 240, 241.
65. May 4, 1963, *Listening In,* 112.
66. Thomas J. Sugrue, *Sweet Land of Liberty: The Forgotten Struggle for Civil Rights in the North* (New York: Random House, 2008), 289.
67. Sugrue, *Sweet Land of Liberty,* 302.
68. John F. Kennedy, June 11, 1963, in *The Burden and the Glory,* 181.
69. John F. Kennedy, June 11, 1963, in *The Burden and the Glory,* 183.
70. John F. Kennedy, June 11, 1963, in *The Burden and the Glory,* 182.

71. John F. Kennedy, June 11, 1963, in *The Burden and the Glory*, 182.
72. Brauer, *John F. Kennedy and the Second Reconstruction*, 263.
73. Rorabaugh, *Kennedy and the Promise of the Sixties*, 115.
74. Quoted in Schlesinger, *A Thousand Days*, 966.
75. Bauer, *John F. Kennedy and the Second Reconstruction*, 279.
76. Bauer, *John F. Kennedy and the Second Reconstruction*, 298.
77. Bauer, *John F. Kennedy and the Second Reconstruction*, 301.
78. Quoted in Bernstein, *Promises Kept*, 108.
79. Quoted in Taylor Branch, *Parting the Waters: America in the King Years, 1954–1963* (New York: Simon and Schuster, 1988), 883.
80. Quoted in Branch, *Parting the Waters*, 883.
81. Quoted in *The Kennedys* (PBS), 1989.

CHAPTER 8

1. Sir Isaiah Berlin, Oral History Interview, John F. Kennedy Presidential Library and Museum Website.
2. Sir Isaiah Berlin, Oral History Interview.
3. Sir Isaiah Berlin, Oral History Interview.
4. Sir Isaiah Berlin, Oral History Interview.
5. Richard Reeves has emphasized this aspect of Kennedy's personality. See *President Kennedy: Profile of Power* (New York: Simon and Schuster, 1993).
6. W.J. Rorabaugh, *Kennedy and the Promise of the Sixties* (Cambridge, U.K.: Cambridge University Press, 2002), 9; Mimi Alford, *Once Upon a Secret: My Affair with President John F. Kennedy and Its Aftermath* (New York: Random House, 2012), 105.
7. Benjamin C. Bradlee, *Conversations With Kennedy* (New York: W.W. Norton & Company, 1975), 148.
8. Tom Wicker, quoted in introduction to the *New York Times, Four Days in November: The Original Coverage of the John F. Kennedy Assassination* (New York: St. Martin's Press), 18–19.
9. Wicker, *Four Days in November*, 19.
10. Quoted in Chris Matthews, *Jack Kennedy: Elusive Hero* (New York: Simon and Schuster, 2011), 328.
11. Caroline Kennedy and Michael Beschloss (eds.), *Jacqueline Kennedy, Historic Conversations on Life with John F. Kennedy* (New York: Hyperion, 2012), 334.
12. Robert Dallek: *An Unfinished Life: John F. Kennedy, 1917–1963* (Boston: Little, Brown and Company, 2003) 476.
13. Ted Sorensen, *Counselor: A Life at the Edge of History* (New York: Harper Collins Publishers, 2008), 122.
14. Kenneth P. O'Donnell and David F. Powers, with Joe McCarthy, *"Johnny We Hardly Knew Ye": Memories of John Fitzgerald Kennedy* (Boston: Little, Brown and Company, 1970), 378–379.
15. Press Conference, November 14, 1963, John F. Kennedy Presidential Library and Museum Website.
16. Ted Widmer (ed.), *Listening In: The Secret White House Recordings of John F. Kennedy* (New York: Hyperion, 2012), 283.
17. Widmer (ed.), *Listening In*, 282.
18. John Bartlow Martin, *Adlai Stevenson and the World: The Life of Adlai Stevenson* (Garden City, N.Y.: Book World Promotions, 1977), 774.
19. Dallek: *An Unfinished Life*, 693–694.
20. Thomas Maier, *The Kennedys: America's Emerald Kings* (New York: Basic Books, 2003), 459–460.
21. Quoted in Dallek, *An Unfinished Life*, 697.
22. Scott Stossel, *Sarge: The Life and Times of Sargent Shriver* (Washington, D.C.: Smithsonian Books, 2004), 298.

23. Sorensen, *Counselor,* 368
24. Quoted in Gerald S. and Deborah Strober, "*Let Us Begin Anew:*" *An Oral History of the Kennedy Presidency* (New York: Harper Perennial, 1993), 451.
25. James Piereson, *Camelot and the Cultural Revolution: How the Kennedy Assassination Shattered American Liberalism* (New York: Encounter Books, 2007), 166.
26. Vincent Bugliosi, *Reclaiming History: The Assassination of President John F. Kennedy* (New York: W.W. Norton & Company, 2007), 769–771.
27. Bugliosi, *Reclaiming History,* 941.
28. Thomas Maier, *The Kennedys: America's Emerald Kings,* 454.
29. William Taubman, *Khrushchev: The Man and His Era* (New York: W.W. Norton & Company, 2003), 604.
30. Arthur M. Schlesinger, Jr., *A Thousand Days: John F. Kennedy in the White House* (Boston: Houghton Mifflin Company, 1965), 1027.
31. Quoted in Philip E. Muehlenbeck, *Betting on the Africans: John F. Kennedy's Courting of African Nationalist Leaders* (New York: Oxford University Press, 2012), 194.
32. Rorabaugh, *Kennedy and the Promise of the Sixties,* 220.
33. Quoted in Muehlenbeck, *Betting on the Africans,* 226.
34. Quoted in Schlesinger, *A Thousand Days,* 1029.
35. Quoted in Thomas J. Whalen, *Kennedy Versus Lodge: The 1952 Massachusetts Senate Race* (Boston: Northeastern University Press, 2000), 182.
36. Theodore C. Sorensen, *Kennedy* (New York, 1965), 758.
37. Rorabaugh, *Kennedy and the Promise of the Sixties,* 203.
38. Rorabaugh, *Kennedy and the Promise of the Sixties,* 237.
39. 1985 Tribute by Ronald Reagan, John F. Kennedy Presidential Library and Museum Website.
40. See Richard Rorty, *Achieving Our Country: Leftist Thought in Twentieth Century America* (Cambridge, M.A.: Harvard University Press, 1998).

BIBLIOGRAPHY

PRIMARY SOURCES

Newspapers and Unpublished Sources

The Papers of John F. Kennedy, John F. Kennedy Presidential Library and Museum, Boston Massachusetts.

Oral History Interviews, John F. Kennedy Presidential Library and Museum, Boston, Massachusetts.

The American Presidency Project, University of California, Santa Barbara. *New York Times.*

Published Sources

Beschloss, Michael (ed.), *Jacqueline Kennedy: Historic Conversations on Life with John F. Kennedy.* New York, Hyperion, 2011.

Bradlee, Benjamin C. *Conversations with Kennedy.* New York: W. W. Norton & Company, 1975.

Chase, Harold W. and Lerman, Allen H. eds. *Kennedy and the Press: The News Conferences.* New York, Thomas Y. Crowell, 1965.

Fay, Paul B. *The Pleasure of His Company.* New York: Dell Publishing Company, Inc., 1966.

Goodwin, Richard N. *Remembering America: A Voice From the Sixties.* Boston: Little, Brown and Company, 1988.

Harrison, Maureen and Gilbert, Steve, eds. *John F. Kennedy: Word for Word.* La Jolla, California: Excellent Books, 1993.

Henderson, Deirdre, ed. *Prelude to Leadership: The European Diary of John F. Kennedy Summer 1945.* Washington, D.C.: Regnery Publishing, 1995.

Kennedy, John F. *Why England Slept.* Wilfred Funk, 1940. Reprint, Westport, C.T.: Greenwood Press, 1981

Kennedy, John F. *Profiles in Courage.* Memorial Edition. New York: Harper & Row, 1964.

Kennedy, John F. *A Nation of Immigrants.* Revised and enlarged edition. New York: Harper & Row, 1964.

Kennedy, Robert F. *Thirteen Days: A Memoir of the Cuban Missile Crisis.* New York: W.W. Norton & Company, 1969.

Kennedy, Rose Fitzgerald. *Times to Remember.* Garden City, N.Y.: Doubleday & Company, 1974.

Krock, Arthur. *Memoirs: Sixty Years on the Firing Line.* New York: Funk & Wagnalls, 1968.

Michener, James A. *Report of the County Chairman.* New York: Bantam Books, 1961.

Nevins, Allen, ed. *The Strategy of Peace: Senator John F. Kennedy.* New York: Harper & Row, 1960.

Nevins, Allen, ed. *President John F. Kennedy: The Burden and the Glory.* New York: Harper & Row, 1964.

O'Brien, Lawrence. *No Final Victories: A Life in Politics from John F. Kennedy to Watergate.* Garden City, N.Y.: Doubleday & Company, 1974.

Strober, Gerald S. and Deborah, H. *"Let Us Begin Anew": An Oral History of the Kennedy Presidency.* New York: Harper Perennial, 1993.

The Warren Commission Report, by the President's Commission on the Assassination of President Kennedy. New York: Barnes & Noble Books, 1992.

Widmer, Ted, ed. *Listening In: The Secret White House Recordings of John F. Kennedy.* New York: Hyperion, 2012.

SECONDARY SOURCES

Bernstein, Irving. *Promises Kept: John F. Kennedy's New Frontier.* New York: Oxford University Press, 1991.

Brauer, Carl M. *John F. Kennedy and the Second Reconstruction.* New York: Columbia University Press, 1977.

Brinkley, Alan. *John F. Kennedy.* The American Presidents series, Arthur M. Schlesinger and Sean Wilentz, eds. New York: Times Books, 2012.

Brogan, Hugh. *Kennedy.* Profiles in Power series, Keith Robbins, ed. Harlow, UK: Pearson Education Limited, 1996.

Bugliosi, Vincent. *Reclaiming History: The Assassination of John F. Kennedy.* New York: W.W. Norton & Company, 2007.

Burner, David. *John F. Kennedy and a New Generation,* 3rd edition. Library of American Biography series. New York: Pearson Longman, 2009.

Branch, Taylor. *Parting the Waters: America in the King Years, 1954–1963.* New York: Simon and Schuster, 1988.

Bryant, Nick. *The Bystander: John F. Kennedy and the Struggle for Black Equality.* New York: Basic Books, 2006.

Burns, James MacGregor. *John Kennedy: A Political Profile.* New York: Avon Book Division, 1961.

Casey, Shaun A. *The Making of a Catholic President: Kennedy vs. Nixon 1960.* New York: Oxford University Press, 2009.

Carty, Thomas. *A Catholic in the White House? Religion, Politics, and John F. Kennedy's 1960 Presidential Campaign.* New York: Palgrave Macmillan, 2004.

Clarke, Thurston. *Ask Not: The Inauguration of John F. Kennedy and the Speech that Changed America.* New York: Henry Holt and Company, 2004.

Collier, Peter and Horowitz, David. *The Kennedys: An American Drama.* New York: Encounter Books, 2002.

Donovan, Robert J. *PT 109: John F. Kennedy in World War II.* New York: McGraw-Hill Book Company, 1961.

Dallek, Robert. *An Unfinished Life: John F. Kennedy, 1917–1963.* Boston: Little, Brown and Company, 2003.

Dobbs, Michael. *One Minute to Midnight: Kennedy, Khrushchev, and Castro on the Brink of Nuclear War.* New York: Alfred A. Knopf, 2008.

Donovan, Robert J. *PT 109: John F. Kennedy.* New York: McGraw-Hill Book Company, Inc., 1961.

Freedman, Lawrence. *Kennedy's Wars: Berlin, Cuba, Laos and Vietnam.* New York: Oxford University Press, 2000.

Giglio, James N. *The Presidency of John F. Kennedy.* Lawrence, K,S.: University Press of Kansas, 1991.

Goodwin, Doris Kearns. *The Fitzgeralds and the Kennedys: An American Saga.* New York: Simon and Schuster, 1987.

Hamilton, Nigel. *JFK: Reckless Youth.* New York: Random House, 1992.

Kennedy, Edward M. *True Compass: A Memoir.* New York: Twelve Hachette Book Group, 2009.

Leamer, Laurence. *The Kennedy Women: The Saga of an American Family.* New York: Villard Books, 1994.

Leaming, Barbara. *Jack Kennedy: The Education of a Statesman.* New York: W.W. Norton & Company, Inc., 2006.

Logevall, Frederick. *Embers of War: The Fall of an Empire and the Making of America's Vietnam.* New York: Random House, 2012.

Mackenzie, G. Calvin and Weisbrot, Robert. *The Liberal Hour: Washington and the Politics of Change in the 1960s.* New York: The Penguin Press, 2008.

Maier, Thomas. *The Kennedys: America's Emerald Kings.* New York: Basic Books, 2003.

Matthews, Chris. *Kennedy and Nixon: The Rivalry That Shaped Postwar America.* New York: Simon and Schuster, 1996.

Matthews, Chris. *Jack Kennedy: Elusive Hero.* New York: Simon and Schuster, 2011.

Muehlenbeck, Philip E. *Betting on the Africans: John F. Kennedy's Courting of African Nationalist Leaders.* New York: Oxford University Press, 2012.

Nasaw, David. *The Patriarch: The Remarkable Life and Turbulent Times of Joseph P. Kennedy.* New York: The Penguin Press, 2012.

O'Brien, Michael. *John F. Kennedy: A Biography.* New York: Thomas Dunne Books, 2005.

O'Brien, Michael. *Rethinking Kennedy: An Interpretative Biography.* Chicago: Ivan R. Dee, 2009.

O'Connor, Thomas H. *The Boston Irish: A Political History.* Boston: Back Bay Books, 1995.

O'Donnell, Kenneth P. and Powers, David F. with McCarthy, Joe. *"Johnny, We Hardly Knew Ye": Memories of John Fitzgerald Kennedy.* Boston: Little, Brown and Company, 1972.

Paterson, Thomas G., ed. *Kennedy's Quest for Victory: American Foreign Policy, 1961–1963.* New York: Oxford University Press, 1989.

Pitts, David. *Jack and Lem: John F. Kennedy and Lem Billings.* New York: Da Capo Press, 2007.

Posner, Gerald. *Case Closed: Lee Harvey Oswald and the Assassination of JFK.* New York: Random House, 1993.

Primary by Robert Drew (1960, 2003).

Reeves, Richard. *President Kennedy: Profile of Power.* New York: Simon and Schuster, 1993.

Rorabaugh, W.J. *Kennedy and the Promise of the Sixties.* Cambridge, U.K.: Cambridge University Press, 2002.

Rorabaugh, W.J. *The Real Making of the President: Kennedy, Nixon and the 1960 Election.* Lawrence, K.S.: University Press of Kansas, 2009.

Savage, Sean J. *JFK, LBJ, and the Democratic Party.* New York: State University of New York, 2004.

Schlesinger, Arthur M. Jr. *A Thousand Days: John F. Kennedy in the White House.* Boston: Houghton Mifflin Company, 1965.

Sorensen, Theodore C. *Kennedy.* New York: Harper & Row, 1965.

Sorensen, Ted. *Counselor: A Life at the Edge of History.* New York: Harper Collins Publishers, 2008.

Stossel, Scott. *Sarge: The Life and Times of Sargent Shriver.* Washington, D.C.: Smithsonian Books, 2004.

Taubman, William. *Khrushchev: The Man and His Era.* New York: W.W. Norton & Company, 2003.

Tubridy, Ryan. *JFK in Ireland: Four Days that Changed a President.* New York: Harper Collins, 2010.

Whalen, Thomas J. *Kennedy versus Lodge: The 1952 Massachusetts Senate Race.* Boston: Northeastern University Press, 2000.

Documentaries

Out of Ireland: The Story of Irish Emigration to America, Paul Wagner (1997).

Primary, Robert Drew (1960, 2003).

The Kennedys. The American Experience, PBS (2011).

Index